Slavery, the State, and Islam

Slavery, the State, and Islam looks at slavery as the foundation of power and the state in the Muslim world. Closely examining major theological and literary Islamic texts, it challenges traditional approaches to the subject. Servitude was a foundation for the construction of the new state on the Arabian peninsula. It constituted the essence of a relationship of authority as found in the Koran. The dominant stereotypes and traditions of equality as promoted by Islam, particularly its leniency toward slaves, are questioned. This original, pioneering book overturns the mythical view of caliphal power in Islam. It examines authority as it functions in the Arab world today and helps to explain the difficulty of attempting to instill freedom and democracy there.

Mohammed Ennaji holds a doctorate in economics and is professor at Mohammed V University in Morocco. A historian, writer, and journalist, he is an active proponent of culture in Morocco, where he organizes various cultural events, including international conferences and festivals. He is the author of several studies and books, including *Serving the Master: Slavery and Society in Nineteenth-Century Morocco* (1999).

Slavery, the State, and Islam

MOHAMMED ENNAJI
Mohammed V University

Translated by
TERESA LAVENDER FAGAN

CAMBRIDGE
UNIVERSITY PRESS

CAMBRIDGE UNIVERSITY PRESS
Cambridge, New York, Melbourne, Madrid, Cape Town,
Singapore, São Paulo, Delhi, Mexico City

Cambridge University Press
32 Avenue of the Americas, New York, NY 10013-2473, USA

www.cambridge.org
Information on this title: www.cambridge.org/9780521135450

First published in French as *Le sujet et le mamelouk: Esclavage, pouvoir et religion dans le monde arabe* by Mille et une nuits, département de la Librairie Arthème Fayard 2007
First English edition published by Cambridge University Press 2013

Printed in the United States of America

A catalog record for this publication is available from the British Library.

Library of Congress Cataloging in Publication data
Ennaji, Mohammed.
Slavery, the state, and Islam / Mohammed Ennaji, Mohammed V University,
Teresa Lavender Fagan.
pages cm.
Includes bibliographical references and index.
ISBN 978-0-521-11962-7 (hardback) –
ISBN 978-0-521-13545-0 (pbk.)
1. Slavery and Islam. I. Fagan, Teresa Lavender. II. Title.
HT919.E548 2013
297.5'675–dc23 2013006874

ISBN 978-0-521-11962-7 Hardback
ISBN 978-0-521-13545-0 Paperback

I wish to thank Aline Schulman and Juan Goytisolo for their kind support.
I am grateful to Régis Debray for the interest he has shown in my work.
I wish also to thank Professor Paul Lovejoy for his kind assistance.
This book is dedicated to my wife Naoual, for her patient support and her radiant smile.

Contents

Foreword

Mohammed Ennaji explores dark corners of Islamic thought in this magnificent and poetic excursion into the fabric of Muslim society. Through the explication of dozens of classical texts by Muslim intellectuals on the meaning and historical significance of power, religious authority, and slavery, Ennaji takes us on an odyssey through the rich intellectual and often mystical traditions that have given substance to the social and intellectual fabric of Islam. While some of the texts have been accessible to scholars who are not fluent in Arabic, the majority are largely unknown outside of Islamic scholarship. Ennaji's discussion engages these texts virtually exclusively, not relying on a secondary literature in English or French that attempts to analyze the intellectual discourse of historical Islam and contemporary politics.

As Ennaji demonstrates, the failure to consider this vast Islamic literature has distorted our understanding of the importance of slavery and servitude in history, not just in the Muslim world and Islamic thought, but more globally, with comparative implications for understanding the impact of slavery elsewhere, from China to Africa and as far as the Americas. Ennaji confronts a deep and sophisticated written tradition within Islam that reveals complex contradictions in the social and political history of the state and society. Ennaji contends that the legal framework, the metaphoric implications of language, and the variety of social expressions of slavery reveal power relationships that permeate the Islamic world. These relationships have generated an ideology of hierarchy that fully incorporates slavery as a fundamental and necessary construct of Islamic society.

A sociologist, historian, political theorist, and linguist, Professor Ennaji reveals a command of disciplines that is astonishing. His sociological perspective is evident in the focus on the hierarchy and social construction of servitude. His knowledge of history informs his contemporary readings of the texts. His appreciation of political theory is the fabric of the study. Through his examination of the meaning of words in Arabic, Ennaji demonstrates how etymology can reveal hidden relationships in expressions of power and hierarchy. He extends this cross-disciplinary exploration into symbolism and metaphor, again as a way of revealing hidden meanings and implicit assumptions about power and authority. In his important earlier study, *Serving the Master: Slavery and Society in Nineteenth-Century Morocco* (1999), originally published as *Soldats, domestiques et concubines: L'esclavage au Maroc au XIXe siècle* (1994), Ennaji demonstrated the importance of slavery in Moroccan society and the complexity of its history. Far from an idyllic and benign view of slavery, *Serving the Master* shows the danger of superficial generalizations and reveals the contradictions in society as exposed through the experiences of soldiers, concubines, and domestic servants who were slaves.

Because the current study involves the examination of Arabic texts, the approach is fundamentally empirical. Ennaji is not concerned with examining how power relationships in Islam have been understood in the scholarly literature of history and Islamic studies; rather, he cites almost exclusively the Arabic texts themselves. He demonstrates a broad and sophisticated knowledge of hundreds of texts that characterize the extensive literature of Islam. Few scholars can match Ennaji's command of primary sources. Through his own literary style, he successfully translates this font of classical knowledge from Arabic first into French and now into English. In providing an intellectual commentary on this extensive library, Ennaji not only provides access to a rich body of knowledge not accessible in French or English but also transcends the Arabic sources through his explication and his juxtaposition of the texts. In effect, Ennaji's commentary itself could be in Arabic, thereby fully engaging the intellectual milieu from which the book derives.

Originally published in French, Ennaji's examination of slavery, the state, and Islam challenges us to think again about the complexities of Islam at a time when it is essential that people throughout the world increase their understanding of themselves in the complex multicultural world in which we live. Ennaji bridges a gap that has discouraged dialogue, both among Muslim intellectuals themselves and between Muslims and others.

Although considerable scholarly attempts have been made to engage Muslim societies in the study of slavery and its meaning, it has been a difficult challenge that has had limited success. The UNESCO initiative to explore the "slave route" has been global in perspective, but it has been far easier to examine the trajectory of slavery in the Americas and its impact on Europe and elsewhere than to engage Muslim countries in the discussion. Silence has been the chosen answer, even though the UNESCO project has always included Muslims representing countries that are predominately or entirely Muslim.

Common misconceptions of Islam have not helped the dialogue. Despite the number of countries that are predominately Muslim or have substantial Muslim minorities, many people think only of the Middle East and perhaps North Africa as Muslim. Hence the issues that Ennaji explores touch the lives and histories of a considerable part of the world. Moreover, the interactions between Muslims and non-Muslims make the exploration of the place of slavery in the history of Islam a global question. Ennaji's intention is to foster intercultural dialogue, focusing on slavery and diversity as issues to be confronted to overcome injustices of the past and present. In the multicultural world in which we live, Ennaji's analytical study promotes interculturalism by demonstrating how the confluence of cultures and the convergence of diasporas form the basis for meaningful dialogue.

Paul E. Lovejoy

Introduction

The Sources and Structures of the Bond of Authority

Islamist literature looks at the issue of reestablishing the original, just State, which rests on the fraternity of believers and on egalitarian principles established by the religion. The issue, which consists of questioning the foundations of such a State at its very birth and throughout the centuries that followed it, is crucial. The present work approaches this point by examining the nature and the foundations of the bond of authority in the Arab world. How can the strength of such a bond and the almost absolute power still held by heads of state today be explained?

To what degree does the genesis of the state account for such a reality? Can we detach the almost mythical state of the orthodox caliphs[1] from the states that came after it and refuse to inscribe it in a historical continuum that the advent of Islam was unable to break?

The present work arose out of a desire to understand an authority that is sometimes fascinating in the mystery that surrounds it but nonetheless terrifying in the abuses it can engender and that, in any case, essentially originates in the reasoning of another age. Social changes in the Arab world call for a knowledge of it without which a solid, coherent social project cannot come to fruition.

This work looks at the question from this perspective. Though in the chapters that follow the opening narrative the book deals with the period surrounding the birth of Islam and the great Omayyad (661–750) and Abbasid (749–1258) dynasties, it is in fact the present that is at issue, out of a desire to better understand the modalities of the exercise of power.

[1] The caliph was the lieutenant of the prophet Muhammad; here we refer to his successors: Abû Bakr, 'Omar, 'Othmân, and 'Ali, whose reigns extended from 632 to 661.

This period was not an arbitrary choice; it is quite simply unavoidable. We cannot avoid a detour through the founding moment. We must look to it in order to understand the present, in which the dead still maintain a grip on the living.

It is clear that the foundations of power in the Arab world have their roots precisely in those times. Therefore we will examine that period closely, not only because that power derives its legitimacy from it, but also and above all because we can most clearly see its genesis there. In Arab societies today, the mechanisms in existence at the birth of that power are practically invisible because they are hidden by the illusion of modernity promoted by institutions that originated elsewhere. Going back to the origins removes such screens. Furthermore, the Arab world is still far from having experienced true political and cultural changes that open the way to democracy and freedom. The strong influence of religion remains one of the major obstacles to this.

The question of the nature of the bond of authority leads to another one, essential in our times: that of the bonds between the religious and political realms. Here I attempt to approach this question in a non-traditional way. Servitude has been a very useful key in unlocking the space of the sacred and in desacralizing the approach to this question, or, to be more specific, by approaching it from the bond of authority. Three types of bonds are thus examined: master-slaves, king-subjects, and divinity-faithful. Passing from one to the other enables us to see the interrelationships and to better reveal the interplay of social and political change by emphasizing how naïve it would be, today, to raise this issue outside of any serious discussion of the place of religion in society, that is, without envisioning any fundamental ruptures.

Examining the relationships between the different levels of authority proves easier within the context of the advent of Islam and through the following period because of the crossovers existing during those times. Indeed, the boundaries between the sacred and the profane during that period were not entirely impermeable. The space of the divine was in the process of being circumscribed; the veil and the prohibitions were not yet mandatory. As for the king, he had not distanced himself from the slave master; he had not yet donned the opaque robe of the caliph and still allowed the true social content of his authority to be seen. In other words, there was still circulation and competition among the civil society, the political society, and the celestial society. This is why we must go back so far to investigate the reality of present-day power, which fundamentally feeds from the same sources while flying the flags of the sacred and democracy. Approaching the question by way of servitude ultimately proves very useful.

Rarely has the question of authority in the Arab world been raised in terms of slavery. On the one hand, this social relationship has elicited little interest in the Muslim world, as Islam has exerted such a fascination that many authors have seen it, if not as an abolitionist religion, at least as being profoundly egalitarian. This perception has closed off any questioning of the nature of power in Muslim societies that would place slavery at its foundation, judging the institution to be unworthy of interest since it was assumed to be of little importance in those societies. Furthermore, a sort of discretion has worked against an unmasked examination of the mechanisms of authority, one that would break down the walls between the different levels of authority – from the celestial society to the earthly political society and on to the civil society – notably through the master-slave relationship. Such breaking of barriers, however, appears essential and fruitful.

Contrary to the widely held opinion, I believe that slavery was a determining aspect of social relationships in the Arab-Muslim world. Provided that it is not approached from the same perspective as for western society, ancient or modern – notably through its essential productive role in that society – slavery proves to be of surprising importance in an approach to social relationships and especially in an analysis of power.

This is why I have chosen this approach. On the one hand, the relationship between Islam and slavery remains largely subject to caution and is often the object of unconvincing shortcuts. Thus, to mention only one essential aspect in the analysis of authority, the question of the freedom and the perspectives of the servile classes in Muslim societies is largely unexamined. On the other hand, numerous indicators lead us to assume that the number of slaves was higher in Arab society than has generally been admitted. But without having to rely on numbers, it seems that slavery acted as a catalyst by setting the tone for the bond of authority in local communities, in which kinship was a powerful link. It formed the major referent in them by imposing servitude in its various facets as a mode of expression in relationships of power. Only through servitude could one measure the degree of proximity to the king. Political language borrows abundantly from the register of servitude, as does that of theology. No lexicon has been better adapted than that of servitude to guide the faithful in the quest to approach the divine.

With the goal of shedding light on the questions raised and being able to fully assess the bond of authority, this work attempts to dismantle the various modalities of domination, constraint, dependency, proximity, connection, and solicitation linking the chief – who despite his title of caliph remained a king in disguise – to his servants. The sources that are consulted prove eloquent. This work goes beyond classical historiography, which says little about the aspects it judges to be of scant interest. Linguistic, literary, and theological collections, by contrast, prove very useful. Examining the language through great Arabic dictionaries enables us to shed light on little-known aspects of the social relationships of power. Words have, in fact, preserved the memory of changed or hidden practices; we need merely to call them into question for these practices to be revealed.

This book is thus focused on the person of the king in his relationship with his servants. The complexity of this figure is presented here in its various aspects, both ordinary and extraordinary. But it is particularly the essential bond of authority, elevating the absolute master, that receives the greatest attention. A strange tale opens the work: it tells of the stormy relationships of a nineteenth-century Moroccan sultan with one of his agents of authority. This first tale, at least in part, orients our approach to the question.

I

The Deadly Lie, or the Death Announcement

Just as the caid's household was settling down for the evening, a man on horseback came galloping up out of nowhere. Foam dripped from the mouth of his mount, exhausted after racing all the way at full speed.

This abrupt arrival stupefied the gatekeepers. The rider burst into the courtyard without hesitation. No one approached him to ask why he had come. There seemed to be no force capable of stopping him. He went straight toward the caid, al-Hâj ʿAbdallah Ubihi. The intrepid messenger had come on behalf of the sultan.

The fortress sank into silence. A sort of paralysis took over the entire residence. Still as statues, the guards and servants from time to time glanced anxiously toward the house. Their vigil took on a tragic tone that was fueled by the last rays of the sun.

The call to evening prayers did not come. The call from the mosque outside the residence usually followed that of the inner mosque. That evening, the call was not heard, as if one had tried to delay nightfall. The *maghrib* (evening prayer) was like a threshold no one wanted to cross. Yet the final rays of daylight were slipping away. One by one, the veil of darkness covered them. Mournful shadows seemed to hover over the grounds. Finally, like an ax, night fell.

Al-ghurûb, or sunset, is a moment of finality. Like other words with the same root, it refers to an end, a limit, a mourning. *Al-gharb* means the extreme of everything, the end of the sun's trajectory, the final stage before night. It is the departure, the distancing, the exile that is also designated by the term *at-taghrib*. In reference to a sword, it means the tip. And in a funereal context, *al-ghurûb* describes tears flowing from the eyes.

As night fell, the chronicler notes, women's cries, tears of mourning and submission, could be heard from inside. The caid had confided in his most intimate circle, who then relayed the message to the rest of the household: "The caid bids you farewell and wants you to know: 'For now, he is going to see the sultan. If he returns, so much the better, and if not, farewell.'"

Al-Hâj ʿAbdallah left. A few days later his death was announced.[1] The news spread like wildfire through all of southwestern Morocco. The caid was practically a viceroy there.

His considerable fortune, including hundreds of slaves,[2] his dense network of connections in northern and southern Morocco, and his renown among all the tribes of the region have kept his memory alive to the present day. He was poisoned by the sultan himself, who offered the deadly cup with his own hands.

But more so than the death of the potentate, it is the sultan's announcement of the demise and the publicity surrounding the death that interest us in this tale. It is rare, in fact, that the death of a provincial chief, let alone its precise date, should be the object of such great attention to the point of being included in official history texts. Numerous provincial chiefs, disgraced for various reasons, were imprisoned and dispossessed without the "media" of the time taking note of them as they did in this case. How can we explain this unusual mode of communication?

THE ALLEGED CIRCUMSTANCES OF THE DEATH

Contemporary history, on the whole, keeps the details of this figure's demise tightly under wraps. It shares the death of the caid and remains silent regarding the circumstances. The tales of this episode have reached us not through any written record but thanks to a rich oral history. It has given rise to more than one version.

The simplest account is that of the local chroniclers. Summoned by the sultan, the caid was thrown into prison in Marrakech. He died there shortly afterward. Mukhtâr Sûsi, the most significant of these chroniclers, reputed to be a fine observer, a native of the region having great knowledge of it, and a former minister of the throne, recounts this version. Succinct, it rejects the assassination hypothesis. After all, at that time dying in prison was common and did not arouse curiosity. Prison,

[1] Al-Mukhtâr as-Sûsî, *Min khilâli Jazûla*, IV, 86.

[2] M. Ennaji, *Soldats, domestiques et concubines*, Balland, 22.

as we shall see, was well known to be death's antechamber. Thus the author's attention was focused above all on the reasons for the caid's departure, less so on him personally than on the regional circumstances he left behind.

A second version tells us more. It comes from a European, Robert Montagne, an expert on the region, in his book on the Berbers and the Makhzen.[3] Sûsi, who had traveled the area by donkey gathering a wide range of accounts for his encyclopedia on the Souss,[4] heard this version but said not a word about it. He no doubt consciously chose to ignore it. Recording oral testimony, even long afterward, after tensions have abated, never fails to entail collateral damage.

Montagne's tale is filled with ruse and treachery. The caid was not summoned to appear before the sultan. No horseman had rushed in to pull him from his fortress at nightfall. His departure for Marrakech would not have caused the alleged mourning; no macabre outcome would have been foreseen at that moment. As was customary, the caid simply went to the kingdom's capital to pay his respects to the sultan and give him gifts, as he was expected to do.

The sultan awaited him in person, not with the intention of thanking him, but to accuse him of high treason. The factual history does not skimp on details. The sultan astounded the caid with supporting evidence before offering him the cup: "Do you prefer to drink this tea in silence, or shall I shackle the great caid Al-Hâj ʿAbdallah and drag him in front of the tribe before I cut off his head?"[5] The accused held out his hand, took the cup of poison without flinching, and went to die in his city residence, where his *qâdi* (judge, serving here as notary), who had accompanied him on his trip to Marrakech, was waiting for him.

Disgrace had befallen the caid without his having caught wind of it. His abrupt fall occurred at a time of intense conflict. Yet he was unanimously respected in the region. An unparalleled mediator, he put all his expertise and contacts to work in order to establish the sultan's authority in southern Morocco, in the Sahara. Thus, in that regard, the sultan should have congratulated himself on his agent's effectiveness. Nonetheless, the caid's fate was sealed. To uncover the reasons for his abrupt and fatal disgrace, we will have to look elsewhere, at the very nature of his relationship with his master, that is, at the bond of authority.

[3] Robert Montagne, *Les Berbères et le Makhzen*, 383.
[4] Al-Mukhtâr as-Sûsî, *al-Ma'sûl*, Royal Printing House, Rabat.
[5] Robert Montagne, *Les Berbères et le Makhzen*, 383.

THE ORIGINS OF THE DISGRACE

The story told by Robert Montagne emphasizes the relationships the caid maintained with a large Moroccan dynasty located farther south of his command, some forty kilometers from the city of Tiznit. The house of Iligh in the seventeenth century counted princes among its ranks. It lost its power with the rise and establishment of the Alaouite dynasty. Its chiefs took flight. History lost sight of their descendants after the destruction of their fortress by the central power. In the nineteenth century, the house came back into view. It regained its glory by playing a considerable role in commerce with black Africa through the Sahara. Its chiefs regained their prestige. They once again amassed considerable wealth. They became so famous that they were believed to have secessionist leanings.

In fact, the house was not as independent of the central power as history would lead us to believe, but that power was far away and was no match for the regional leaders. They found themselves with room to maneuver. Thus the chiefs of the house of Iligh played with their quasi-independence and cultivated their image as all-powerful chiefs, uncontested masters, at least among the local populations.

It was that image, Robert Montagne claims, that caused the death of the caid. He supposedly maintained close ties with the chief of the rebel house and upon his visit was received with such pomp that the event has endured in the popular memory. But no trace of this encounter is found either in published sources or in unpublished archives. However, despite the lack of written documents, nothing seems to repudiate this anecdote that is deeply anchored in the popular memory. Its date coincides with a hypothetical armed confrontation between the forces of the house of Iligh and the army of the crown prince at that time.[6]

That would have been enough, as the seeds of suspicion had been sown. Fate took care of the rest: a messenger from the caid misdirected a letter that was intended for the lord of Iligh. Curiously, the missive fell into the hands of the sultan; it convinced him completely of his servant's crime. According to another version, far from having misdirected the letter, the messenger took care to send it directly to the sultan. In fact, the path of the letter is unimportant. In either case, the sultan was omniscient and all-powerful, and luck was always on his side.

[6] M. Ennaji, "Discours politique et gestion des conflits," in *L'amitié du prince*, 86.

A QUESTIONABLE DEATH

Regardless of the circumstances of this episode, history is untruthful in the details. For the caid did not die! He lived for several more years in Marrakech after the supposed date of his death. This is a proven fact. Official documents after 1868 testify to this.[7] Later documents confirm the information.[8]

The historiography deliberately lied: how could the caid's fate have escaped court historians? Such a thing is highly improbable. The caid ʿAbdallah was such a well-known figure at the time that no high-level person could have been unaware of his activities; he had been one of the sultan's inseparable companions, a prodigious lord, constantly giving to the royal entourage and especially to the scribes.

So it is hard to understand how the chroniclers could have been so mistaken about his death. The declaration of his death in 1868 by the voices of authority had the appearance of a public announcement. It solemnly notified the servant people of the death of one of their own, while leaving the motives and means to be filled in by rumor.

But what kind of death was it? In the Arabic language, death is the opposite of life. It is the opposite of the principle of life. A dead land is one whose vital resources have been exhausted. Every thing dies when it stops moving. Thus the wind dies when it is calm, and a man dies when he lets sleep overtake him. Man also dies in a situation of decline or degeneration. The word by extension designates "difficult situations such as poverty, humiliation, begging, old age, and disobedience."[9] The prophetic tradition teaches that Satan was the first to die because he was the first to disobey. "To die" thus can also signify leaving the circle of servants to join the rank of infidels.

Satan would have died from that curse. Recall that the word "death" also means "deadly." Did the fallen Adam die? Of course! He died chased from paradise and from the world of immortals, forced at Satan's instigation to enter the world of mortals. In one tale of this episode, he leaves paradise at dusk. It is said that he died for having succumbed to temptation, for having broken the pact that connected him to God, and for having lacked resolve when facing the demon.[10]

[7] *Kunnach* 47, Royal Library, Rabat.
[8] Including a local work by al-Saddiqi, *Tarikh al-Sawira*.
[9] Ibn Mandhûr, *Lissân al-ʿArab*, II, 92. Henceforth *Lissân*.
[10] The Koran, 20:115–127.

Wasn't the caid guilty of the same crime? He allowed himself to become friends with a renegade, an outlaw.[11] The renegade in question, Ḥusayn Ben Hâchem, the chief of the house of Iligh mentioned above, refused, like Satan, to follow the royal order and to bend, following established rules, to the local agents of authority, that is, to the king's representatives. Arguing his sharifian ancestry and symbolically bearing the name of one of the grandsons of the Prophet, he refused to bow down to an agent of authority having more modest origins.

The caid ʿAbdallah would have been incapable of resisting the temptation. He was on the borders of the zone fully under the prince's control. He officiated over the border lands, in contact with unsettled tribes and practically autonomous chiefdoms, over an uncertain territory where authority wavered. He was at the crossroads of irrigated farmlands, the privileged domain of royal authority, and the edge of the desert, where recalcitrant communities could strike and then disappear without leaving a trace. He was on the border between the realm of servitude and the chasm of disobedience. In other words, he was between life and death. A delegate in negotiations with Ḥusayn, due to his diplomacy and his status, he moved in places the master avoided. His supposed leanings toward the chief of the house of Iligh managed to convince his superiors of his crime. The caid thus had listened to Satan. He had given into temptation and failed to obey orders. His disobedience led to his fall. As a result, he had to die.

METAMORPHOSIS

To die politically, of course. History confirms this indirectly through a tale by a court historian, ʿAbdarrahmân Ibn Zaydân. He provides precious information about the matter, though the facts might go unnoticed in the course of the story.

The historiographer does not formally challenge his predecessors. He does not bother to explicitly correct the supposed date of the caid ʿAbdallah's death, but he gives precious details about the circumstances of the event. According to him, the caid was in open conflict with the prince Mawlay Ḥassan, who was irritated by the great solicitude his father, the sultan Mohammed ben ʿAbdarrahmân, showed toward the great caid,

[11] M. Ennaji and P. Pascon, *Le Makhzen et le sous al-Aqsa, la correspondance de la maison d'Iligh*, CNRS, 1988, 14–15.

essentially making him a viceroy of the southern provinces. Allying himself with other rising potentates in the region, the prince undertook to put an end to the caid's good fortune. He took advantage of the agitation of the tribes.

We could, of course, discuss forever the true motivations for the decision to bring down the caid. The country was undergoing profound changes in the nineteenth century. The rise of new tribal chiefdoms due to European commercial penetration exacerbated rivalries among the established caids and those who had recently become wealthy through business. It seems incontestable that the caid ʿAbdallah fell victim to his competitors' rise in power. It is also certain that the breaking up of vast areas of command, such as his, was part of an overall movement. But these basic tendencies, despite their strength, only partially illuminate the underlying reasons for the supposed death of the great caid.

The oral tale, rich in minute details, is of great help here. It happens to recount a strange fact that no historian bothered to point out and that only Robert Montagne noted. The father of the caid ʿAbdallah, ʿAbdelmalek, had supposedly received as a gift from the sultan Mawlay Slimâne (1792–1822) a concubine slave girl who came to him pregnant! The awkwardness of such a "scoop" banished it from the portrait sketched by the historiographers. The information, true or untrue – it doesn't matter – opens the door to many ambiguities. The caid ʿAbdallah, son of that slave and strong in the sultan's affection for him, could have taken advantage of dynastic rights in the same measure as the prince Mawlay Ḥassan.

In any event, the sultan, or his son, put an end to his career as a great governor. He stripped him of his responsibilities and went so far as to announce his death publicly. In fact, as we have seen, he did not die. He was transferred to Marrakech, where he entered into the personal service of the prince, who placed him in his corporation of ablutions,[12] made up exclusively of slaves, unlike other corporations.[13] The caid ʿAbdallah was black, which went perfectly with his new status. He was henceforth relegated to the rank of slave. The metamorphosis was complete. The royal message was crystal clear: service to the king demanded an unfailing loyalty, such as a slave owes to his master.

[12] Ibn Zaydâne, *Ithâf*, II, 117.

[13] M. Ennaji, *Soldats, domestiques et concubines*, 160–163.

A FAMILIAR DEATH

In fact, as far as we are concerned, the exact date of the caid's death does not really matter. Historiography abounds with erroneous dates of death. Rarely are deaths dated with precision. We often do not know dates of death for important figures, as written recollections quite often prove to be curiously deficient in this area. Strictly speaking, this omission is surprising in the case of clerks familiar with written testimony. Many notaries and jurisconsults spent their entire lives inscribing dates on acts of ownership, sale, or inheritance, yet died without those near to them feeling obliged to note their date of departure. The great familiarity people had with death perhaps explains this. Death was always right around the corner. Its crushing presence haunted one's consciousness. People dreamed of death at night, when it would appear in varied and often terrifying forms. In a vision attributed to the Prophet Abraham, the angel of death appeared to him "as a black man, with dark hair, smelling badly, dressed in black and with fire and smoke coming from his mouth and nose."[14]

The year of the presumed death of the caid ʿAbdallah had been particularly terrible. It was a horrible year, following so many others, a year of desolation and death. People had suffered cruelly from famine; they ate what they could find, to the point of eating human flesh. Death took a large portion of the population. Cadavers lined the roads, and parents left their children, abandoning them to their fate, to flee elsewhere.

Death is synonymous with forgetting. The anonymity of cemeteries in those lands was significant. Death, ever present, struck entire families without mercy. Added to the deaths were those who vanished into nature, reappearing only in abundant tales. Entire lineages became extinct in that way. Death thus attacked the very foundations of memory.

And so what was another death in this morbid landscape, even that of a great caid? False dates of death were abundant. Often, in cases of falsification, the death was postdated. This happened at the end of the nineteenth century with the death of the sultan Hassan I, which his chamberlain kept secret for several days, giving him time to take the necessary measures, in complete calm, to install on the throne his successor, the prince ʿAbdelʿaziz.

The dates of the deaths of many agents of authority or of sultans' servants were also deliberately falsified to allow time for at least part of the

[14] Ghazâli, *Ihyâʾ ʿulûm ad-Dîn*, V, 65.

deceased's estate to escape the grasp of the central authority. The reason for this was that the goods acquired during a term of office were theoretically supposed to return to the central government, and upon the death of agents of authority, notaries were sent to their homes to perform a meticulous accounting of their estates. Thus there was always a race against the clock as soon as the authorities learned that an agent was dying. The family of the dying man in turn took great care to hide valuable property from the notaries. One can understand that in such a situation, dates of deaths played an important role. Consequently, one may question those that are mentioned in official documents.

The issue is different in this case. The caid ʿAbdallah, whose death had been announced, was still alive. While it was normal to avoid announcing a death in order to pretend someone was still alive, here it was the life that was kept quiet. Either voluntarily or involuntarily, historiography participated in this lie. It accredited the hypothetical death of the caid to his arrival before the sultan in Marrakech, despite the evidence of his "survival."

A SYMBOLIC DEATH

The news of the death was a warning in the form of a coded message. Death was a deliverance for the pious and a punishment for heretics.[15] The caid whose "true death is yet to come"[16] was no longer recognized in life except as dead. He was constantly faced with his death. He had crossed the threshold of his own death by order of the king and was annihilated as a social being. His new status as slave was established by his absence. He was his antiphenomenon, a shadow being surrounded by light.[17]

The caid's death was a theatrical death. It was a virtual production of the zone of power and the relationships that prevailed there, that must have prevailed there. Beyond the adversity, beyond the tribes and their own dialects, beyond the mountains and valleys, the authority of the king called the dissidents back to order and pronounced the executionary order of death in a language understandable to all. Henceforth no one could foster sedition without being exposed to his wrath. Unconditional

[15] Ibid., V, 42.
[16] Vladimir Jankelevitch, *La mort*, Flammarion, Paris, 32.
[17] Michel Guiomar, *Principes d'une esthétique de la mort*, 77.

submission and obedience were the rule in the closed space of the master and the slave.

The announcement regarding the caid ʿAbdallah restored order to the situation: it reminded people of the absolute power of the king. It revealed the profound nature of the relationship that the king demanded from his servants and his subjects, which could be summed up in a word: servitude. A great figure of the state had been brought back into line. His servitude was made public. His placement into the corporation of ablutions made this clear. In addition, his black skin reinforced this obvious fact, which was almost natural in a society where the huge majority of slaves were black.

He was brought back from the distant regions to the bosom of the king, installed in proximity to the king himself, where his servitude was more obvious than elsewhere. Such a status was accompanied by death, that is, by a complete effacing, by a dissolution of the servant in the service of his master. This is what the king conveyed to his entourage and his servants by the announcement of the caid's death.

The extraordinary power of the king, ratified by public opinion, in other words his power over life and death, is indeed the truth of the story of the caid ʿAbdallah. Henceforth, this edifying story reveals one aspect of the relationships of power in the Arab-Muslim world, that of the bonds that tied servants to the king.

2

The Battleground of Servitude

An Illusory Freedom

In the exercise of power, servitude was often vague in the relationships between the king and his "free" servants, who enjoyed an elevated rank in the workings of the state and the prestige that accompanied this. In the story of the caid ʿAbdallah that we have analyzed, the inclusion of a high dignitary into a corporation of palace slaves revealed the true nature of the status of "free servants." More than a punishment, it constituted a clarification of the relationship of power. An analysis of this relationship to the king will be the focus of the following chapters. But first we will examine the relationships to freedom that were maintained by statutorily servile groups during the period following the advent of Islam. What possibilities did the Muslim state offer them? Did it allow them to escape their status? In other words, what was their relationship to freedom, both in theory and in reality?

The following tale, told by the prophet Muhammad, deserves a close look:

In the Jewish marketplace, the prophet al-Khadîr, whose face radiated purity and goodness, encountered a slave who had agreed to pay his master a sum of money to be set free. To earn the money, the *mukâtab* [as the slave in question was called] was begging.

"Alms, may God bless you!" implored the slave.

"I believe in God," answered al-Khadîr, "and nothing happens unless He decrees it. I have nothing to give you."

The *mukâtab* repeated:

"Alms, may God bless you! because your face is good and I had high hopes for you."

And al-Khadîr repeated, word for word, his previous reply. The beggar did not get discouraged:

"I beg you, in God's name, give me alms."

And so the prophet bowed to him:

"I believe in God, and nothing happens unless He decrees it. I have nothing on me to give you, unless you take me by the hand and sell me."

The man asked if such a thing could really be done. The Prophet agreed. And the sale was made.[1]

What persistence the slave showed in his quest for freedom! But what difficulty in succeeding, and at what a price! Al-Khadîr was, however, the thaumaturgist prophet. This tale of his encounter with the slave under contract is highly enlightening and powerfully revealing.

In the arrival of the prophet, the slave saw the light marking the end of his dark night. The highly awaited alms would finally buy him his desired freedom. But either by coincidence or by divine decree, he encountered the prophet in the marketplace, where the implacable law of commerce imposes its diktat.

In the end, the slave was set free, but only at the price of the prophet's servitude. The problem of setting free, of the abolition of slavery, and of freedom is bluntly raised in this tale, where it is least expected. It is unveiled before the jurisconsult, pushed far back into a vague past, disguised in tales of prophets, wrapped in legends outside the articles of law.

This tale is of primary importance. More than the events of history, more than the miracles of al-Khadîr, it expresses the essence of the vision that the prophet Muhammad seemed to have of the fate of the institution of slavery in light of the constraints entailed by its status as a social organization. If we read between the lines, it tells of the impossibility of dealing with slavery in a radical way.

At the beginning of his mission, during difficult days, Muhammad maintained very close ties with many of his black companions. The notables of his people, the merchant aristocracy of the Quraysh, criticized him strongly for "surrounding himself with slaves." The tale attributed to al-Khadîr was not foreign to the experience of nascent Islam.

We will attempt to look in detail, insofar as the sources allow us, at the question of freedom in Islam as seen from the perspective of its opposite: servitude. What were the motivations for freedom in the Muslim religion? How can we pose the question of freedom in the face of an extension of slavery? Did one become truly free following the formal act of liberation?

[1] Ibn Kathîr, *Qasass al-Anbiya*, 396, and at-Tha'labi, *al-'Arâiss*, 232.

PROPERTY VERSUS THE *SÂIBA*

The prophet Sâlih's camel was an established miracle.[2] It wandered freely in the pastures of the Thamud[3] and quenched its thirst in their watering places. It was the living proof of the truth of a Messenger who had warned his recalcitrant people of the danger of any profanation concerning it, as is said in the Koran:

> Serve God, my people, for you have no god but Him. A veritable proof has come to you from your Lord. Here is God's she-camel: a sign for you. Leave her to graze at will in God's own land and do not molest her, lest a woeful scourge should take you.[4]

This camel, free to wander where it wished, could well be the ancestor of the Arab *sâiba*. But what is the *sâiba*?

In pre-Islamic society, a man who had returned from a long journey, recovered from misfortune, escaped a trial, or returned safe and sound from war showed his gratitude to the gods by taking the reins off a camel. He would then say: my camel is *sâiba*. But such a sacrifice did not depend only on the will of shepherds and on happy outcomes. A camel who gave birth to ten females in a row without any males among her offspring became a *sâiba*, that is, free to roam.

No watering hole or pasture was denied it. Regardless of the need, it could no longer be used as a mount. Only her offspring and the passing guest drank her milk, and it was to be thus until her death. A mark at the base of the animal's neck indicated its status. When it died, its youngest acquired its status; it was called the camel with the split ear (*al-baḥîra*) because its ear was split, and like its mother, it wandered freely.

There was a similar status for males, that of *al-ḥâmi*, the protector, conferred upon an established reproducer, the dispenser of abundant offspring expected to protect him.[5] The male who had sired ten females,

[2] Sâlih is one of the five Arab prophets according to a *ḥadith* that is attributed to the prophet Muhammad.

[3] A people mentioned in ancient texts and in the Koran with their prophet Sâlih, often identified with the Nabateans. Cyril Glasse, *Dictionnaire encyclopédique de l'islam*, Bordas, Paris, 1992, 392.

[4] The Koran, 7:72. See Zamakhchari, *Kachâf*, II, 115 et seq. The fragile balance between the sedentary oasis dweller and the livestock owner, between crops and herds, in a desert space where water is rare seems the key to such tales. Translator's note: English-language translations of the Koran are from *The Koran*, translated with notes by N. J. Dawood, London, Penguin, 1999.

[5] Tabari, *Tafsîr*, V, 88.

without interruption, or whose offspring had been fertile could earn that status. He then became a pure stallion who was used only for that purpose.[6] In fact, without dwelling any further on the conditions for attaining these statuses and on the multiple versions relating to them, it is above all their content and its social implications that are of interest to us.[7]

The verb *sâba* means to walk briskly. *Sayyaba* suggests the act of unfettering. From there we derive the condition of the *sâiba* animal. The word indicates not only the animal that leaves its shelter, but also everything that moves freely on the earth. Uncontained floodwaters are so named, as is the snake that slithers aimlessly. Yet everyone is aware of the dangers of a blind and impetuous river; it must be contained. Can such a precious resource be allowed to slip away, far from gardens and watering troughs, in a desert thirsty for water? As for the wandering snake, it symbolizes temptation, sin, unsubmissiveness ... These are the connotations.

Sâiba camels were sacred. As offerings to the gods, they could circulate through or outside of tribal lands without anyone stopping them.[8] They were left to their own devices on the territory usually off limits to animals, around campsites, without anyone seeking to profit from them. The servants of the sanctuaries used their milk as alms to feed passing travelers and pilgrims.

They constituted goods that the populations devoted to pious works.[9] The motives for such sacrifices are unimportant; the important point was that "people imposed restrictions on themselves in the enjoyment of their animals."[10] They deprived themselves forever in a gesture of definitive renunciation. Islam strongly denounced these practices and categorically prohibited them. The rupture with the ancient divinities partially explains the new prohibition. Concerns that were strictly linked to the restructuring of the modalities of the sacred and the rationality of a more obvious merchant logic were no doubt also a part of the prescribed measures. The sense of private property was proven in any case to be more important in Islamic society than in earlier times.

For there was only one step from the sacred to the profane. Like animals that could graze "unbridled," the slave in pre-Islamic society could achieve the status of *sâiba* if such were the will of his master. He then became a freedman who could no longer be constrained by any servitude

[6] Ibid., V, 92.

[7] Ibn Hichâm, *As-Sîra*, I, 126, henceforth *As-Sîra*.

[8] Tabari, *Tafsîr*, V, 91.

[9] *Lissân*, VI, 45.

[10] Tabari, *Tafsîr*, V, 93.

whatsoever, a free man in the full meaning of the term, who was given the title of *sâib*[11] and not *mawlâ*, the classic freedman later established by Muslim law. The *sâiba* slave constituted the highest degree of liberation that existed in the Arab world. He was in fact free, subjected neither to the *walâ'* or the right of patronage, nor to blood obligations, nor to the right of inheritance that the former master could claim on his property.[12]

This form of liberation was to be eliminated. Every freed slave was henceforth to be indebted for the *walâ'* to his former master. He remained in a situation very similar to that of a slave.

Sâiba left a deep mark on Arab political language. The word, still frequently used today, has become the equivalent of "dissidence" and "revolt." Born of a generous gesture of renunciation and sacrifice, the word has become associated with a questioning of the power of masters. The action that originated as a gift given by the master came to designate a unilateral breaking of a contract by a servant. The nature of the sacrifice, deemed illicit, transformed the gift into a revolt, no doubt to better erase its original meaning.

Within the framework of the new state, in which servitude would play a fundamental role, freedom became an indivisible privilege of the dominant groups. It was necessary henceforth to prohibit the inferior servile classes from possessing it. Thus to claim *sâiba* for a freed slave was to transgress established boundaries in the Arab-Islamic world. Freed slaves became the dependents of their former masters. This bond has been the object of strong resistance, echoes of which can be found in literature. The great black poet Bachâr protested it, maintaining that there was no *walâ'* but that which was owed to God.[13] He was executed by one of the Abbasid caliphs.[14]

Sâiba was not the only form of liberation; other less radical forms existed that enabled masters to maintain control of their freed slaves.

A PRECARIOUS LIBERATION

If Islam eliminated the status of *sâiba*, it also rejected other, less generous forms of liberation, notably the *ṭalq*, a sort of temporary or reversible liberation in which the master retained the possibility of taking back

[11] *As-Sîra*, II, 11–12, and III, 8.
[12] Tabari, *Tafsîr*, V, 88. See the section on the *mawlâ* in chapter VI, p. 121 et seq.
[13] *Aghâni*, III, 131 and 200.
[14] *Aghâni*, III, 241–244.

his former slave. *Ṭalq* presents striking similarities with repudiation, or *ṭalâq*, which constitutes a variant of it.

A repudiated woman was called *ṭâliq* or *ṭâliqa*. The word, when applied to a camel, meant the one that was sent out to pasture or the one freed of restraints and left to graze freely.[15] *Ṭalâq* thus refers to freedom; it relates to a gift, the work of an all-powerful master. The wind is thus a *ṭalîq*, that is, something freed by God, who always holds the reins.[16]

The term is used to describe camels' long walk toward watering holes. When these animals are led to a distant water source, the first night, when the members of the herd are gathered, is called *taḥwiz*.[17] Two days before reaching the water source, the animals are released; this is the day of *ṭalâq*, of releasing, when the camels are left free to wander and graze. Finally, on the last night, called the *qarab*, the thirst that has become severe is quenched by the nearby water.[18] In the end, the freedom granted to the camel is temporary. It is free only during the journey. The word designating repudiation thus relates to a passing rather than total freedom. The repudiated woman is in the same situation as the prisoner who, freed of his chains, is still confined to his cell,[19] as are those captives "who were seized without being chained."[20] *At-ṭalâq*, from which comes the word for repudiation, indicates bindings of rope or leather[21] that Arabs commonly used.[22]

This sort of liberation thus did not indicate total, complete freedom. If the condition of a captive, *al-asîr*, was initially synonymous with being bound and derives its very name from that of the chain (*isâr*), ultimately the term for a captive was used for anyone who, even unbound, was deprived of freedom of movement. And a woman, it seems, was in that condition. Thus when the Koran speaks of the servants of God who "give sustenance to the destitute, the orphan, and the captive, saying: 'We feed you for God's sake only,'"[23] it places the captive, the debtor, the prisoner, and the woman in the same category.[24]

[15] M. Ennaji, "La belle et la bête," in *L'amitié du prince*, 63.
[16] On these aspects see *Tâj al-ʿArûss*, XIII, 301–308.
[17] Al-Akhtal, 180–181.
[18] At-Tha'labi, *al-ʿArâiss*, 236.
[19] Al-Jawhari, *As-Siḥaḥ, tâju al-lugha wa siḥaḥu al-ʿarabiyya*, IV, 272, "someone is imprisoned *ṭalqan*," that is, without chains.
[20] *Diwân al-Ḥutay'a*, version of Ibn Sikkite, 270.
[21] Kûrâ', *Al-Munjid fi al-lugha*, 254. On bindings, see Ibn Durayde, *Jamharat al-lugha*, 113.
[22] *Al-ʿIqd al-farid*, I, 65, henceforth *ʿIqd*.
[23] The Koran, 76:8.
[24] Râzi, XV, Part II, 217, which Tabari does not mention, *Tafsîr*, XII, 360.

The marriage contract, which is considered to be an appropriation of the woman by the husband (*tamlik*), reinforces this point of view.[25] She is in fact given to him as a *hadiyyun*, literally an "offering" like those that were made in sanctuaries,[26] a word also used to describe a captive.[27] Calling the captive an offering is explained by the fact that the offering goes from one person to another,[28] and more precisely, that it goes from low to high, that is, from the slave who offers it to his master.[29] The sexual act, the single moment uniting a man and a woman, is at the same time an expression of the strongest division. *Al-waṭ'u*, the scholarly word favored by jurists to designate coitus, means to kill and to trample upon, which is the highest form of scorn and servility.[30] As in the servile relationship in general, the woman is there, crushed and showing no resistance. She belongs completely to the master, like the servants of the prince who exist only for him. Even the wedding ceremony, or *al-ʿurs*, refers to the violence of the initial conquest. Bedouin tribes would stop on the occasion of a wedding to put up a tent so that the union could be consummated (whence the expression for a wedding: "to build upon her," that is, to set up the tent). *Al'-ars* is the central pillar that holds up the tent. The term also refers to the act of chaining up a camel. Servitude is immediately proclaimed, for the name of the ceremony (*al'-urs*) translates, moreover, the gesture of the stallion jumping upon the female camel, bringing her down to the ground willingly or by force (*al-i'tirâss*).[31] The relationship of submission and servitude is no better expressed than by the lexicon of marriage and repudiation. The woman is brought to her knees.

Doesn't the Prophet advise believers to take care of women because they are "captives in their hands"?[32] As for his wife 'Aisha, she doesn't mince her words, speaking of marriage in harsh tones: she openly calls it "slavery," pointing out to a Muslim man that he should "choose well to whom he will give his beloved daughter as a slave."[33] The chronicle relates wives' declarations that are filled with complaints to whomever

[25] Ibn Sikkite, *Islâḥ al-Mantiq*, 254.
[26] At-Tha'âlibî 'Abdallah Ibn Muhammad, *Fiqh al-lugha wa sirru al-ʿArabiyya*, Dâr al-Jîl, Beirut, 1998, 190.
[27] Ibn Durayde, *Ichtiqâq*, 428.
[28] Râzi, IX, Part I, 74, and also VI, Part I, 102.
[29] Râzi, III, Part I, 128.
[30] *Tâj al'Arûss*, I, 278.
[31] Ibn Sida, *Kitâb al-ibil*, in *Al-Mukhassass*, II, 167.
[32] *ʿIqd*, VI, 86, also Ibn Sikkite, *Kitâb al-alfâdh*, 238, and Kûrâ', 259.
[33] *ʿIqd*, VI, 86.

will listen to them. Thus that of Asmâ' al-Achhaliyya: "We women are all prisoners and are forbidden any initiative."[34]

Repudiation was consequently only a liberation that did not open wide the doors of freedom. The repudiated woman "can be legally brought back to the slavery of marriage," specifies the jurisconsult.[35] This reversible liberation certainly influenced classic liberation in Islam: the former master kept the right of patronage over the liberated one. It greatly concerned captives, who, when they were granted freedom without a ransom, thus remained marked by their passage into captivity and the servitude that resulted from it. This was still happening at the beginning of Islam. Thus a close companion of the Prophet said to him, among other things: "I tell myself to free [*uṭliqu*] my slave."[36] To be more precise, let us say, "to let go, to liberate my slave from his chains." Those who were converted to Islam by force were part of this category. Such was the case of the Meccans called *at-ṭulaqâ'*: they were infidels conquered by force, and for this reason they could, theoretically at least, be reduced to slavery without being in a position to legally contest it. They had been conquered, had set down their weapons, and had taken refuge like women, says the chronicle. Thus they were not truly liberated and were not allowed to go wherever they wished.[37] Upon the death of ʿOthmân, the caliph ʿAli said: "There is no longer anyone but me and Moʿâwiyya, and I consider myself better suited than he [for the caliphate] because I am a companion of the Prophet at Medina whereas he is a Bedouin; I am a cousin and son-in-law of the Prophet whereas he is a *ṭalîq*, the son of a *ṭâliq*," that is, a dependent not completely free and thus not qualified to reign.[38] He then wrote to Moʿâwiyya telling him that "he was among the precarious liberated ones who did not have a right to the caliphate."[39]

Far from the presuppositions of the prevailing ideological discourse in Islam on the equality of people and particularly of believers in business matters, the reexamined history of the formation of the Muslim state sufficiently shows that freedom was a crucial aspect of social legitimacy and a strategic weapon in the conquest of power. The question is to what extent freed slaves, theoretically liberated, in fact benefited from freedom and enjoyed its advantages. Granted, the problem is fundamentally

[34] *Tâj al-ʿArûss*, VII, 393.
[35] Râzi, XVI, Part II, 143.
[36] Râzi, VII, Part II, 52.
[37] Râzi, XVI, Part II, 143.
[38] *ʿIqd*, IV, 280.
[39] *ʿIqd*, IV, 306.

a question of the social evolution of freedmen, but it is appropriate, first, to review the measures established by public authorities with the intent to uphold the initiatives of liberation.

ISLAM, PUBLIC TREASURY, AND EMANCIPATION

What policy did the nascent Muslim state adopt with regard to the liberation of slaves? What means did it employ to that end? The Koran is explicit regarding the distribution of public funds:

> Alms shall be only for the poor and the destitute, for those that are engaged in the management of alms and those whose hearts are sympathetic to the Faith, for the freeing of slaves[40] and debtors, for the advancement of God's cause, and for the traveller in need. That is a duty enjoined by God. God is all-knowing and wise.[41]

First came the poor, who were not completely penniless but could play a role notably in war; then came the needy who held out their hand to passersby. Then there were the tax agents and "those from whom one hoped for favors." This latter group was that of chiefs of Arab tribes, and powerful Jews and Christians whom the Prophet handled by giving them gifts.[42] Assistance for emancipation came after these categories. The expense in question was normally to be allocated, according to most authors, to contractual freedmen, to complete the sum necessary for buying their freedom. It was a sort of fund for assistance toward liberation.

More than inciting believers to liberate their slaves, it served above all to solidify a liberation procedure that was already being used. Thus it did not include any measure that would undermine the institution of slavery. Moreover, why earmark considerable funds for such a purpose? What were the reasons for such a choice? What strategic interest did it represent when the concern for connecting with the dominant groups appeared to be so important?

And first, how can we explain the place of liberation in the apparent order of the wording of the verse? The question of priority has

[40] Translator's note: "Freeing of slaves" is given in the French edition of this book as "*l'affranchissement des nuques*" (literally, "the liberation of necks"). The author makes the following note on the French-language translation of the Koran: "The translation … (with the revision by Sobhi Elsaleh) is here 'buying back captives [*rachat des captives*],' which is inexact because they were not the only ones concerned. Masson translated it as 'liberation from the yokes [*l'affranchissement des jougs*],' but I prefer translating *raqaba* as 'necks' [*nuques*] in order to remain in the Arabic context."

[41] The Koran, 9:60.

[42] This practice was abandoned by Abû Bakr; Tabari, *Tafsîr*, VI, 400.

been discussed by jurisconsults on the basis of technical criteria. Thus Zamakhchari, basing his theory on linguistic considerations, favors the last four categories, that is, slaves to be freed, travelers, the mujahideen, and pilgrims in difficulty. But his argument seems weak, for according to other jurisconsults, his criteria do not establish a hierarchical order but take into account only the differences between the categories. The first, in fact, consisted of people who themselves collected the sums intended for them, whereas for others, the money was spent for their benefit without them taking care of it themselves.[43]

A fundamental debate sheds light on this and enables us to measure the importance attributed to the extension of freedom. The canonical tax (*zakât*) was instituted with the goal of reaching two objectives: to help Muslims in difficulty on the one hand, and on the other, to spread and establish Islam. The latter, primordial goal required giving to the poor and to the rich according to the needs of the moment, with the important thing being not the one or the other, but the interest of the religion.[44] Nothing then expresses a will to expand emancipation. Ibn ʿAbbâss, cousin of the Prophet and one of the most frequently cited Muslim authorities, did not enthusiastically endorse the allocation of legal alms for the freeing of slaves. "There is nothing bad," he said, "in liberating by dipping into the funds of the *zakât*."[45] In this regard, Tabari is more explicit:

> God made legal alms an obligatory duty for the one on whom He imposed it, and who pays it from his funds without expecting a benefit on earth as compensation. Now, the one who frees a slave using legal alms in turn earns the patronage, *walâ'*, over the liberated one, and he will have then derived profit from his alms.[46]

Such a result logically casts doubt on the value of an act of charity that is supposed to be pious and disinterested!

In fact, the hierarchy of priorities shows how little the authorities were interested in freeing slaves. In this order from the Koran, the priority goes first to one's family, then to Muslims without resources or support:

> Righteousness does not consist in whether you face towards the East or the West. The righteous man is he who believes in God and the Last Day, in the angels and

[43] *Kachâf*, II, 273–274. Ibn ʿAbbâss, the orthodox caliphs, and the companions of the Prophet gave priority to the poor. The imam Châfiʿî considered the eight categories to be equal.

[44] Tabari, *Tafsîr*, VI, 401,

[45] Ibid.

[46] Ibid.

the Book and the prophets; who, though he loves it dearly, gives away his wealth to kinsfolk, to orphans, to the destitute, to the traveller in need and to beggars, and for the redemption of captives.[47]

Each society indeed has its priorities; the all-powerful God, Râzi comments, favored the close family, then orphans, and finally the needy. And this was because the great affliction caused by the privation of children of food and drink is more intense than that provoked by an adult's inability to meet these needs. As for the traveler in difficulty, he could be rich while pretending to be in great need. "He put the contractual slave last because the abolition [*izâla*] of slavery is not on the order of the greatest need."[48] This statement requires no commentary.

As for his own slaves, the master was not allowed to give them a share of his *zakât*, no more than he was allowed to give it to his father, his mother, or his children.[49] Considered to be members of the family and thereby deprived of the right to the *zakât* of the master, the slaves nonetheless became foreigners as soon as the question of inheritance was raised.

Regarding the use of public funds, not only were the public authorities unconcerned with enlarging the scope of freedom, but it is important to stress that they hardly took freed slaves into account in the redistribution of wealth. Freed slaves were ignored. They did not draw from the register of public expenses (*diwân*). They were once again considered to still belong to their former master's household. Such a position, in limbo between two places, compromised their interests and in the end managed to exclude them. The register of expenses included the Banû Hâchem – a Meccan clan to which the prophet Muhammad and his cousin and son-in-law, the caliph ʿAli, belonged – and then their family, followed by the first faithful. Without dwelling on the order of priority in the allocation of the canonical tax, if we look closely at the acts of goodwill that the Muslim was required to perform, slaves were scarcely better off. The compassion of the wealthy person, like that of one who is less well off, must be extended toward his family and, among them, first, the poor and the traveler in difficulty.[50] "Your alms for the needy," says the prophetic tradition, "are [simple] alms, whereas those intended for a family member count doubly, for they are at the same time alms and a renewal of ties

[47] The Koran, 2:177.
[48] Râzi, III, Part I, 36.
[49] Râzi, XVI, Part I, 44.
[50] The Koran, 30:38.

of blood."[51] In some verses bearing on charity, slaves are not mentioned.[52] And, in any case, the position they occupied did not procure them a revenue that would put them in a position to envision being freed.

> Serve God and associate none with Him. Show kindness to parents and kindred, to orphans and to the destitute, to near and distant neighbours,[53] to those that keep company with you, to the traveller in need, and to the slaves you own.[54]

The slave thus comes after the preceding categories.[55] Support for free people seemed to be more important than that for the servile classes. The rank assigned to the related neighbor, to the foreign neighbor (in other words, belonging to another religion, according to some commentaries), and finally to the traveler in difficulty illustrates the lack of eagerness to come to the aid of a slave. In the verse cited above, one could not even argue for his belonging to the family, since the family comes first. Such logic suggests that the servile classes were considered to be very well exactly where they were. It could only increase the disparities between free men, slaves, and freed slaves.

THE NEW HEIRS

According to the chronicle, women and children did not have the right to an inheritance during the pre-Islamic period. Only the adult male line, that of warriors, inherited[56]: "Only he who has fought with his spear, defended his land and taken spoils will inherit from his kin."[57] Furthermore, people had the right to make a testament, that is, to bequeath a portion of their goods to whomever they chose.[58]

Islam challenged such practices. It abhorred the "horizontal" distribution of property, and thus of power and influence. As the founder of the state, it was the natural ally of the family. Close relatives were favored, not only for inheritance but also for benefits of all sorts. Wealth and

51 *Kachâf*, I, 217.

52 "They will ask you about almsgiving. Say: 'Whatever you bestow in charity must go to parents and to kinsfolk, to the orphans and to the destitute and to the traveller in need.'" The Koran, 2:215, and also 30:38.

53 Related, according to some, through blood or religion. *Ibn al-sabîl* is the distressed traveler, or the guest. *Kachâf*, I, 217; Râzi, XIII, Part I, 109; Tabari, *Tafsîr*, VI, 396.

54 The Koran, 4:36.

55 Tabari, *Tafsîr*, IV, 80–87.

56 Tabari, *Tafsîr*, III, 616, and Râzi, V, Part I, 158.

57 Râzi, V, Part I, 158.

58 Tabari, *Tafsîr*, V, 106.

its advantages henceforth circulated vertically. In this hierarchy, relatives were located just after God, and kin of the male lineage came first.[59]

This implied a closing up of the immediate family, which became the legal and exclusive heritors to the exclusion of more distant members of the lineage. This exclusion occurred in stages, with a reduction of rights and customary advantages granted to the extended family, to clients, and to freed slaves, who saw theirs diminished little by little as ties of dependency were defined more strictly.

At the advent of Islam, inheritance was based on kinship and on pacts of alliance, which included two variants: alliance under oath (*al-ḥilf*[60]) and adoption. Initially the foundations of inheritance were not questioned. On the contrary, Islam strengthened them and even added to them. Thus, the unbreakable ties that connected the close followers of the Prophet made them each other's heirs, to the detriment of relatives, and faith, in the context of exile, cemented these ties. In addition, fraternization, the pact that the Prophet himself sought to establish between followers, was a reason for inheritance. One may imagine that such measures, which would subsequently prove to be temporary, truly benefited refugees of low extraction, in that they opened unexpected avenues of social promotion for them. A number of freed slaves, especially those close to the Prophet, enjoyed them before the question of inheritance was settled once and for all to the benefit of the family circle: "according to the Book of God those who are bound by ties of blood are nearest to one another. God has knowledge of all things."[61] Here we see a decisive change in Islam's attitude toward slavery. Almost extreme on several levels at the beginning, through the militant practice of recruitment by the Prophet and the spirit of a minority and necessarily close-knit community of believers operating outside the pressure of the dominant society, if not against it, Islam subsequently endured the constraints of the social game and adapted to them.

The new measures put tighter social relationships into place and seriously slowed the mobility that the increased wealth of the empire could have permitted. Those who did not belong to the powerful lineages had more difficulty succeeding and climbing the social ladder. The contesting of agreed-upon donations outside the family circle, justified by alliances or through other contractual relationships that up until then were

[59] Râzi, III, Part II, 22.
[60] The ally inherited a sixth. Râzi, V, Part II, 69.
[61] The Koran, 8:75.

common, was a rude blow to freed slaves and the emancipation of slaves in general. Three social bonds conferred the right to inherit: kinship, marriage, and *wala'* (the relationship between the master and his freed slave). Thus the master inherited from his freed former slave without the latter benefiting from the same opportunity in return.[62]

In order to avoid an abrupt elimination of the former practices, which carried the risk of rupturing clan-based bonds of solidarity, which were always useful, it was recommended that the division of inheritance be performed so as to include former allies, dependents, and noninheriting relatives: "If relatives, orphans, or needy men are present at the division of an inheritance, give them, too, a share of it, and speak kind words to them."[63] Small objects and food were thus offered to overcome the grievances of those concerned, whether they were notables or the needy. Records indicate, however, that the change was not easy. Accounts from the period report situations in which those excluded from inheritance still had access at least to the division of money, of metallic coins.[64]

Contrary to the prevailing discourse and to beliefs that are still very strong today, to give to the poor at the expense of threatening the familial patrimony or to liberate at the approach of death was not seen as a praiseworthy gesture: "Let those who are solicitous about the welfare of their young children after their own death take care not to wrong orphans. Let them fear God and speak for justice."[65] The believer had the sacred duty to think of his own. He was not to give in to the remorse that assailed man at the end of his life and inclined him to give abundant alms. He was not to say to a dying man: "Give your goods as alms, liberate and give for the love of God."[66] On the contrary, duty called upon the Muslim to clearly mention what he possessed and to bequeath only to the benefit of close relatives who did not have the right to inherit.[67]

Thus, there was no question at the moment of extreme unction of bequeathing one's goods as charity might command! The will of the dying encountered legal limits in this domain. A man might have freed the six slaves that he possessed and that constituted his only fortune. The Prophet decided otherwise in the name of the law. After drawing lots,

[62] The master, if he had liberated his slave himself, or the one who had freed the slave from slavery. Râzi, V, Part II, 70, and Part I, 165 and 169.

[63] The Koran, 4:8.

[64] *Kachâf*, I, 467.

[65] The Koran, 4:9.

[66] Tabari, *Tafsîr*, III, 612.

[67] Ibid.

two of them were confirmed in their new status as freed men and the four others were returned to slavery, as the master was not legally free to bequeath more than a third of his goods.[68]

Post mortem, or *tadbîr*, freeing of slaves, scarcely mentioned in the literature, took a hit from this. This type of liberation already had weak credibility. It was considered by its very nature to be an unstable pact, one in which the benefiting party could have little confidence.[69]

Legislation on inheritance eroded both the freeing of slaves and the rights formerly held by the freed. The freed slave was *mawlâ* (pl. *mawâli*). He shared this title with many others, including his master. This similarity induced by a misleading proximity concerning the content and implications of the respective statuses was in a certain sense a chimera maintained by the language. The term conveys a strong relational proximity arising from kinship, alliance, submission, and authority, which hid the respective positions of each of the parties. But the fiction does not eliminate the issue. One may, in fact, justifiably ask what these different statuses under the same name had in common. Equal proximity should normally entail an equal right to inheritance.

Some scholars went in this direction and maintained the right of the freed to inherit from their former master. Contrary to popular opinion, such a version exists, drawing its argument from a verse in the Koran: "To every parent and kinsman We have appointed heirs [*mawâli*] who will inherit from them. As for those with whom you have entered into agreements, let them, too, have their share. Surely God bears witness to all things."[70] We see an echo of this in a tale by Ibn ʿAbbâss, according to which the Prophet granted inheritance to a freed slave whose former master had left no heirs. What better proof of his rights! Not so, argued the jurisconsults, who explained that this inheritance should go to the Muslim community: the Prophet, in this case, had only drawn from the public treasury to come to the aid of an unfortunate.[71] The social reality and the will of the dominant groups, the latter apparently proving to be very attentive to the yield of the law, thus won out over the earlier egalitarian yearnings.

Thus there was a true marginalization of freed slaves by the fact that they were deprived of the dividends resulting from the expansion of the

[68] *Lissân*, X, 234. For the jurisconsults each of the slaves should normally be freed in proportion to a third of his value.

[69] Or *walth*; *Tâj al-ʿArûss*, III, 279.

[70] The Koran, 4:33.

[71] Râzi, *Tafsîr*, V, Part II, 70.

empire. By consigning them to the lowest rung of the social ladder and denying them the fruits of conquest and access to the means of production, such a measure could only weaken the ability of freed slaves to increase their social standing. Freed slaves were also kept at a distance from the society of free people: it was in fact frowned upon and openly discouraged to enter into marriage with freed slaves, in order to preserve their status, to keep them "pure" in their servitude.

SLAVE WOMAN, FREE MAN – A DISPARAGED UNION

A certain ʿAbdallah Ibn Rawâha introduced himself to the Prophet. He owned a black slave woman whom, in anger, he had slapped. Contrite, he told this to the Messenger of God, who asked him: "What is she, ʿAbdallah?" To which the latter replied: "Oh, Envoy of God, she fasts, prays, does her ablutions perfectly and recognizes that there is no God but Allah and that you are His Envoy." And the Prophet exclaimed: "She is a believer!" This convinced the man to free her and take her as his wife. But this action subsequently earned him the unanimous reprobation of his fellow Muslims.[72]

This is because marriages with women – or men – who were slaves or of servile origin were not approved. However, marriage between female slaves and free men was one of the means of emancipation.[73] But the master who took a wife from among his slaves was mocked. The disapproval of such unions, furthermore, enclosed the freed slaves, especially black ones, into social ghettos, thereby reinforcing the hold of their former masters upon them. Whereas parents and guardians were obligated to see to the marriages of free men and women of marriageable age, it was simply suggested, that the same be done for slaves. To marry off a male slave, given that the master was required by the arrangement to feed him, could only diminish his returns. The marriage of a female slave, in spite of the dowry given to the master in that case, was in no way obligatory.[74]

Countless reasons discouraged potential candidates from such unions. First among such considerations was the inherent instability of marriages with slave women. If her master decided to put her up for sale, the contract would be compromised to the point of necessitating a forced divorce.[75]

[72] Tabari, *Tafsîr*, II, 391.

[73] Not only because the slave mother was freed, but according to Châfiʿî the marriage of a slave with an Arab did not produce slave children. Ibn Kathîr, *Tafsîr*, I, 624.

[74] Râzi, XII, Part I, 186.

[75] Tabari, *Tafsîr*, V, 9.

The master could intervene in situations over which the couple had no control. Thus, a certain jurisconsult, though his opinion was not unanimously held, cited six forms of divorce for the slave woman, including sale, liberation, and gift.[76] Thus such a marriage was not advised. Among free people, only the poorest could resign himself to it, and even then, he was like a starving person being forced to eat the flesh of a cadaver.[77] Wisdom dictated abstaining from it: "but if you abstain, it will be better for you. God is forgiving and merciful."[78]

A free wife was obviously the ideal. She and those like her were better protected, through their freedom, from the conduct that female slaves adopted. They were entirely made for marriage, the goal of which was to have children. The goal of keeping a concubine, on the other hand, was purely for pleasure, which explains the fact that one could get rid of a concubine when one so desired, which was not the case with a free wife.[79] It is clear, in fact, from an exegetical perspective, that slave women were known for constantly entering and leaving (*kharrâja wallâja*[80]), and for being repugnant and of careless appearance. The free woman, however, was preserved from these faults; she was surrounded, protected, and veiled.[81] In good society, the slave was modeled after the girl of the street, immodestly associating with men and shamelessly participating in prostitution.[82] The slave was synonymous with *baghiya*, or a woman with a bad life; when people called out to her children in the street, they were reminded of that title. Despite the discourse on equality, in the dominant opinion, the one that held sway in everyday life, a union with a slave woman came close to adultery.

This burden that was placed upon the servile class worked against its social advancement and its liberation. The bestowing of freedom was meant to reward, above all, slaves of irreproachable morality. But the female slave was considered intrinsically bad, incapable of facing her duties and unworthy of confidence.[83] As a woman, and a slave on top of

[76] Tabari, *Tafsîr*, IV, 9. On the question of sale and its discussion through the case of a freed slave (by the name of Barira) by 'Aisha, the wife of the Prophet, who was given the choice between divorce or remaining with her husband. Tabari, IV, 9.

[77] Tabari, *Tafsîr*, IV, 18.

[78] The Koran, 4:25.

[79] *Kachâf*, I, 459.

[80] The expression also means "wily" if not "treacherous." J. B. Belot, *Vocabulaire Arabe-Français*, Beirut, 1899, 958.

[81] Râzi, V, Part II, 46.

[82] Râzi, V, Part II, 48.

[83] Râzi, VI, Part I, 12.

that, who could be bought and sold like merchandise, she represented a lack of judgment: "Because she combines these two qualities, she is considered not to belong to the class of rational beings."[84]

Such words created a dividing line between free people and people of the servile condition. A dominant class in the process of forming and establishing itself looks after its interests and its property, including its slaves and dependents. Thus there was to be no confusion resulting from the proximity and intimacy that slavery imposed between masters and servants: this intimacy was not to entail a conversion to kinship alliances. The similarities between these bonds were praised; however, they did not have any positive effect for the slaves or freed slaves. The denunciation of unions with blacks no doubt conveyed the concern with maintaining intact the breeding ground of servitude. The line of demarcation was in fact clearly drawn, even apart from the question of unions. The act of freeing a slave and the deeper meaning of this act were not forebears of true freedom.

TO SET FREE: THE *RAQABA* IN QUESTION

ʿItq raqaba, taḥrir raqaba, or *fak raqaba* – these are the expressions most commonly used to designate the act of freeing a slave. Literally, they mean to save a neck, to free it. *Raqaba* is a term that designates the nape of the neck, the lower part of the neck. The word is borrowed from the lexicon of observation, of watching, of surveillance. This body part is located on the upper section of the body, similar to the height at which a sentinel stands. For this same reason one says: God has freed the nape of his neck, as if it could oversee the punishment it observes. The woman who powerlessly witnesses the agony of her dying children is called *raqoube*.[85]

But just as one word hides another, the *raqaba* recalls *al-riqb*, the rope that is put around the neck of an animal, just as it recalls *al-qabr*, which signifies a grave.[86] The word also designates the preferred place where the warrior should strike his blow: "When you meet the unbelievers in the battlefield strike off their heads and, when you have laid them low, bind your captives firmly."[87]

84 Râzi, XII, Part I, 71.
85 Râzi, VIII, Part I, 132.
86 Ibn Durayde, *Kitâb jambarat al-lugha*, I, 323.
87 The Koran, 47:4. Translator's note: The translation of the Koran used in the French-language edition of this book has "frappez-les à la nuque" (literally, "strike them in the neck") here.

More concretely, the liberation of the neck first designated the freeing of the captive before it acquired the general meaning of emancipation. Indeed Arabs dealt with the captive by tying his hands to his neck with a leather cord, a rope, or some other material. When the term was broadened, one spoke of liberating the hands from the neck.[88] *Fak raqaba*, to free the neck, means to undo the knot that ties the hands of the prisoner to his neck. Finally, the neck came to designate the person himself.[89]

In the language of freeing slaves, one spoke of *ʿitq* (or *fak*) *raqaba* and also *ʿitq nasama*. The first term seems to mean the complete liberation of a slave, whereas the second designated paying a portion of the total price of a sale in which other associated masters participated.[90] Râzi suggests that it is possible that *fak raqaba* refers only to the fact of saving one's soul from the flames of hell by devoting oneself to worship, for that is indeed "true freedom."[91] This leaves a number of unanswered questions regarding recommendations for freeing slaves. To take these into account, let us examine a few types of contracts for emancipation in order to assess the incentives put into place before questioning the degree of liberty granted to the one freed.

THE CONTRACTUAL FREEDMAN

While Abû Mûsa al-Achʿari was delivering his Friday sermon, a man in the assembly stood up and spoke to him out loud: "O Emir, make people help me!" Friday is the day of assembly for Muslims and a day of great piety. The man in question was a contractual freedman, a *mukâtab* who lacked the resources to earn his freedom.[92] This recalls the tale of al-Khadîr in which the Prophet, speaking initially of *mukâtab*, then used the word "beggar" to describe the same man, the same status. Does this mean that for slaves wishing to buy their freedom, begging was often their only recourse to obtain the money?

Al-kitâba means writing, recording. The word designates the written act of contractual emancipation.[93] The *mukâtaba*, which designates

[88] Tabari, *Tafsîr*, V, 28.

[89] Ibn al-Athîr in *Lissân*, I, 428.

[90] Râzi, XII, Part I, 190. At birth the child is *nasama*, as soon as he rolls onto his stomach he is *raqaba*, and at the age of prayer he is *mûmina* (a believer); Tabari, *Tafsîr*, V, 29.

[91] Râzi, XVI, Part I, 168.

[92] Tabari, *Tafsîr*, VI, 401. On the question of whether aid should come from the master or from the Treasury of the Muslims, see IX, 312–318.

[93] *Lissân*, I, 700.

the same contract, is literally the exchange of writings. The master and the slave both agreed in writing. The master: "I engage myself in writing toward you that you will be free at the end of the payment of the agreed-upon amount and you have engaged yourself in writing to me to pay that." One notes that the benefit of the action goes to the master: he is the agent whereas the slave is passive.[94] Obviously, it is not the initiative of action that is at issue here, but the master's right of property, the master remaining, in any event, the benefactor dispensing freedom. But it is possible that the origin of the name, still in the same spirit, is the obligation of a written contract, the slave not being in a position to pay his obligation immediately since he did not have his own property. It is also possible that the origin is the term *al-katb*, that is, the fact of tying, of holding tight, bonding one tightly to the other, as the master and the contractually freed slave were bound by the sums to be paid as provided for in the contract.[95]

In practice, the two parties agreed on a specified number of terms for the payment, at least two, according to the dominant tradition. The caliph ʿOthmân, furious at a slave who wanted a contract, yelled at him: "I will be extremely tough on you. I will contract with you for your freedom with a payment in two terms."[96] The agreement could also include a specified task to carry out, for example a well to dig or a building to construct. It even happened that the slave under contract would provide another slave to his master in exchange for his liberation. In any case, the *wala'* (right of patronage) belonged to the master by reason of his compassion and the favor granted to his servant.[97]

As long as the amount fixed was not paid in full, freedom was not acquired: "The contractual slave remained a slave as long as he owed even a dirham" to whomever it was due.[98] The duration of the agreement granted the slave a sort of reprieve. Through it he acquired an economic autonomy that made him a master of his income and that authorized him to receive legal alms, prohibited to slaves, from his owner. During this period of temporary reprieve, the master theoretically did not have the right, for example, to sleep with a female slave benefiting from such a contract, and more generally to use her as he wished.[99]

94 Ibid.
95 Râzi, XII, Part I, 188. Only Abû Hanifa admits the possibility of immediate one-time payment.
96 Râzi, XII, Part I, 188.
97 *Kachâf*, II, 232.
98 Râzi, XII, Part I, 191.
99 Râzi, XII, Part I, 189.

Was such a contract of liberation an action that God imposed on the believer? The sacred text seems not to call for a charitable act but to order it: "As for those of your slaves who wish to buy their liberty, free them if you find in them any promise and bestow on them a part of the riches which God has given you."[100] The majority of commentators maintain, however, that it was only a question of incentive. All have supported the prophetic tradition according to which "the property of a Muslim is licit only if he agrees [to give it up] willingly."[101] Since nothing obligated a master to give his slave to someone else who was disposed to free him, nothing forced the master, either, to agree to a slave's request to buy his freedom. The slave was passive; the terminology leaves no doubt about that.

The master was not obliged to grant a discount to his contractual slave. The *kitâba* was a contract of exchange in which equivalence was the rule (*mu'âwada*); it was not a contract of sale, although some considered it a contract of buying back.[102] It is highly plausible that in the beginning it was presented, due to a lack of monetary currency, as a pure exchange of services. All things considered, the formula of a contract of sale would have rendered the master's right of patronage problematic. Further, the ability of contractual slaves to earn their living and the need for them to prove their honesty made them complete partners. Thus the Koranic prescription to "give to them" means rather "lend to them"; at least that is what Abû Hanifa suggests. Others believe that it concerns the aid to be provided them after they were freed.[103] We saw, when we examined the canonical tax, that this aid remained a pure vision; it was never applied to slaves. From these considerations arises a great fragility of the contractual liberation agreement, which had little chance of being expanded. How could emancipation have become a significant tendency in that period? These two points are not the only ones to darken the perspectives for the extinction of slavery.

A FREED MAN VERSUS A FRIVOLOUS OATH!

It happened, in fact, that an individual might give an oath in haste and later regret his action. Freeing a slave was one of the means by which he could absolve himself of such betrayal.

[100] The Koran, 24:33.
[101] Râzi, XII, Part I, 189.
[102] *Lissân*, I, 698 et seq.
[103] Râzi, XII, Part I, 233.

God will not punish you for that which is inadvertent in your oaths. But He will take you to task over the oaths which you solemnly swear. The penalty for a broken oath is the feeding of ten needy men with such food as you normally offer to your own people; or the clothing of ten needy men; or the freeing of a slave. He that cannot afford any of these must fast three days.[104]

The emancipation was to involve, in this case, a slave who was physically able, in a position to earn a living, and mentally stable. The repented betrayer nevertheless had the choice between three options: to feed ten poor people his usual food,[105] to clothe them, or to free a slave. Whoever lacked the means to feed his own for a day and the following night had the possibility of fasting for three days. Apart from the latter case, the first three options were equivalent for Muslims.[106]

This equivalence seemed to make to distinction between rich and poor. The affluent notable was not obliged to free a slave in order to expiate a frivolous oath. No explicit injunction or even any incentive leaned in the direction of prioritizing emancipation. Tabari emphasizes that "all the scholars of the great cities, the ancients and the moderns among them, agree in maintaining that expiation by other means than emancipation was completely justified for the rich."[107] One can henceforth legitimately doubt a preference by betrayers for emancipation. Râzi is explicit on this subject:

Being the easiest and the most available means, food came first. That was linked to the will to draw attention to the fact that the All-Powerful was concerned with easing and facilitating for believers that which was part of their obligations. And finally, food was preferable because the free poor person might lack it without being able to find someone to come to his aid, which could not fail to be harmful to him. As for the slave, his master was obligated to feed and clothe him.[108]

This is yet more proof that freedom was not a primary objective in Muslim society at the time. People were concerned with free people more than with freedom; they were preoccupied with consolidating their dominant social position. This preoccupation was coupled with a severe and systematic marking of the servile statuses, or those recognized as such.

104 The Koran, 5:89.

105 Not the worst nor the most refined food. The best meal advised under the circumstances was bread, meat, and sauce, or bread mixed with butter or dates. Tabari, *Tafsîr*, V, 18–19; Râzi, VI, Part II, 64.

106 Tabari, *Tafsîr*, V, 29–30.

107 Tabari, *Tafsîr*, V, 30.

108 Râzi, VI, Part II, 65.

However, these categories continued to play a growing role with the expansion of the Muslim empire. How did the profits resulting from its expansion affect their status? To what degree did the gains generated by the empire favor the expansion of the realm of freedom? In what way were the spoils of war put to use in this direction?

THE PORTION OF SPOILS DEVOTED TO FREEING SLAVES

If the public treasury was not overly concerned with freeing slaves, if the sums generously earmarked as alms and compassion were not destined for the enlargement of the realm of freedom, what happened to the spoils of the Muslims' wars? Different versions agree on the absence of special funds earmarked for the liberation of slaves.

Spoils of war were divided into five equal parts. Four of them went to those who fought for the faith. The remaining fifth was then divided into four parts: "one fourth went to God, to His Envoy and his family ... the next fourth went to orphans, the third to the poor, and the last to travelers needing assistance."[109]

The caliph Abû Bakr took away the share going to the Banû Hâchem or the clan of the Prophet, reminding them: "Let us give to the poor one among you, let those who are still single among you be married, and let those among you who have no servant be served."[110] Which in truth did not promise to reduce the number of slaves!

In any event, the inferior classes – the slaves, workers, and poor artisans who followed the army into a campaign and ran all the risks – did not participate in the division of the spoils.[111] Far from supplying any sort of fund to free slaves, the spoils of war became a sure means of developing slavery. Since the divine message encouraged the enjoyment of unforbidden things, the realm of slavery could only grow. Beautiful captive women seduced the warriors of the faith. This phrase addressed to them is attributed to the Prophet: "Go to war; you will have as your spoils the girls of the Blond," an allusion to the beautiful Byzantine women.[112]

As for the thorny question of captives, it did not fail to cause problems. Before Muhammad, prophets did not have the right to them, according to the chronicle.[113] If the expansion of Islam was the main objective, why

[109] Tabari, *Tafsîr*, VI, 250; see also the Koran, 8:41.
[110] *Kachâf*, II, 215.
[111] *Lissân*, XII, 446.
[112] Tabari, *Tafsîr*, VI, 387.
[113] Tabari, *Tafsîr*, V, 289 and 291, and Deuteronomy 12:13–18 and 20:10–14.

be burdened with infidel captives? The taking of captives as spoils had its supporters but also its detractors, including the caliph 'Omar, at the time a companion of the Prophet, who planned to cut the throats of any captive he found on his way. Speaking to the Prophet, he said:

> Oh, Envoy of God, what do we have to do with these spoils? We are men fighting for the religion of God so that God will be obeyed!

And the Prophet replied:

> If we had been punished for that, no one else's life would have been saved except yours.[114]

The logic of a pure and disinterested jihad thus did not leave people indifferent. Voices other than that of 'Omar were heard.[115] The concern shown at the outcome of the battle of Badr as to the fate of the captives is indicative of a certain confusion. The text of the Koran instructing the Prophet is sufficiently eloquent: "A prophet may not take captives until he has fought and triumphed in the land. You seek the chance gain of this world, but God desires for you the world to come. God is mighty and wise. Had there not been a previous writ from God, you would have been sternly punished for what you took."[116] However, the ascent of the dominant groups and the concern with forming a state apparatus surpassed such considerations. Koranic legitimacy seemed to have calmed the tensions. One had simply to distinguish between good captivity (in enemy territory, that of the *ahl al-ḥarb*) and bad, which could involve Arabs.[117] Wars of conquest were, in such a context, to increase the number of slaves.

In spite of the reluctance to allocate public or private funds for freeing slaves, what was the life of a freed slave like? What true perspectives of freedom were offered to him? And what did it mean to be free at that time?

THE FREEDMAN, THE PURE, AND THE IMPURE

What does the word for free, *al-ḥurr*, refer to? Did the freed slave really achieve such a status? *Ḥarra*, a verb designating the action of becoming

[114] Tabari, *Tafsîr*, V, 291.

[115] The Prophet is said to have given a similar response to Sa'd Ibn Mu'âd, Tabari, *Tafsîr*, VI, 291; on the same question see also XI, 307–308.

[116] The Koran, 8:67.

[117] *Kachâf*, II, 324.

free, covers two different realities: one bearing on true liberty, or *ḥurriya*, that of the individual not suspected of servile origins; the other, expressed by the derivative *al-ḥarâr*, is that of the freed slave.[118] The collective memory was very careful to keep these distinctions in the public mind.

Following the word "freedom" in the context of the time, one becomes aware of its complexity and of how different it was from the concept that modern societies have of it. *Al-muḥarrar*, literally the liberated, named the freed one. The same word is used in the Koran to designate, in the practices of Judaism, a person devoted to prayer and in the service of a synagogue, freed of all earthly servitude – this is the *nadhr*, a wish that parents addressed to the divinities to put their children in their service, and to which the Virgin Mary was subjected.[119] She said: "Lord, I dedicate to Your service that which is in my womb. Accept it from me. You alone hear all and know all."[120] These children were a sort of pious work, a renunciation for the benefit of the religious institution. When they came of age, the children concerned had the choice of rejoining the world or remaining in their function. *Muḥarrar* (liberated) here is far from the concept of freedom in and of itself; the freedom is relative to the servitude dictated by duty toward ones' parents.[121]

Ḥarrara designates the cleaning up of a text, the operation that consists of correcting it, purging it so that no error remains, cleansing it so that it becomes pure. Freedom is thus that purity. *Ḥurr* clay is that which contains no grains of sand or stone, no black mud or any other impurity. Thus the free man is the purely free "who is entirely for himself and who is dependent on no one."[122]

Purity is the essential point of the notion of freedom. No spot or vice is allowed in such a situation. The adjective that gives consistency and reality to freedom is *khâliss*, that is, pure – and, by chance, also white. Cleaned, purified writing becomes a *mubiadda*, a document the obvious whiteness of which proves that is no longer subject to doubt.

Does this mean that the freed slave was not pure? Granted, emancipation carried out within the rules of the game granted access to a new status that was meant to be that of a free man. The Koran, evoking this transformation, uses the expression *taḥrir raqaba* five times,[123] *fak raqaba*

118 *Lissân*, IV, 177–185.
119 On *nadhr*, A. de Biberstein Kazimirsky, *Dictionnaire Arabe-Français*, II, 1231–1232.
120 The Koran, 3:35.
121 *Kachâf*, II, 349.
122 Râzi, IV, Part II, 23.
123 The Koran, 4:92, 5:89, 58:3.

once,[124] and *riqâb*,[125] the plural of *raqaba*, three times. These expressions show that it thus favored the technical aspect of the freeing of a captive rid of his chains. A precarious emancipation rather than true freedom! The word *taḥrir*, the one most commonly used, refers to the state of *ḥarâr*, not to *ḥurriya* or freedom clearly differentiating the free man from the freed man! The Arabs of the time "did not [really] free their *muḥarrar*."[126]

This is a remarkable lexical precaution! Nowhere does the Koranic text speak of *ʿitq* on this subject. It reserves this adjective for the house of God, the *Kaʾba*, called *al-bayt al-ʿatîq*,[127] which can be translated as "ancient house," but this is only one of the accepted meanings, and others are more revealing. This one highlights the origin; it signifies the ancient in all things. It is the master in a certain sense, the first, as the *ʿatîq* horse or thoroughbred racer is. The word can mean the most beautiful, the most generous, which only further reinforces its nobility. Applied to the *Kaʾba*, *ʿatîq* also means the house that God saved from the tyrants, the meaning that Tabari favors. Other more concise scholars prefer the meaning of a house that no one has ever owned and where nothing belongs to anyone.[128] Preeminence, beauty, and purity were everything. One could not use such a noble adjective to describe people of doubtful origins! Granted, elsewhere the freed man was called *mûʾtaq*, *ʿatîq*, or *ʿâtiq*, but not once in the sacred text.[129]

What produced such purity? What established its difference? Was it nobility, origins, nature, or faith? Râzi asserts that "people and human souls are of contrasting essences and differ in their qualities. Some are good, others evil. And the same is true for intelligence and stupidity, freedom and servility, nobility and lowliness, as well as other qualities."[130]

The free was the *khâliss*, the pure. The human being at creation was conceived by God to be master of things: "He created for you all that the earth contains."[131] The status of slave altered and disturbed the human condition. This is why liberation was meant to be a sort of purification through the elimination of the ownership of another, which altered the

124 The Koran, 90:13.
125 The Koran, 2:177, 9:60, 47:4.
126 *Fâʾiq*, I, 409.
127 The Koran, 22:29, 22:33.
128 Tabari, *Tafsîr*, IX, 146.
129 *Lissân*, X, 234.
130 Râzi, VII, Part I, 14.
131 The Koran, 2:29.

human condition.[132] But the purification in question was only virtual. The pure free remained unique, irreplaceable, that is, inaccessible. We cannot avoid citing in this regard the teaching of the sura whose name means "Purity": "Say: 'God is One, the Eternal God. He begot none, nor was He begotten. None is equal to Him.'"[133]

How to repair the damage caused by a reduction to slavery? Râzi mentions three sorts of damage: alteration, lies, and finally defectiveness, the imperfection that evokes the idea of debris. Slavery was a sort of defectiveness.[134] Man is born to serve God; if he disobeys, he is punished with slavery.[135] And disobedience, like original sin, is inherent in man and accompanies him throughout his earthly journey.

Inequality was thus present, as in other societies of the time. "And marry those among you who have no husband."[136] The Koran addresses with this statement the community of free Muslims, according to many commentators, thereby establishing a distinction between statuses.[137] In Muslim society, slavery was one of the manifestations and fundamental constituents of the social organization. The very existence of believers and infidels irreparably induces the dichotomy between free men and slaves, two contradictory and complementary statuses. There could be no infidels without believers, no paradise without hell, no free men without slaves. Human beings, similar in their corporal constitution, differed in their qualities, by reason of God's will to put his creatures to the test.[138] More explicitly, "in their essence, human souls differ in their qualities. There are those who are intelligent or stupid, others who are free or base, others who are noble or ignoble. Each of these statuses may vary in its intensity."[139] The degree of humanity was judged with regard to faith. Humanity and reason were faith and obedience.[140] Questioned on men, Hassan, son of the caliph ʿAli, said: "We are men, our allies are menlike, and our enemies are monsters."[141]

In this context, the concept of freedom remained restrictive and inevitably did not encompass all of society. One of the Prophet's freed slaves, who adored him to the highest degree, came to visit him. Saddened not to

[132] Râzi, V, Part II, 186.
[133] The Koran, 112.
[134] Râzi, VI, Part I, 117.
[135] Râzi, VI, Part II, 91.
[136] The Koran, 7:32.
[137] Râzi, XII, Part I, 186.
[138] Râzi, VII, Part I, 85, and Part II, 12.
[139] Râzi, IX, Part II, 90
[140] The Koran, 7:179.
[141] Râzi, XVI, Part II, 144. *Nassnâss* means to be fabulous, one-legged.

have approached him for a long time, and fearing that death would take him, he said to him: "I feared I wouldn't see you above, because if I am allowed to go to paradise, you will be among the prophets and I among the slaves!"[142] This perfect believer was obsessed by his servile destiny, which was only reinforced by its representations. The permanence of servitude weighed heavily on one's mentality.

Ibn ʿAbbâss said that "every man will have a house, a family, and slaves in paradise."[143] On the most distant horizon, slavery was always there. A curse and a trial on earth, slavery in the afterlife gave coherence to a divine judgment that rewarded the faith of the believer. In the delights of paradise, covered with satin and brocade, the chosen ones, compensated for their efforts, will drink from crystal goblets. "They shall be attended by boys graced with eternal youth, who to the beholder's eyes will seem like sprinkled pearls."[144] These were the *ouildâne*, or slaves of paradise, who were the children of infidels on earth.[145] Slaves were eternal children considered to be legal minors.

INCAPABLE OF BEING FREE

Service required youth and strength. The slave, even of mature age, was called *fatâ*. Let us be clear: the word did not refer to physical qualities but to intellectual and moral ones, thereby signifying the slave's judicial incapacity and absence of mature judgment. Thus there was a lack of consideration for the elderly slave, "for in the image of the adolescent, one did not respect him the way one respected adults."[146] A minor even at the oldest age, the slave could only be dependent, placed under the direction of a guide, a guardian, or a master. This fiction of youth, and thus of the lasting minor status that even an adult age never overcame, consecrated slavery into permanence.

Slaves of paradise were *ouildâne*, a word that carries the double meaning of child and slave without creating any ambiguity. The slave was *mûkhallad*, a word designating among Arabs the one of an advanced age who has kept his dark hair and his teeth intact, symbols of freshness and vigor.[147] Attributes such as earrings gave him a feminine look, symbolic

142 Râzi, V, Part II, 136.
143 Râzi, XIII, Part II, 223.
144 The Koran, 76:19.
145 A debated issue; see *Kachâf*, IV, 695.
146 Râzi, V, Part II, 49.
147 Tabari, *Tafsîr*, XII, 369–370.

of an eternal submission. He was an incapable subject. His field of social mobility was limited to the servile space to which everything, from rights to morality, from representations to the color of his skin, confined him. The paradigm of servitude was unchangeable.

On the level of principles, equality was foremost a question of faith. And indeed, it seems that here, again, the incapacity of the slave placed in doubt his ability to pray to God without prejudicing his master. The slave was not able to apply himself assiduously to religious duties, being first held to the duty of obeying his master. Emancipation was indeed a pious work insofar as it put the slave in a condition to devote himself to obeying God.[148] Though some commentators recognize in the slave the quality of witness, eminent masters specify that, a witness being obligated to appear, nothing guaranteed that a slave would do so, not being master of his person. Freedom thus figured among the conditions for being able to testify.[149]

We are far from the myth that says that the initiatives for freeing slaves were strongly supported and that equality prevailed among believers regardless of their status, their ancestry, or the color of their skin. The increase in the entourage of the powerful and the central place of freedom in the access to power worked together to enclose the servile group in its social status. The proof is evident in the care that the language took in listing the different categories that this status encompassed.

A TENACIOUS SERVILE MEMORY

If expanding the realm of freedom was not a central and urgent preoccupation, the dominant groups made the freedom of their members a precious privilege to defend. Freedom was defined by noble origins, by the purity that only ancientness, conveyed by memory, and power endowed. Freedom was indeed that of people in place; it was an attribute of places and their masters. Tha'lab alleges concisely that he who is "born of Arab parents"[150] is free. Hence the eagerness of those in power to clarify the social structure and to free Arabs in situations of slavery. For kidnappings and wars between tribes often resulted, even for the notables, in captivity and reduction to slavery. Paying ransom usually remedied the situation but did not always succeed.

148 Râzi, IV, Part I, 99. Ibn Charih, Ibn Sirîne, and Ahmad consider the slave a witness worthy in the eyes of the law.

149 Râzi, V, Part II, 186.

150 *Lissân*, IV, 182.

Thus the caliph ʿOmar undertook to bring the situation back to order. For him Arabs could not be the objects of appropriation: "We have no intention of depriving anyone of property that was in his possession before the advent of Islam, but we will determine the value of the people concerned as we do for the price of blood and wounds.[151] And he set the price at five camels (in another version, two slaves) per head, which the relatives would give or guarantee to those who held ownership of the person. A policy of appeal for the liberation of former slaves of Arab origin was thus launched. It was pursued by ʿOthmân, who proposed as the price two camels, and then by others, sometimes setting sizable amounts. The Muslim public authorities adopted a clearer policy here. The incentive or even the order to free slaves of Arab origin was motivated by the dominant group's growing awareness of the necessity of establishing its hegemony, of asserting its superiority and its homogeneity by getting rid of any trace of servitude. The established precaution concerned only the respect for the property of others within a merchant society in which private property was sacred.

In this way, slavery was endowed with a rationality that more closely conformed to the new rule. The slave would be the Other, and the Arab became synonymous with freedom. To avoid any ambiguity, in the case where an Arab had a child with a slave who did not belong to him – a morally condemnable act – he had the right to take his free son in exchange for two slaves. Thus, for a slave who became free, two others became slaves. Liberation – for in this case, true emancipation was not at issue – meant not a widening of the realm of freedom, but the assertion of a group defending that of its own. Such practices could only stimulate demand in the slave market.

If the memory of freedom preoccupied the dominant group, servitude, by contrast, was relegated to the other pole, among groups whose origins were doubtful, who thus became the holders of it. *Al-ʿajamî* was thus the "foreigner," the one without perfect mastery or pronunciation of the Arabic language; he was also the slave rounded up from elsewhere, the non-Arab.

A line of demarcation was thus drawn between men free by virtue of their "roots" and those who obtained their liberty by emancipation. One was expected to avoid entering into an alliance with the latter. The very pious caliph ʿOmar Ibn ʿAbdelʾaziz said: "Only the Arab who is insolent and lacking piety and recognition to God takes a wife from among the

[151] *Lissân*, XI, 632.

mawâli. And only the *mawâli* who seeks a bad reputation takes a wife from among the Arabs."[152] The remnants of servitude that persisted with the liberated thus ensured a hard life and classified the freed slave in an inferior group, still servile in many respects, that of the second-order free or *haratine*, as they are still called today in the Maghreb.

Besides the man who was free in his essence, social classification occurred according to the relationship to servitude, through the evaluation of a distance to servitude, by the greater or lesser degree of purity, by its intensity. Let us review the social statuses that denoted a direct or indirect relationship, close or distant, with slavery to determine the weight of the memory of servitude in representations of the time.

Al-laqîṭe was the foundling whose mother and father were unknown. He shared his obscure origins with the slave. The term also designates a base man. A related word serves to name the freedman who then found himself relegated to the lowest social level. *Al-mâqiṭe* was the slave of the *laqîṭe*; and *al-sâqiṭe*, the slave of his slave. Here we are in the bowels of society, in the most distant depths. Yet even at the bottom of the deep dark depths, we do not lose the sense of the hierarchy, and rankings were assigned. *Al-nâqiṭe* (and *al-nâqile*) designated the slave of the freedman. Even as the master of slaves, the freedman was never able to set himself apart from servitude: he and his dependents were marked with the seal of baseness and enclosed in a relationship that belonged only to them, freedom not being of their world. The obvious concern with distinguishing slaves possessed by freedmen from those held by noble groups, aimed, without a doubt, to weaken the status of the freedmen rather than that of their slaves. It was the maintenance of their marginalization that was at stake.

Al-milṭu was the man with unknown and no doubt mixed origins. He was the one that time left without a name, deprived of means and family, and covered with shame, like the plucked bird whose destiny he shared.[153] A thief, unworthy of confidence, he should be avoided.

Al-sa'âfika were despicable men belonging to the lowest levels of society. Not Arabized, and the descendants of slave parents, they could only eke out an existence, having scarcely left servitude and not even speaking the language of the masters.[154]

152 *Lissân*, VIII, 234.
153 *Lissân*, VIII, 392.
154 Ibn Sikkite, *Kitâb al-alfâdh*, 349.

The freed man and the slave were sons of *baghiya*, prostitutes, the term most commonly used to describe a woman in slavery.

Al-ʿabanqass was the one whose paternal and maternal grandmothers[155] as well as whose wife were slaves.[156]

Al-falanqass (or *falqass*) had the same servile ancestry as the *ʿabanqass*, but his wife was Arab, that is, free. His direct ancestry was made up of the freed, or of a freed father and an Arab mother. Thus the second generation of freed people still bore the mark of servitude. An alliance through marriage to Arabs was a sign, no doubt, of a certain wealth that caused *al-falanqass* to be called the worst kind of miser.[157]

The same scorn was heaped on the *al-hajîne*, that is, the individual whose father was Arab and whose mother was a slave, according to Ibn Sikkite, whereas they were both freed according to Ibn Mandhûr.[158] A despicable and insulting status, *al-hajîne* also designated a bastard horse. A family or tribe stripped of glory was given that title.

Al-maḥyouss is the one who had a mother and a grandmother who were slaves; the term was synonymous with a bad mixture.[159] It foretold of ruin for Arab families who were tempted to enter into an alliance with such an individual. Referring to one of a freed father and a mother of relatively better birth, the term was reputed, in the dominant opinion, to be synonymous with delinquency and malediction. An odor of sin hung around his family, who would be stricken, as an evil omen, with contagious illnesses.

Finally, the *mukarkass* was "surrounded everywhere by slave women."[160] The dictionary tells us that he descended from a line of two or three generations of slaves: "The mother of his mother, the mother of his father, the mother of the mother of his mother, [and] the mother of the mother of his father were slaves."[161] He was profoundly set in slavery. His title evokes the repetition that, like an eternal call to order, established his status. The word also designates the one in chains whose feet are always shackled.

But there was a worse status. The *musba'* was descended from seven generations of slaves; he was the servant left to fend for himself in nature,

155 *Kitâb al-alfâdh*, 348.
156 *Tâj al-'Arûss*, VIII, 351.
157 *Tâj al-'Arüss*, VIII, 403.
158 *Kitâb al-alfâdh*, 348–349.
159 *Tâj al-'Arûss*, VIII, 255.
160 *Kitâb al-alfâdh*, 348.
161 *Lissân*, VI, 196.

who lived like the animals with which society associated him. Through him, kinship was established with the animal, making the exit from slavery all the more problematic.

Servitude thus had a depth that made it a reservoir of dependents of all sorts at the disposal of dominant groups. Freedom and servitude formed the flip sides of the bond of authority. But knowledge of this bond leads us beyond the master-slave relationship; it spreads to all the servants of the king as well as to his subjects. Thus, having started with slavery, we will now examine the meaning of servitude and its importance while questioning the relationships that could be defined by reference to it.

3

Open-Air Servitude

Rarely has the question of authority in the Arab world been dealt with in terms of servitude, and even more rarely in terms of slavery. In fact, the social relationship in question has been of little interest in the Muslim world. Islam has exerted such a fascination that many authors have seen it, if not as an abolitionist religion, at least as a profoundly egalitarian one. This attitude has a priori discredited the path toward questioning the nature of power in Muslim societies, which was not considered pertinent since the institution of slavery supposedly had very little weight in those societies. A sort of discretion has also worked against a candid examination of the mechanisms of authority that breaks down the walls between the different levels of authority from celestial society to the political society on earth and on to the civil society, notably through the master/slave relationship. Such a decompartmentalization appears, however, essential and fruitful.

SERVITUDE AND ADORATION

The Arabic word *ʿabd*, "slave," comes from treading on the ground to trace a clear, smooth path like the asphalt roads of the present. To crush, to smooth, to suppress any agitation, any resistance, is the profound mechanism of slavery. The idea of treading is essential here because along with the use of force both convey the same scorn. Applied to a camel, which is called *muʿabbad*, the word is used to designate a mangy animal, covered with tar and put in quarantine.[1] That is, metaphorically, an

[1] Ibn Chajari, *Mâ ittafaqa lafdhuhu wa ikhtalafa maʾnâhu*, 288.

isolated individual, kept outside the group without the protective bonds of which he might take advantage.

This image of trodden ground expresses extreme domination. The desired and appropriate attitude for prayer and for the invocation of God is to be in humiliation and debasement, like a desolate land.[2] The dominated and servile man was the same as the portion of earth tramped by one's feet, which is crushed under the weight of one's body; he was "beneath," in the full sense of the word.[3] The poet Abû al-ʿAtâhiya, having offered the caliph al-Mansûr some shoes, regretted not being able to sew his own cheek to the sole so that al-Mansûr could walk on it to glory.[4] The people below, *al-tuḥut* – which would normally be translated as individuals of lowly condition – were, for the jurisconsult, "those who are under people's feet," which is more in line with the strict definition of servitude, whose meaning it renders faithfully.[5] It is said in prophetic tradition "that when God removed [expulsed] Adam from paradise, he threw him with force onto the ground," thus reminding him of his status as a slave of God. In its very origin, the relationship of authority, inaugurated by this abrupt degradation, proves to be fundamentally servile.[6]

The word *ʿabd*, the only concept able to render at the same time the idea of ownership and the obedience that results from it, is used in the sense of "creature," a term encompassing all men in their relationship to God. The "creation" aspect is also found in the relationship between master and slave, in the formation to which the latter was subjected. Further, the reduction to slavery was considered to be a re-creation, allowing the crushed, conquered one to avoid death. One's relationship to God being of a superior level, the caliph ʿOmar Ibn ʿAbdelʾaziz says in a funeral speech: "May God cover with his mercy every slave whether he be free or slave, man or woman."[7] Thus there was a general and superior servitude that linked man to God.

But this celestial servitude, although of a superior nature, was conceivable only in terms of the earthly relationship that existed between master and slave, a relationship that remained a tangible reference. First, it was important to rid the earthly relationship of its imperfections and blemishes in order to reach the highest level of servitude. The hold that

[2] Ibn al-Athîr, *Nihâya*, II, 4, henceforth *Nihâya*.
[3] *Jamhara*, 950.
[4] Jâhiz, *Bayân*, 475, henceforth *Bayân*.
[5] *Fâʾiq*, I, 148.
[6] *Nihâya*, IV, 232.
[7] *ʿIqd*, IV, 399.

forced ownership offers within the framework of slavery was turned into an unconditional attachment, a sort of gift of oneself. Commenting on the command not to raise one's voice before the Prophet, as the slave sometimes did in front of his master, the jurisconsult emphasizes the difference in attitude that one must have before two masters from very different levels of authority. The attachment to one's master was synonymous with a complete forgetting of oneself. The relationship of servitude, which borrowed its model from a private social bond, in this case that of slavery, was transposed into the public realm with the adjustments that this entailed. Such a transposition of course reinforced the position of the master, the focus of general interest.[8]

With the advent of Islam, the *ʿibâda*, of which the accepted equivalent term is "adoration," was reserved for God. When another master was associated with God as a divinity, the relationship was of this order. The term did not, however, apply only to divinities. In fact, it is important to remember that the posture of "adoration" owed much to the lexicon and the reality of the social relationships of the time.[9] It was not the fruit of the invention of a radically new, sui generis relationship without an equivalent in the past, nor was it specific to a relationship with the gods. The *ʿibâda* was defined as "extreme submission and is due only at the price of the most complete charity, and for that reason is for God alone."[10] Obedience was to a lesser degree due as much to God as to men.[11] "*Al-ʿibâda* is the greatest degree of obedience and submission, whence the use of a derivative of the word to designate a thick, dense, perfectly woven cloth."[12] It expressed "the action that aims to exalt others" and constituted the apex of consideration. It was derived from slavery or *ʿubûdiyya*,[13] and brings us, in spite of its divine resonance, imperceptibly back to earth.

The *ʿibâda* was above all recognition for the primordial act of charity, the giving of life: "I brought you into being when you were nothing before."[14] We can now understand what "to crush" and "to trample" meant: to reduce the individual to nothing, as if to put him to death, leaving him in existence only as a creation of the master. Slavery recalls death in its function as a renunciation of the self, as an offering of one's

[8] Râzi, XIV, Part II, 98.
[9] *Kachâf*, I, 639.
[10] Ibn Hilâl, *al Furûq*, 243.
[11] Ibid., 245.
[12] *Kachâf*, I, 23.
[13] Râzi, I, Part I, 196.
[14] The Koran, 19:9.

person as a tribute of surrender to the other. It was a question of submission (*tadhallul*), in the sense of giving way in the face of power without putting up any resistance, to be as malleable as required. Applied to an individual, it designated a lowly and servile being. We are now in the realm of pure servitude.[15]

The lexicon of slavery proves to be the only one capable of conveying the weight and intensity of such an attitude. The representation of authority in Arab society, well before the advent of Islam, made it synonymous with servitude. A certain person, reputed to communicate with heaven, asserted that "those who are on earth are the slaves of the one who is in heaven."[16] Here "heaven" should be understood as nobility, the loftiness that it thus conferred, and the authority that resulted from it. The adorer was in a situation of complete servitude. He relinquished any initiative in the face of complete power, "that is, he is like a weak slave who does not hold his own destiny in his hands." Beyond any charity, it was the approval of the master that became the object of adoration.[17] The reference to earthly servitude is constant and unchangeable.

Adoration was a common practice between the dominant and the dominated, between masters and servants. "Arabs call any individual who submits to the king his slave, or if one uses conventional language, his adorer. This is why the people of Hira are called *al-'ibâd*, because they obey the kings of Persia."[18] That is, the term used for the subjects of the king would subsequently be applied exclusively to believers in their relationship to God. It is reported that certain tribes who converted to Christianity agreed to adopt the name of "adorer" instead of *'abîd*, which more directly and more crudely meant "slaves."[19] Even after the advent of Islam, the signs of servitude in the modes of expression of obedience to the Muslim commanders, going as far as prosternation, were not always seen as acts of condemnable heresy, insofar as they were considered examples of the adoration of God through obedience to his lieutenants on earth.[20] Thus there was a close relationship between the *khidma*, or service to the king, and the *'ibâda*, or divine adoration. The two did not differ strictly in their nature but simply as a matter of degree.[21]

[15] *Tâj al-'Arûss*, XIV, 252–256.
[16] *Majma 'al-amthâl*, II, 171.
[17] *Kachâf*, II, 280.
[18] Tabari, *Tafsîr*, IX, 217.
[19] *Jamhara*, 299.
[20] Râzi, XII, Part II, 50.
[21] Râzi, XIII, Part II, 85.

There have been many attempts to distinguish the different levels of servitude, both in their content and by considering the various masters involved. One speaks of *ʿabd mamlouk*, literally the slave as property of a man, in order to establish the use of the word *ʿabd*, taken alone, to mean adorer. The Prophet recommended using another word for private slavery, encouraging masters to use the expression "my boy" to call their slave.[22] One even finds *ʿabd mutlâq*, in the sense of an absolute slave, to convey the content of a relationship to God.[23] But such specifications in fact have remained without effect. The term *mamlouk* was already used to distinguish between the person who was legally reduced to slavery and the one who was made a slave unjustifiably.

The constant reference to slavery to more clearly bring out the content of the bond of adoration does not help to avoid the confusion whose true importance we must measure at a time when slavery was a fact of everyday life. The strength of this bond was stressed with an insistence that constantly referred to social relationships. Thus we have the evocation of the day of resurrection in the Koran: The verse "when the earth is crushed to fine dust"[24] picks up the image of slavery defined as trampling, a stamping upon solid earth. The word is applied to the individual who possessed a slave in servitude for three generations. The slave was given a name derived directly from the word for "dust" (*al-turtub*), that is, from the nothingness that was suggested by his prolonged servile submission.[25] This annihilation of the subject, pushed to the extreme, was promoted as a means of celebrating the nobility of the master.

LIKE A DOCILE CAMEL

Voluntary servitude was praised. Thus one author notes the difference between the individual who was considered base due to circumstances or to the actions of someone else (*dhalîl*, *dhalûl*) and the one who lowers and debases himself as a sign of recognition.[26] Jâhiz, on the other hand, comparing merchants with servants of the sultan, praises the qualities of the former and notes that it is "otherwise with those who have an intimate relationship with the sultan and who are close to him by serving

[22] Ahmad Ibn Hanbal, *Musnad*, II, 558, 609. The Arabic words are *fatâ* and *ghulâm*. We may also recall here the use of *sayyid* instead of *rabb* for the master.

[23] Râzi, IX, Part I, 105.

[24] The Koran, 89:21.

[25] *Tâj al-ʿArûss*, I, 321–326.

[26] Ibn Hilâl, *al-Furûq*, 274–275.

him. They are covered with lowliness, and their currency is flattery. Their hearts beat only for those whose slaves they are, and they are filled with fear and accustomed to servility and its corollary, greed."[27]

Constraint was a determining element in the relationship of servitude.[28] The slave, as an accomplished model of the servile subject, was in fact classified among animals, *al-dawwâb*, in particular among the beasts of burden used for the lowest of work. Grouped in this category were "camels, cows, donkeys, and slaves [*raqîq*], men and women."[29] One of the names for a slave was *qaynan*,[30] a term that designated the placement of chains on a camel's legs.[31] Brute force was the generator of slavery, which it attempted to legitimize over time by dehumanizing its victims. The pure free man was contrasted to the pure slave, or *'abd zulma*,[32] recognizable physically by his branding, like an animal, visible by his split ear proclaiming his anchoring in servitude.[33]

Branding protected property and gave its insignia to nobility and to servitude. It could be symbolic when it was related to a community, notably through the debasement of and control over its essential intermediaries. Thus, regarding tribes, it was said that "appropriating their lords and the powerful among them is the same as branding them permanently between the ears." The importance of branding derives from the fact that it relegated the individual or the group to the condition of animals, in which its indelible sign imprisoned them. It established the difference between the master and his slave, between the king and his servant. As a visible sign, it instilled among men the difference in nature contained in the perfect bond of servitude, like the bond that connected earth and sky. Branding the neck with a hot iron – one of the prerogatives of nobility among the Arabs – and branding the hands, a symbol of strength, were signs of extreme debasement that a master could inflict on those he owned. An Omayyad governor of Bagdad by the name of al-Hajjâj thus branded a group of people from black Africa, an act that left a deep, long-lasting impression. The poet al-Farazdaq, speaking of someone who insulted him for being an Arab, wrote: "If al-Hajjâj had been alive for him, he would have branded his palms with a hot iron."[34]

[27] Jâhiz, *Rasâ'il*, II, Part IV, 255, henceforth *Rasâ'il*.
[28] Al-Ansâri, *an-Nawâdir*, 87.
[29] At-Tha'âlibî, *Fiqh al-lugha*, 22.
[30] Kûrâ', 315.
[31] *Islâḥ al-Mantiq*, 398.
[32] *Ichtiqâq*, 175, or *zanma*, adds *Tâj al-'Arûss*, XVI, 322.
[33] *Tâj al-'Arûss*, XVI, 328.
[34] Mustafa 'Alyane, *Charh diwân al-Mutanabbi*, I, 166, henceforth *Mutanabbi*.

The terms that designated the king's subjects and the animals in a herd had a common etymology. The same word designated the commander and the shepherd, *al-râʿi*, even if some authors differentiate the two positions through use of the plural form.[35] The word "people," in the sense of a group, comes from the same root, *al-raʿiya*. Since the camel and the horse were vital resources for desert tribes, one can understand how leading a herd, which demanded experience and know-how, inspired the government of a human community.[36] In this the political world found one of the justifications for constraint through the use of force.

And animals were classified according to their degree of obedience. The *rayyid* camel was the one that resisted being tamed. *Al-ʿasîr* was the animal that presented certain difficulties in its taming. *Al-qadîb* was the one that proved to be stubborn, rigid, and unbreakable. *Al-ʿarûd* was the animal that showed a ferocious resistance.

The caliph ʿOmar, one of the founders of the state, advocated praising and welcoming the obedient one, constraining the one that dragged its feet and slowed down the group, calming and talking to the agitated one that did not know what it was doing, and finally, beating the *al-ʿarûd*. The recalcitrant quadruped gave its name, in modern political Arabic, to the opposition, *mu'ârada*. The "opposing" animal was "the one that is stubborn in its head and submissive in its body." It was the beast of burden over which the rider had no mastery, the one that refused to carry out orders.[37] It was like the haughty man, refusing to obey.[38] Submission of the body, as the caliph recalls, referred to slavery: the master was thought to possess the body but not the soul of the servant. This ownership established the right to punish one's slave. Punishment by the king consequently found its legitimacy here: to be part of the herd required obedience.

The most highly praised model was that of the completely submissive animal. The Prophet defined believers as "easy and soft like the docile camel."[39] Tradition insisted on the virtues of submission: "Those among you closest to me on the day of the resurrection," says the Prophet, "will be those who have the softest character and are the most submissive"; as

[35] *Ru'ât* primarily designates agents of authority, and *ru'yân* designates shepherds for some authors.

[36] *Tâj al-ʿArûss*, XIX, 465–468.

[37] *Tâj al-ʿArûss*, X, 71–75.

[38] Ibn al-Mubarrad, *Al-Kâmil fi lugha wa al-adab*, I, 81, henceforth *Al-Kâmil*.

[39] *Fâ'iq*, I, 61.

for the prideful, they would receive no consideration.[40] Submission was a matter of degree. The example of the Yemenites is mentioned: they were familiar with monarchic authority and "were very sensitive and very soft and of unfailing obedience." The invoked obedience was connected to the image of the extreme slitting of an animal's throat, which consisted of cutting so deeply that one reached the spinal cord.[41] Exemplary obedience was a gift of the self, complete sacrifice. The position of the believer in prayer was a constant symbolic reminder of this.

Submission was the promptness of the servant to respond to the commands of his master. This is illustrated in one of the most widespread prayer formulas exalting the name of God and praising him: "*Subḥân Allâh*." The formula means "to go to God quickly and submit oneself to his orders with the most extreme diligence." Used first in the service of earthly masters, the word is a derivative of the word "swim," that is, an aquatic mode of locomotion where the movement of the hands is the driving element and the flat posture is that of absolute prostration. The Prophet's horse, during the battle of Badr, was called *Sabḥa*: it showed a remarkable extension of its forward limbs (hands) while running.[42] Nothing could better illustrate speed in the execution of orders! The formula used at the royal court is more laconic and uses no parables: *a-sam' wa tâ'a*, in other words, the almost automatic ability to listen and to obey.

IN THE SERVICE OF THE MONARCHY

Beyond ties of blood and with a view to maintaining them, servitude was the bond that suited monarchic power the best. It was the perfect model for the king's mood swings and his unpredictability. The bond of servitude had an elasticity that allowed it to resist the tensions it could be subjected to. The slave, as property, was matter that one could shape as one wished, like clay, until he conformed to the wishes of the master – that is one of the definitions of the verb "to possess" in Arabic.[43] His nature was one that did not protest against abuse. His desire to earn his master's approval or to get closer to him made him like a transfixed lover bending to the demands of his beloved. Servitude thus turned the relationship

[40] *Fâ'iq*, I, 8.
[41] *Fâ'iq*, I, 82.
[42] *Tâj al-'Arûss*, IV, 76–78.
[43] *Tâj al-'Arûss*, XIII, 649.

of authority into an arbitrarily controllable bond of which the king was the center despite the many intermediaries that necessarily came between him and the servants who were not in his immediate proximity. The servant was subject to the will of the prince, and the latter in return heaped his goodwill upon his servants, which earned him fear and consideration. If disgrace befell the servant, he had only to solicit his master's pardon: "Pardon, pardon! And I, unjustly too, must grant it you!"[44] Such theatrically forced clemency in fact added a new link to the invisible chains that held the servant.

It was as if the servant was drained of his own substance, his entire person given over to the king. His rank and prestige increased in proportion to his self-effacement. It was a game of shadow and light that made him more present through absence in his henceforth established nature as a man of the king. He and his master were like connected vessels. A high-ranking state official was reminded: "The commander of believers took you exclusively for him ..., he speaks through your tongue and takes and gives through your hand ... and the more he adds to your elevation and your worth, the more you must add to your fear and consideration of him."[45] Greatness thus was transmitted through its opposite, debasement. This is why servitude was so desired in high places. As proof of this, some agents avidly delved into the lexicon of servitude, without it even necessarily corresponding to their status, in the sole aim of getting closer to the king. They gave themselves titles such as *khadîm*, *ʿabd*, and *mawlâ*, willingly proclaiming themselves to be in extreme servitude of the king.[46]

The most coveted servitude was that owed to very powerful kings. It belonged to the preferred circles where the master resided and where the servant was completely dedicated to adoration, like the angels closest to God. The master was so powerful that he was never in need of servants; like God, he was the dispenser.

It was reported that a servant who offered a gift to the king as a symbol of his submission declared to him: "O commander of believers, the more delicate and fine the gift, when it goes from the small to the great, the more elegant and beautiful it is. And the more considerable and imposing it is when it goes from the great to the small, the more useful and elevated it is."[47] What could the servant, the creation of his master, give? "If I offer

[44] Shakespeare, *Richard III*, Act II, Scene I.
[45] *Jamharat rasâ'il*, IV, 139.
[46] M. Ennaji, *Soldats, domestiques et concubines*, 153.
[47] *Jamharat rasâ'il*, IV, 170.

my person, it is already your exclusive property. I looked over the best of what I have, and I realized that it came to me from you."[48]

One of the most powerful figures of the Abbasid kingdom, Yahya Ibn Khâlid the Barmecide, disgraced and imprisoned, said he suffered from nothing except the absence of his master. "Your slave," he cried out to the caliph, "has seen death with his own eyes for being sadly afflicted by your anger, O commander of believers. And this not in the hope of some mercy, but from the fact of being kept away from you. My family and my property are yours and came from you, and they were in my hands only as a loan and the loan must now be repaid."[49]

LEVELS OF ADORATION-SERVITUDE

Without his master, the servant was nothing. The *'ubûdiyya*, literally slavery, was of course humiliation and debasement. Slavery must, however, be situated in its social and political context, not considered in the absolute. It was tempered by the status of the master: the more noble he was, the less humiliating the servitude was, and the more it resulted in enjoyment and happiness. The exultation and the intoxication of the adorer of God, the pride of the courtier, and the lofty allure of the slave who belonged to a powerful master are illustrations of this.[50]

The commentators have distinguished several levels of adoration-servitude. The first is the one in which the adorer aimed through his submission to avoid a punishment. The second is that in which the adorer anticipated a reward or benefit for his adoration. At those two levels, the master was not adored for himself, and the servitude was consequently imperfect. The third level consists of adoring God in his capacity as creator, the adorer then being legitimately his slave; he adored God and served him because of that: "The divinity imposes the imposing presence and power, the *'ubûdiyya* imposes submission and debasement."[51] This final level is the most complete servitude.

Arabs brought small statues representing their idols with them on their journeys. "What greater glory than that of being with one's adored!" Debasement from the point of view of the servant was to be kept far from the king[52]; proximity, on the other hand, was a privilege. Among

[48] *Jamharat rasâ'il*, IV, 246.
[49] *Jamharat rasâ'il*, III, 192.
[50] Râzi, I, Part I, 197.
[51] Râzi, I, Part I, 202.
[52] Râzi, XIII, Part II, 8.

the angels, those who "dwell with God give glory to Him night and day and are never wearied."[53] They did nothing else, and nothing could distract them. They formed a distinct category encompassing the most noble and the greatest, forming the inner circle.[54] It was the highest level of servitude and was similarly found in the entourage of kings. The servants in the entourage were delighted not by the largesse they received but from being seen by the king, by being one of his elect. "Thus, if the very considerable king throws an apple at one of his slaves before all the other slaves present, the latter feels great joy, not from having received the apple, but for having had the privilege of such a distinction."[55]

Proposed by the imam Râzi to describe divine proximity and its different circles, curiously inspired by a very earthly logic of proximity, the grid with different levels of servitude that structured the relationship of the king with his subjects had seven categories,[56] recalling the seven celestial levels. The chaste were the closest of all the servants. They were not only around the king, but with him.[57] Infallible, sheltered from any subversion, they were removed from the rest of society to live fully in the royal universe without any other bond than the one to their master, for whom they lived. Their similarities with the angels of the first rank are striking. Chastity here was synonymous with extreme political castration, as those involved had no other claim than a love of their king and his reflected attention. Pure individuals, fashioned by the royal will, they took pride in no other bond; servitude was their raison d'être, they were its pure product.

Next were the elect. Servants hand-picked and in direct contact with the king, but not being with him, they received the distinction bestowed upon them by royal friendship and proximity. They made up one of the most distinguished components of the *khâssa*, a group that contained courtiers and state dignitaries.

The virtuous were not part of the first circle and were not personal companions of the king. They were nevertheless the most faithful, respected and endowed with a proven know-how that made them advisers and counselors, as is said in the sacred text: they were "those who listen to [His] precepts and follow what is best in them."[58]

[53] The Koran, 41:38.

[54] Râzi, XIV, Part I, 112.

[55] Râzi, VIII, Part II, 14.

[56] Râzi, XI, Part I, 193.

[57] The jurisconsult thus distinguishes the *ʿindiyya*, which assumes more distance than the *maʾiyya*, in *Tafsîr*, XI, Part I, 34.

[58] The Koran, 39:18.

Then came the nobles who belonged to the upper classes of society and occupied important positions in the kingdom. Next were the servants of redemption, who were all intimates of the king belonging to different circles, but in a state of disgrace, momentarily distanced, who awaited the opportunity to return to service and once again frequent the halls of the palace. The common servants were by far the largest category, encompassing the servants of the sultan assigned to carry out specific tasks. Despite their modest status, they, along with soldiers, formed the most visible shield for the king. Finally, the supplicants were the common subjects of the king, his *ra'iya*. They were reduced to soliciting benefits and his help through servile supplication: "I am near. I answer the prayer of the suppliant when he calls to Me."[59] These were the *souqa*, that is, people subject to the kings,[60] called by a term that suggests the souk because people brought their merchandise and notably their beasts of burden. Let us emphasize that even today in southern Morocco the black former freedmen are called *issouquin*, which indicates the weight of servitude contained in the word that, already in old Arabic, was the opposite of freedom and nobility. This is how the subjects of the kings were viewed.

Following a revolt by the people of Medina against Yazid, the son of Mo'âwiyya, one of his lieutenants who reestablished control of the city ordered the inhabitants "to swear allegiance as slaves of the caliph who would decide everything that concerned them, and they swore allegiance to him."[61] *Al-ra'iya* is unambiguous, meaning the herd; *râ'i*, a word designating the shepherd, was also a synonym for leader or chief. It implied know-how and political sense regarding business, either public or private, as is mentioned in the hadith.[62] The word itself is not found in the Koran, but its meaning is there.[63] The dictionary reports that, most often, to distinguish the meaning "chief" from the meaning "shepherd," the plural was used – *ru'ât* for governors and *ru'yân* for shepherds. As for the subjects, they were called *al-ra'iya*. The term seems to have been applied to the *'âmma*, no doubt because it sounds like "quadruped." The nobles or *khâssa* kept their distance with regard to this prejudicial branding. The quadruped was by nature an inferior being, lending its back to the dominant bipeds; the upright position was in fact one of the characteristics of chiefs in Arab society.

59 The Koran, 2:186.
60 *Lissân*, X, 170.
61 *'Iqd*, IV, 356.
62 kullukum râ'in wa kullukum masùlun 'an ra'yatih.
63 The Koran, 57:27.

Servitude was born first in the relationship of person to person, through physical strength and primitive violence. The symbolic evocation of the hand is very instructive in this regard: not only does it indicate servitude, but it better clarifies what remained unsaid in the relationship between the king and his subjects. So many contacts involving the hand and apparently peaceful in the royal protocol of our days in fact have a history filled with violence.

WITH HEADS, AND NOT WITH HANDS

"To have the upper hand" on someone is to have authority over him.[64] That authority is even more obvious when one speaks of a person's treatment "at the hands" of another. Someone's "right-hand man" is his support and his ally.

"To give from the hand" is an expression that raises more questions; one says *'an yad*, that is, with consent. Granted, one gives from one's hand only with consent or, as in the present case, after having been driven to do so. The expression is cited in the Koran on the subject of payment of a tax (*jizya*) by the dhimmis, and it has caused a lot of ink to flow: "Fight against such of those to whom the Scriptures were given as believe in neither God nor the Last Day, who do not forbid what God and His apostle have forbidden, and do not embrace the true Faith, until they pay tribute out of hand and are utterly subdued [*'an yad*]."[65] Most commentators nevertheless insist on the actual modalities of the payment: "to give from the hand" then seems to consist of not delegating the task to anyone else, but presenting oneself personally, arriving on foot and not on horseback, to pay the tax. These details highlight the status of the subjected one, who lowered himself and showed his gratitude for having been spared by his conquerors. The servile status indeed was born out of desolation, out of having been conquered and dominated, and finding oneself in the hands of one's master – not face to face with him, but having to raise one's eyes to see him. The slave could not delegate; his position was to be on his knees in front of his owner.[66]

From such expressions, which belong to everyday vocabulary, we see that the language of the hand was a language of power that spoke to the relationship between the conqueror and the conquered. "To show one's hands" means to give up, and for a powerful one, to ask for the favor of

[64] Shakespeare, *Richard II*, Act III, Scene II.
[65] The Koran, 9:29.
[66] *Kachâf*, II, 46.

serving as a vassal: "O king, don't kill me," cries a notable, "I am your guide on the land of the Arabs and here are my hands as proof of the submission of my tribe."[67]

But this very familiar organ of submission and domination could also manifest revolt. To engage in dissidence was literally called "to remove one's hand from obedience" or even "to pull off the rope of obedience from the neck." Both cases suggest that the initial state was that of servility, comparable to the condition of a captive. The plural of captive is *asrâ*, a word that designated the captives that one held with one's hands; the plural of the plural, even more intense, is *asâra*, which designated captives bound by both the neck and the hands.[68] Two conditions, two phases of captivity, of which the hand was primordial: one hand held the captive and the other bound him. We will return later, even more concretely, to this very "manual" aspect of domination.

The language of the hand served first to express the bonds of personal domination within the framework of a limited community, such as a household, before it came to symbolize a general constraint exercised over increasingly larger groups. This is why servitude proves to be the decisive key that sheds light on the mechanisms of the genesis of power in the Arab world. The Koran illustrates this point by stressing that "there is not a living creature on the earth [whom He does not hold by the hair]."[69] The top-knot, *al-nâsiya* in Arabic, designates the hair that grows on the top of the skull. To tie one's hair above the forehead, during battles, was a highly regarded act of bravado and invitation to fight.[70] And to clearly mark someone's debasement and submission to another, it was said that "he has his hair between the hands of the other." Hence the common practice of cutting off the *nâsiya* of the captive that one planned to release out of concern for clemency and to keep the hair as a sign of victory.[71] It was a symbolic scalping, in a certain sense.

Other expressions confirm the status of the hand and its close connection with power. "To be in the hands of someone," *bayna yadayh*, is another illustration of this, even if the content of the expression is subject to disagreement. Some render it as "to kneel before authority"; in

[67] *As-Sîra*, I, 46.

[68] Râzi, II, Part I, 157.

[69] The Koran, 11:56. Translator's note: The translation of the Koran used in the French-language edition of this book has "il n'existe aucun être vivant que Dieu ne tienne par le toupet" (literally, "there exists no living being whom God does not hold by the hair") here. In the English-language version, the reference to hair is missing.

[70] *Kachâf*, II, 285, note 3.

[71] Râzi, IX, Part II, 12.

any event, it was indubitably to be in front of authority. Note that the expression was also used for God and his prophet. An author advances that the hands, in the expression in question, designated the chief's right and left sides.[72] Râzi is more explicit. For him, to say that "a person is in the hands of another" indicates first that those concerned were in the presence of each other, but that one of them occupied a noble position whereas the other had a base status. In his opinion, the one who took his place next to another forced the first to turn his head to give his instructions, which never happened with a king. On the other hand, one who was in another's hands, that is, in front of him, did not force him to make such an effort, thus befitting the status of a master. The one who was in the hands of another was in fact his servant. He was like an object in the master's possession, to be used as he saw fit.[73]

KISSING THE HAND

Expressions that allude to the hand, which are still used today and which can be found in court protocol, were endowed with a servile content that reaches back to the time when physical constraint in the relationship of the dominant and the dominated was direct and personal. The hand, the symbol par excellence of power, was the organ that conveyed allegiance. It punished, first directly, then by delegating to other hands; it gave; it distributed honors; it received firsthand the recognition of its supremacy by dignitaries. Like God, the one who held supreme authority held the privilege of the right hand, which granted pardons and privileges, and delegated his left hand, which was the instrument of repression, to his subalterns.

The recognition of authority that is called allegiance was performed from hand to hand, a testimony of the primary surrender, of the submission originally imposed through physical strength. The kiss placed on the hand of the chief was an organic attribute of power. It betrayed the initial violence of the origins that all organized power later struggled to hide, to mask the founding battle. To kiss the king's hand then became a natural gesture. Popular wisdom says: "The kiss of the imam is on the hand, that of the father on the head, of the brother on the cheek, of the sister on the chest, and finally of the wife on the lips."[74] One kissed the elevated hand, the hand that gave, the hand of the lieutenant of the Most High on earth,

[72] *Kachâf*, IV, 341.
[73] Râzi, XIV, Part II, 96.
[74] *'Iqd*, II, 100.

which was, like the hand of God, above those of the common man. Let us recall, incidentally, that the low hand was not only that of the beggar; it was also that of the rebel who refused to obey.

One kissed the noble hand (*charifa*). The *charaf*, that is, the sheriff-like status acquired by the descendants of the Prophet (after the advent of Islam), was applied in the beginning to physical space: it designated a landscape overlooking others, a "high place," to use the language of the court and thereby stress its origins. The *charaf* was later employed in the domain of kinship: it still denotes a strategic topographical position, no longer spatial but social.

Kissing the hand is an ancient custom. Chroniclers report that Muslims kissed the hand of the Prophet. They did the same with the caliphs, as is reported for 'Omar. A witness claims to have seen a man go before 'Ali, the son of Husayn, son of the caliph 'Ali, the son-in-law and cousin of the Prophet: he "kissed his hand and placed it on his eyes." Kissing the hand of the descendants of the Prophet scarcely seems to have raised any problems: "It is thus that we were required to act with the descendants of our Prophet," admits a faithful.[75]

To kiss the hand of the chief was to pledge allegiance, but was also to ask for his blessing. One kissed the right hand, the seat of power, thus recognizing its due. It is said in the Koran: "Had he invented lies concerning Us, We would have seized him by the right hand and severed his heart's vein."[76] That hand, called the hand of the very fortunate chief, was the seat of prosperity, *al-yumn*.

According to prophetic tradition, the black stone was the right hand of God, and an author notes that it was fitting to kiss it, as one did the hands of kings at the time. Hand kissing, a legacy from long ago, emphasized the status of the organ that tied and untied. In the first wave of monotheistic rationality, the caliph 'Omar is said to have hesitated before kissing the black stone. He then complied with the ritual, saying that "he did it only because he had seen the Prophet do the same."[77]

THE HAND THAT GIVES

The hand is the organ that touches. Asking, begging, and imploring were first accompanied with gestures of the hand. The beggar seized the hand

[75] Ibid.
[76] The Koran, 69:44–45.
[77] An-Nassâi, *Sunan*, 147, XXIII, and Ahmad Ibn Hanbal, *Musnad*, I, 22.

of the solicited authority, from which comes the name that still exists today for the beggar, *al-multamiss*,[78] "he who touches" – a word that today has given us *al-multamass*, or "petition."

The hand that one implored and that gave had the ability, through the very gift that it conceded, to sustain solicitors attached to its good will. The hand of the giver had a certain innate sense of a double accounting. The one who gave had "a long hand," according to a well-known expression. The wives of the Prophet, having asked him who among them was the closest to him, were told: "The one among you who has the longest hand." It was reported to be Sawdâ due to the abundance of her alms.[79] To see the power that giving endowed, one need only look to the centrality granted to the saints by virtue of their alms – evidence of their mastery of the circuit of redistribution. (Let us note in passing that *at-tawwal*, a word from which the Arabic term for "length" is derived, designated the rope that enabled the master to keep hold of his animal while allowing it to graze far from him – again a question of bonds![80]) But let us go back to the wives of the Prophet: Sawdâ physically had a long arm; however, most commentators assert that it was Zaynab who won even though she was the most petite. Jâhiz, obviously immovable, thought that she won because she gave as alms the fruit of her work, that is, the product of her hand![81] The hand thus had the power to multiply. It was the weapon that controlled the means of production.

Giving was thus an investment; a renunciation in the present with the expectation of receiving in the future; a reinforcement of the power of one's hand, like that of Zaynab; and an assurance of power itself. By giving to others, I have a hand on them, *li yadun ʿalayhim*, "I hold them in my hands." The constraining and grasping hand thus lurked in the shadow of the charitable hand. Charity, in Arabic, is *as-safad*, from the verb *safada*, which means "to give"; but *safada* also means "to tie" or "to bind with a rope." The act of giving thus tightened the bonds of dependency, which gradually turned into servitude. The term *as-safad* has a synonym, "bond," which the Prophet confirms in declaring that "He who gives you charity enchains you."[82] A king, when asked about the meaning of a land concession he had granted to a poet who had not always

[78] *Tâj al ʿArûss*, VI, 209.
[79] An-Nassâi, *Sunan*, 59, XXIII.
[80] *Lissân*, XI, 413.
[81] *Bayân*, 486.
[82] *Kachâf*, IV, 93.

demonstrated tenderness toward him, responded: "I granted it to him to kill him and his reputation."[83]

The gift granted without immediate and apparent gain was the one that imposed the heaviest return in terms of servitude. It debased the one who received it, reducing him to a low status. It was the gift made with the back of the hand, *ʿan dahri yad*, an expression that brings us right back to the kiss applied to the back of the hand. The gift from the back of the hand called for submission, servitude; it was the poor who "ate off the backs of people's hands."[84] The back of one's hand was not shown as a greeting; it was offered to a solicitor to kiss.

ON PROSTRATION, OR THE ROLE OF THE HAND IN PRAYER

We can see the degree to which hands revealed social positions and relationships of power. Such was the case in relationships to God and to the king. In heavenly matters, one need only follow the prayer ritual to be convinced of this.

Al-Masjid is the word used to designate the space set aside for prayer, that is, the mosque. The plural form, *masâjid*, also designates the limbs and body parts on which the faithful lean when prostrating themselves. The verb *sajada* means "to kneel." Prostration involves seven parts: the two feet, the two knees, the two hands, and the face.[85]

The Prophet, in prostrating himself, put his knees on the ground before his hands, and in getting up, he raised his hands before his knees.[86] But the Prophet, the elect of God, had an exceptional status. He ordered his faithful: "When one of you prostrates himself, you should place your hands [on the ground] before your knees, and not kneel like a camel." Unlike the man, we are told, the camel, like other quadrupeds, has knees at the level of its hands, that is, on its forelimbs.[87]

If we look closer, the kneeling man still has his hands free. Even diminished in the posture of a kneeling man, he is still capable of opposing resistance, if only by holding his head up in front of him. But to be prostrate is to submit oneself completely; it is practically to annihilate oneself. According to the jurisconsults, the slave was never so close to his master as when he was bowing down. The prostrated individual was in the

[83] *Aghâni*, VII, 151.
[84] *Tâj al-ʿArûss*, VII, 168.
[85] Râzi, XV, II, 144.
[86] An-Nassâi, *Sunan*, 38, 12.
[87] Ibid., 18, XII.

greatest debasement. In prostration, one aspired to achieve proximity to God (*wajh al-qurbiya*). The posture of the prostrated slave was invocatory; he was a beggar, and God loves beggars. His debasement was complete when he placed his face on the ground, in the dust, thereby rejoining the species' humble origin in clay. The man affixed to the ground, full of dust, was in extreme poverty; this is one of the definitions of the creature reduced to complete nakedness. He was thus in prostration: this is the first posture of obedience that God demanded following the creation of Adam, and it is similarly the occasion of the first disobedience, that of Satan.

It is understandable that the prayer ritual is the object of so much attention. The greatest care is taken to leave nothing to chance and to have the various parts of the body contribute, each according to its rank and the symbolism that is connected to it. The hand has the most important role. Thus God said to his Envoy: "Pray to your Lord and sacrifice to Him."[88] According to one of the versions reported by the exegetes, the Envoy then asked the archangel Gabriel about the meaning of the verb *naḥara*: "What is this sacrifice, *naḥira*, that God asks of me?" And the archangel replied: "It is not a sacrifice [in the usual sense], but he orders you to raise your hands at the moment of prayer each time you exalt his name [*takbira*], each time you bow [*ruku'*], each time you arise, and when you are prostrate. ... This is how we pray and how the angels of the seven heavens pray, and the ornament of prayer is to raise your two hands after each exaltation of the name of God."[89]

The hands therefore constitute the center of the ritual. Another version explains the *naḥr*, or "sacrifice," by the fact that the two hands are placed at the top of one's chest during prayer: "To raise your hands at the beginning of the prayer is the gesture of the one who seeks protection and refuge in God, and putting the hands on one's chest is the gesture of humble submission."[90] The term, with which so many commentators have struggled, designates the part of the chest between the base of the neck and the sternum where one slits a camel's throat, and from that, we get the act of immolation itself, the putting of the beast to death. Before the advent of Islam, there was an ancient tradition among Arabs to pray to their divinities and bring animals as offerings.[91] This evocation of sacrifice explains the attitude that was to be adopted before God: the forgetting of oneself

[88] The Koran, 108:2.
[89] Râzi, XVI, Part II, 121.
[90] Ibid.
[91] Abû Tayyeb Lûghaoui, *Chajar ad-Dur*, 135.

and annihilation before God are symbolized in prayer by the term denoting sacrifice, which the very ritual of prayer illustrates. Whence comes the advice to the faithful who symbolically offer their chests for immolation, which we take to mean those who face Mecca chest first as a gift of obedience to the all-powerful God. They endeavor to occupy the first rows at the mosque in order to be the first givers. The first to arrive is the one who achieves the greatest sacrifice.[92] *Al-muhajjir* designates the first to arrive; the title that recalls that of *muhâjir*, the companion of the Prophet in the Hegira.

Thus hands play a central role in this sacrifice. Zamakhchari suggests that it consists of placing the right hand on the left hand, in other words, to surrender! The right hand covering the left hand conveyed the praiseworthy intentions of the faithful servant by virtue of the extant social code. And if requesting a favor always entailed debasement, the same was true of invoking God. And the hand revealed the servant's degree of need. The Prophet never raised his hands except in supplicatory prayer.[93]

THE DARK SIDE OF THE HAND

The hand thus had two sides: dominant and dominated, high and low. The *jawâriḥ* were man's body parts, particularly the hands and feet.[94] They were so named because man obtains his subsistence thanks to them, and they hold the memory of that quest. The term was also applied to certain goods that man possessed, such as reproductive female animals, because of their offspring and the profit that resulted from them; the camel, the mare, and the slave woman all belonged to this group. It comes from the verb *jaraḥa*, which clearly refers to a wound. Earning one's means of subsistence was often accompanied by violence. *Jawâriḥ* also designated carnivorous animals and birds of prey; the word bears the imprint of that violence, of that primary accumulation enabled by brute strength. One does not speak of blows by the hand for nothing! In societies where the hunting of game and men was practically a profession, where the spoils of the razzia were the object of daily trade among tribes, where brutal force was publicly praised, the hand was indeed the decisive organ that conquered one's enemies, dealt the mortal blow to the beast, and captured as many beautiful women as possible. It seems, moreover, that

[92] An-Nassâi, *Sunan*, 59, 10.
[93] Ibn Mâja, *Saḥîḥ*, IX, 17.
[94] *Tâj al-ʿArûss*, II, 423.

jâriḥa (singular form of *jawâriḥ*) initially designated only the hand before it came to encompass other parts, that is, to be more explicit, before the hand fell into anonymity among the other body parts.

Derivatives of the same root say a great deal about the violence contained in this vocabulary. We see that a word such as *ḥaraj* designated, among other things, the stretcher on which the wounded and dead were carried. Death was thus hiding in the midst of the language, one side of the word unveiling what the other side was hiding. Death was there to recall the reality that social and cultural evolution would try to hide. *Jariḥa*, or "active member," has lost, over the years, any traces of the blood and killings of earlier ages. It recreated itself from scratch, creating a costume of respectability in societies where one could henceforth earn a living by exercising any activity; the brutal and naked exploitation, the violent stripping, and the murder of the other were relegated into the darkness of night.

Fears of the night that evoked death were not without reason. The Prophet said: "If someone among you awakens at night from his sleep, he should not put his hand in the vase [understood to mean the water of ablutions] before washing it three times, because no one among you knows where his hand has spent the night."[95] Thus, during the night, the hand wanders as it pleases! During the short death that is a man's sleep, the body part in question thus overflows with life and wanders to places unbeknownst to us! A traitorous body part, moving of its own accord, it is a vestige of our primal, uncontrolled animal nature that dwells in us without our knowledge and is unveiled only in the hour when we lose awareness of our acts and gestures.

We can understand that the night might be accused of being an unbeliever and a renegade (*kâfira*) – the unbeliever was the one who hid things and kept them from sight. To wash one's hands three times upon awakening thus was not only a way of purifying oneself but also a way of keeping one's distance from the nocturnal wanderings of the hand or ridding oneself of them. The sacred text says, as a threat addressed to the unbelievers, that the punishment of fire awaits them as the cost of what their hands have done.[96] Normally, the hands do only what the heart commands. Jâhiz clarifies in this regard that the body parts that carry out a man's thoughts are to man what the masses are to the elite[97]: the force of will is what subdues them and makes them act as one wishes.

[95] An-Nassâi, *Sunan*, I, 1.
[96] The Koran, 8:50–51.
[97] Jâhiz, *Rasâ'il*, II, 36.

A HAND ON GOODS AND MEN

The carnivorous hand, if we permit ourselves the expression, endowed he who had the means to use extended powers over men and their property; it turned him into an owner, then a lord, and even, perhaps, if his power grew, a king. In considering ownership, are we not fully in the domain of power? God, the king, and the slave master were owners, each in their own way. Ownership and the servile relationship that it established present an essential common element in decoding the bond of authority.

The root of the word for "ownership" in Arabic alludes to strength and vigor. This root, which gives us *malaka*, that is, "to possess," when read backward becomes *lakama*, a contemporary word that is familiar to boxing fans: it means to strike someone with one's fist. The hand, or in other words strength, played a primordial role in the formation of ownership: *fi yadi* yields the expression "in my hand," or "in my possession." To come into possession of something means to obtain it by force. *Al-malku*, *al-mulku*, and *al-milku*, words all synonymous with ownership, have as a primary meaning to possess a thing and to be in a position to have it for oneself alone,[98] which means having the force to take it for oneself and to defend it.

Regardless of what is said about the ideological foundations of power, mastery and the consolidation of a material base are determinant in its origins and even more so in its survival. Originally, he who had a house and slaves to serve him held the title of king. Ownership of men and property were the first marks of royalty. Mastery over vital resources was also a path to royalty. Such was the case with the control over water, which gave the right to the title. *Al-ayâd*, the plural form of "hand" that means strength, originally designated the low wall erected around a pool of water and a house in order to protect them: the allusion to the hand, which conveyed an accumulation of work and the organization of a defense, is evident here in the building of infrastructures indispensable to power.

The indispensable instrument for the accumulation of goods, the hand was even more indispensable in the control and command of men. To control the manpower, to surround oneself with servants, and to have control over reproduction through the domination of women were, in this perspective, fundamental issues. From this perspective, the slave was the *mamlouk* or the appropriated man. Strength, in this case the strength

[98] Râzi, I, Part I, 24.

of human arms, was primordial – in fact the royal path – to take possession of the slave. The hand was the fearsome weapon of servitude and domination. Regardless of the profile of the slave, the work of the hand was present, either clearly displayed or hidden in the shadows.

According to the commonly accepted meaning, the term *ʿabd mamlaka* was used for a man recently reduced to slavery, the one newly bought without confirmed servile ancestry. The misuse of the hand is obvious here: the reduction to slavery could not occur through a legal act of acquisition; there occurred no trade, which could silence the relationship of strength and the hunt for a man. This profile is tightly connected to royal power.

The case of the *al-ʿabd al-qinn* is different; he was a slave whose parents were already in the hands of his masters. But upon closer inspection, the word *qinn* seems to come from *qinya*, that is, *mulk*, and is related to other words that refer to binding, or the chain and its placement around the hands.[99] A rapid incursion into the language destroys any legalistic vision of the servile relationship and reveals the clanking of chains and the brutal grasping of the hand.

References to slavery in the Koran give the seat of honor to the hand. *Mulk al-yamîn*, literally "what your right hands possess," in the sacred text designates slaves. The expression is strictly reserved for slaves and is never used for other goods[100] – not only because slaves were specific goods but also because of their strategic role in the access to and consolidation of power.

Another reference to slavery in the Koran is *raqaba* or its plural form *riqâb*, which designates the neck – terms that we have already mentioned in reference to the freeing of slaves. Here we are dealing with the conquered hand, the other side of the hand. The mention of the neck comes from the fact that the hands of the captive were tightly bound to his neck, which explains that the chain was called *jâmiʾâ*, that is, something that joins. Freeing oneself from it meant untying the knot around the hands and the neck – whence the expression used for liberation, *fak raqaba*.

Neither strength, in the framework of forced servitude, nor greed, in that of voluntary servitude, can explain the extent of royal servitude. This is because royal servitude also obtained its numbers through the social constraints that sent many individuals into the hands of the powerful. Strength in fact took hold of the individual in difficulty who was asking

[99] *Islâḥ al-Mantiq*, 398; Asmaʿî, *Muʿjam al-ʿAsmaʿî*, 341.
[100] Ibn Hilâl, *Al-Furûq*, 207.

for support. Servitude came to be entrenched in a social milieu that established a dynamic favorable to its exercise, a dynamic that engendered a being susceptible to servitude.

THE INDIVIDUAL IN THE CHAINS OF SERVITUDE

Servitude devoured individuals deprived of strong bonds of solidarity. Such was the *mufrij*, the outsider without bonds of kinship or alliance to call upon. "One does not leave in Islam an individual without family or patronage,"[101] says the prophetic tradition. The isolated man, led to the land of Islam by the vicissitudes of fate and lacking support there, was socially dead if he did not put himself into a relationship of servitude, according to his intellectual or professional capacities, whether with people of modest means, with the powerful, or, if he had the opportunity, at court.[102] The same was true of individuals isolated through circumstances, who were reduced to begging and were forced to attach themselves to groups or families in order to escape destitution.

The state of perfect servitude was that in which the connection to the master was exclusive. The individual had to be deprived of ties with any anchor or base that could feed the desire for independence in him; he had to be lowered and debased. At the time, the outsider, the man without lineage, without family, held the lowest and least coveted status.[103] The person of low status was compared to inedible mushrooms that men crushed under their feet. A parasitic plant, having neither roots nor leaves but attaching itself to tree branches, it was cursed by the poet: "It is the *cuscuta* with neither leaves nor roots, nor zephyr nor shadow nor fruit."[104] Like it, the isolated individual attached himself and sought protection; for him servitude was a way out, even a blessing. In the case of a man who was found and helped by another, who then went to inquire of the caliph ʿOmar regarding his status, history retains the caliph's very clear edict: "He is a free man and you have his patronage." It was a strange freedom indeed, earning him the fate of the freed slave.[105] The master was the providential savior in the absence of close or distant family.[106]

[101] *Jamhara*, 463.
[102] Al-Haroui, *Gharîbu al-ḥadîth*, I, 29.
[103] *Majma ʿal-amthâl*, I, 361.
[104] *Majma ʿal-amthâl*, I, 362.
[105] Al-Haroui, *Gharîbu al-ḥadîth*, II, 65.
[106] *Jamharat rasâʾil*, IV, 280.

Al-manbûdh, the illegitimate child, was a rootless parasite, like the isolated palm tree or the palm tree that grew from seed without having been planted. In the beginning, the prophet Muhammad was given that name by his tribe, who wanted to diminish him.[107]

Al-munqati' designated the individual cut off from everything, without support, as though he were physically handicapped, as the name suggests. Wars, famines, and displacements of tribes engendered these types of men.

The *nazi'*, the one who was pulled out, was the person whose mother had been raped. *Al-ḥamîl* was the one whose mother had been brought from the land of the infidels while carrying him in her womb.[108]

One who was simply an outsider was the *gharîb* or the *attawi* – a word that designated one who had arrived alone; this term also evoked death, illness, and misfortune.[109]

All these statuses bore witness to the diversity of destinies that gave rise to such situations.[110] These processes of individualization were not accompanied by the possibility of either economic or social autonomy – this latter category was unthinkable at the time. These statuses were visible in groups in the process of disintegrating; they illustrated how difficult it was to survive outside the group and the resistance that arose before the phenomena of marginalization. *Al-za'nafa* was a part of a whole, necessarily incomplete, that is, without internal coherence that could endow it with autonomy. The term was used to designate a minuscule tribe, incapable of surviving because of its reduced size, that attached itself to a larger tribe. It was not a complete tribe: it could include individuals without real or fictitious ties of kinship; it sought to connect to another community. Endurance in this harsh environment unfavorable to the minor structures of sociability necessarily arose through an alliance with larger structures or with powerful authorities.[111]

The process of generating individuals was, however, not just the result of chance due to wars and catastrophes. It could also be the outcome of specific destinies of very diverse people who had taken leave of their original communities. We are speaking here of people with confirmed social know-how, *dâhiya*, endowed with a remarkable political sense,

[107] *Tâj al-'Arûss*, V, 400.
[108] *Tâj al-'Arûss*, XIV, 170–171.
[109] Al-Haroui, *Gharîbu al-ḥadîth*, II, 118; *Tâj al-'Arûss*, XIX, 134.
[110] Tâj al-'Arûss, XI, 474.
[111] *Tâj al-'Arûss*, XII, 150.

who eagerly went in search of a position that better corresponded to their talents.

For all of these people, servitude was a way out that served a wide range of functions: it was a way to reintegrate the displaced. Whether they were simple servants, workers who needed to earn their bread, or enterprising individuals who were stifled by their community framework, they would find a place in servitude.

The expressions that conveyed these phenomena are riddled with the violence of the shock that pulverized the compact group that had survived only by its very unity, reducing it to individuals who were isolated and directionless, dispersed far from one another. The expressions stress the scattering and reveal the changing of statuses, notably the reintegration into the social milieu by means of servitude. Speaking of dispersed peoples, texts call them *ʿabâbîd*: the word crudely recalls enslavement and the status of slave, or *ʿabd*.[112]

The king fed on this erosion of social structures, which he accentuated by war and usury. He gradually dominated them by mastering their foundations. On the one hand, he established and consolidated his control over the chiefs; on the other, he opened his doors to the "dregs" of society that the work of erosion had produced, as well as to nobles who had been marginalized in the internal competition of their tribes. These individuals were found in great numbers in the royal entourage; they were called intruders and were constantly cursed by the families of the kings.

The exclusivity that servitude assumed is best highlighted within the framework of adoration, which took its referents from slavery. "Those who have distanced themselves from the world have won," said the Prophet. These were the *mutafarridûn*,[113] the "individualized," whose status was highly lauded; individuality opened the path to solitude with the one adored, which was one of the foundations of the monarchical State of servitude, for it implied escaping all networks of dependency, both horizontal and vertical, to benefit only the master. Former pacts of allegiance were called into question with the intent of making the new masters into incontrovertible supports.[114] As we have seen, even within the family, which saw its dimensions notably reduced through the new regimentation of inheritance, the authority of the father was diminished in favor of God and his lieutenants: "[R]emember God as you remember

[112] *Kitâb al-alfâdh*, 41.
[113] *Tâj al-ʿArûss*, V, 158.
[114] Tabari, *Tafsîr*, IV, 58 and 386–387.

your forefathers or with deeper reverence."[115] It was necessary to reinforce the nascent central authority.

Thus one attained pure obedience, which was the fantasy of kings.[116] The logic of servitude was pushed to the extreme: the only filiation praised was that of the master, with the individual becoming an essential piece in the construction of the kingdom. In this fantasy, society was pulverized: no other bond held in the face of the one that could overshadow it as on the day of the resurrection: "[O]n that day their ties of kindred shall be broken, nor shall they ask help of one another."[117] The king's objective was to diminish the subject, to weaken him, to reduce him to impotence, to annihilate in him any will for resistance and autonomy while keeping him active. The status indicated is indeed slavery, in which the servant was extracted from normal social bonds of kinship as well as being removed from other influences.

Such control by the king over his subject, real or anticipated, represented a considerable change in the dominant relationships within pre-Islamic Arabia. In this society, royalty in fact had a tendency to stretch the bonds within the group; it opposed the tribal community whose members were very closely bound and that was characterized by a remarkable integration of the outsider. "The tribe of Quraysh, which was the Prophet's tribe, was beneficent toward the *mawlâ* [the dependent], whom it treated practically like one of its own" – just like other tribes.[118] Ibn Hichâm, regarding a certain Sâlem, presented him as a dependent of Abû Hudayfa, whereas in reality, he was a former slave, freed according to pre-Islamic practices that could grant complete freedom to a slave; the man was later adopted as a son by the above-mentioned patron.[119] The description of his situation shows well what separated the pre-Islamic world from the new society. In the latter, the solitary individual was in a precarious state, which necessarily threw him into the arms of the powerful. One may legitimately raise the question of the greater capacity for integration in pre-Islamic society than in the society that would follow. It is striking to note that within the most renowned families, former slaves were adopted as sons.[120] The phenomenon was sufficiently powerful in its message to

115 The Koran, 2:200.
116 *Nihâya*, III, 465.
117 The Koran, 23:101, and Râzi, XII, Part I, 106.
118 *Al-Kâmil*, II, 725.
119 *As-Sîra*, II, 479.
120 One speaks of *istalqaha*, which means to be affiliated with someone as a son; the word also means to fecundate, to enseminate, *Aghâni*, I, 326; another term, *al-ibtitân*, is also used, II, 260.

mark a difference and to suggest that the space for liberty was rigorously closed to individuals lacking the means to establish their belonging to Arab families. Servitude was thus the only path to reintegrate into society and to escape social death, if not death itself.

SLAVES OR SUBJECTS OF THE KING: NO ONE IS FREE IN THE VALLEY OF ʿAOUF!

The possession of slaves in tribal societies existing in a hostile environment was a sign of wealth, if not of opulence. "Slaves were an ornament and not possessions," notes a chronicler.[121] A notable, a companion of the Prophet, who was asked about poverty, replied: "Do you have a wife you are going home to? Do you have a house to live in? Then you are among the rich!" And the possession of slaves opened other social horizons, as a jurisconsult liked to recall: "What is royalty if not a mount, a slave, and a house?"[122] The quote is also sometimes attributed to the Prophet.[123] In other words, royalty consisted of the vassal, the soldier, the mount, and the shadow of the home that would provide a very fortunate threshold to God (*a-sudda alʾâliya billâh*)!

Domestic power was the core, the primary and fundamental foundation of royalty, or *mulk*: "to be master of oneself, one's goods and one's household,"[124] the obligatory first step. Next came another indispensable condition for acceding to the opposite side of servitude: not being dependent. The king was "he who has goods that prevent him from having to fulfill undesirable obligations."[125] When the sons of Israel were saved from the slavery to which the Copts had reduced them, their freedom was named *mulk*, or "royalty,"[126] thus showing how much that condition was defined by its opposite: servitude. The bond between slavery and royalty is explicitly highlighted in the Koran when it speaks of the queen of Sheba: "When kings invade a city they ravage it and abase the mightiest of its people."[127]

The reference to slavery had as a clear objective to highlight the free status of the dominant groups. Owning slaves was not automatically

[121] *Al-Kâmil*, I, 385.
[122] Ibn Kathîr, *Tafsîr*, II, 52.
[123] Tabari, *Tafsîr*, IV, 509–511.
[124] Ibn Kathîr, *Tafsîr*, II, 52.
[125] *Kachâf*, I, 607.
[126] Ibid.
[127] The Koran, 27:34, and Tabari, *Tafsîr*, IX, 515.

synonymous with access to chiefdom, as illustrated by the experiences of slave masters of common origin or *souqa*. Thus we find the one who "endured trials, was master and slave, gave orders, and received them" without that making him a king. In royalty, servitude worked in a single direction; the king belonged unfailingly to the realm of masters and not to those of subjects. A clearly established barrier on the ladder of power thus distinguished masters from others.[128]

The reference to slavery better renders the depth of the king-subject relationship. "No one is free in the valley of ʿAouf!" says a proverb inspired by the story of a petty king who "ruled by force over any person who appeared in his valley, to the point that all the inhabitants were at the level of slaves because they obeyed him blindly."[129] It illustrates the message of the bond of authority within monarchical power.[130] Slavery also functioned, in representations, as one of the obvious signs of power: "A black servant abruptly entered my house and told me to get dressed, so I knew that he had done so on the order of a governor or a king."[131] The degree of enslavement of populations revealed the measure of power and glory. Subjects addressed their king in no other way than by saying: "We are your slaves ready to hear and to obey."[132] Thus a warlord received from his tribe "the oath of king, his crown, his greeting, and the obedience that was his. His power was such that subsequently he forbade access to any space under the clouds where pasture was forbidden, took hunting grounds that did not belong to him, decreed that no other herd could drink with his, that no fire would be lit along with his!"[133] We find many examples of tribal chiefs like this lord, none of whose subjects "had the freedom to rent a camel or to work without his permission; no land could be defended without his order."[134]

The king was completely different from his subjects. He was foreign to them in his origins and by virtue of his extraordinary nature. In the tribal milieu, this foreignness preserved the segmental social balance, avoided the difficulties that such a milieu opposed to the emergence of an uncontested absolute authority, and resolved the dilemma

[128] *Islâḥ al-Mantiq*, 407.
[129] *Majma ʿal-amthâl*, II, 279.
[130] This was ʿAouf Ibn Muḥallam Ibn Dhuhl al-Chibâni, who was called that because of his nobility and power, *Nihâya*, I, 363.
[131] *Aghâni*, XXIII, 83.
[132] *As-Sîra*, I, 47.
[133] *ʿIqd*, V, 202.
[134] *Aghâni*, V, 39–40.

of the apparent contradiction between servitude and kinship. The king was naturally external to the society of his governed. It was thus that the notables of a tribe seeking a supreme chief resolved their problem: "We have decided to enthrone a king ... and he cannot belong to one of our tribes out of fear that the others would refuse, which would lead to a conflict. Therefore we call upon a *tuba*ʿ [king belonging to a royal line of Yemen], upon whom we will confer our rule."[135] The path was then open to relationships other than those that existed between members of the same clan or the same tribe. Servitude acquired an immediate legitimacy in the relationship between foreigners, whether they were so due to their origins or for statutory reasons.

BEHIND THE SUBJECT, THE DEPENDENT SLAVE

According to certain commentators, the *mamlaka*, which today would be translated as kingdom, means "the power of the king and his authority over his subjects," thus describing the bond that united them and that some indeed render as slavery.[136] The word is, in any case, clearly related to enslavement. Generally, in representations of the time, command was linked to strength and to control over men. The term *ḥâkim*, "representative of authority," is derived from *ḥakâmatu*, which designates the metal noseband attached to the straps of the collar and affixed to the animal's muzzle. The term is used in prophetic tradition to illustrate man's relationship to God: "There is no man who is not held by the noseband."[137] Such control assumes a very constraining bond for the subject. Thus, "when a king held power over a territory thereby reducing its inhabitants to slavery, he then exercised over them the same power as over his own slaves."[138] That is, he could choose among them those he deemed best for his service and those he wanted to give away. Even better, Jâhiz drew a parallel between service to a master and service to a king, calling service to kings "perfect servitude" that consisted of anticipating, of never committing a blunder, and of demonstrating vigilance in order to diligently execute orders.[139]

The parallel was not purely speculative: conflicts of jurisdiction were common between the two authorities, that of the master and that of the

[135] *ʿIqd*, V, 210.
[136] *Tâj al-ʿArûss*, XIII, 648.
[137] *Nihâya*, I, 420.
[138] Al-Haroui, *Gharîbu al-ḥadîth*, II, 78.
[139] *Bayân*, 392.

king, when it came to applying punishments to slaves. The jurisconsults offer differing opinions on this subject.[140] For Jâhiz, "obedience to the king is different from obedience to the chiefs [of tribes]. The king in fact possesses the bodies of the people, who keep for themselves the choice of their feelings. It is the same with the *mawâli* and with slaves."[141]

This was indeed the situation that prevailed in monarchies at the advent of Islam. A certain al-Ach'ate Ibn Qays sought support from the caliph ʿOmar against the people of Najrân, his former subjects before Islam, who henceforth refused to obey him. Called upon, they replied: "We were *mamlaka* slaves and not *qinn* slaves." The *qinn* was the slave who was owned from father to son, whereas the *mamlaka* slave was originally free, enslaved by force not following a war, a kidnapping, or a purchase but simply by constraint.[142] The caliph decided in favor of the argument of the enslaved populations.

Our work focuses on the nature of the servile bond between the king and his subjects, not on its legality. In fact, untying the existing bond of servitude was an essential factor in the struggle with powers that dominated up until that time and whose foundations had to be eroded. Regarding private slavery, the right of ownership was not questioned, the principle retained by the Muslim leaders being "What is in his hands cannot be taken away."[143] Thus the numerous people at the foundation of the considerable chiefdoms were targeted. For those powerful petty kings, the legitimate ownership of those who were "placed in their house, at their service" was recognized without examination of how they were acquired, and the rights over "those who were abandoned to themselves and who paid the *kharâj*"[144] were denied. In other words, the process consisted of reassuring the master within the domestic framework and of delegitimizing his royal hold over men.

The new caliphal power henceforth operated within a framework that was otherwise more structured and ideologically more refined. The caliph ʿAli juxtaposed the former masters with a more vast dependency: "We have conquered you thanks to these reds," he declared to a former king, meaning by that the *mawâli*.[145] This meant that the act of liberating a population from servile subjection to the king did not aim to eradicate

140 Râzi, XII, Part I, 126.
141 Jâhiz, *Rasâ'il*, II, 188.
142 Al-Haroui, *Gharîbu al-ḥadîth*, II, 78.
143 *Lissân*, X, 491.
144 *Fâ'iq*, I, 397.
145 Al-Haroui, *Gharîbu al-ḥadîth*, II, 158.

the bonds of servitude, but attacked potential competitors who were still powerful, whose troops they sought to disperse: it was reported that a notable visited ʿOmar accompanied by four thousand slaves![146] This eloquent procession indeed recalled the high stakes of mastering the networks of servitude.

The distinction was made between private slavery and royal slavery. The new power recognized as a slave any individual serving within the palaces of the kings and the great tribal chiefs, whereas those on the outside who paid the *kharâj* were declared free.[147] The true objective of this distinction was to deprive the former kings of their subjects, not to decree that the reduction to slavery was illegal, as one might be led to believe by a quick scanning of the sources.

Slavery was the explicitly recognized principle of the monarchy, of the state. This was conveyed in deeds by enslavement through force and by the payment of a tribute, the *darîba*. The tale of Hujr, father of the great poet Imru'û al-Qays, is an example of this. When the tribe of the Bani Assad refused to pay the tribute, Hujr took its notables and beat them to death. They were henceforth called the "slaves of the club,"[148] an expression that subsequently became the symbol of all forced submission.[149] The *darîba*, in modern, classical, and popular language, is the word that designates taxes. Initially a tax imposed by force on the subjects by the king – the quality from which it earned its name – the word meant "to strike" and also designated the sword.[150] The tribute in question was the bearer of violence that could lead to death.

In fact, if the interior slaves paid their due in work, those of the exterior paid it in kind or in coin (*kharâj* or *darîba*).[151] The *kharâj* or *darîba* was the product of the slave; his *ghilla*, or fruit, was the profit that he procured for the master; one then spoke of *ʿabd mukhârij*, an expression that can be rendered as "tributary slave."[152] The tribute was paid periodically to the master in money or in kind, as was also the case for prostitute slaves.[153] Enslavement following conquests and the submission

[146] *Naqa'id*, I, 39. This was Samayfa' Ibn Nâkûr al-Kulâ'î.
[147] Al-Haroui, *Gharîbu al-ḥadîth*, II, 242.
[148] *A-Chi'ru wa chu'arâ'*, I, 105.
[149] *Bayân*, 431.
[150] Jamhara, I, 315; *Majma ʿal-amthâl*, II, 490.
[151] Al-Haroui, *Gharîbu al-ḥadîth*, II, 242; *Kharâj* or *kharj*, *Lissân*, art. *kharj*. One also speaks of *itâwa* connected to the tribute paid by the foreigner; see *Al-Kâmil*, I, 328.
[152] Al-Haroui, *Gharîbu al-ḥadîth*, I, 393; *Lissân*, I, 544. Some linguists make the distinction between the *kharâj* or *fay'* and the *kharaj* or *darîba* or *jizya*.
[153] Al-Akhtal, 374.

of populations was conveyed by payment of the tribute, which was the sign of the new status.[154] This vocabulary was adopted, after the former royalties, by the nascent Muslim state. The caliph ʿOmar thus imposed on peasants a tribute that was called *kharâj* because it was tied to the produce of the earth, which was also the case of lands conquered without resistance, which became *kharâjiya* lands.[155] Speaking of populations of the Book who were subjected and converted, and evoking the modalities of their insertion into the fiscal system by the payment of the *kharâj*, al-Hajjâj says: "They are our slaves from father to son, and when a slave converts to Islam, does that absolve him from paying the tribute to his master?"[156]

ESCAPING ROYAL AUTHORITY

This detour on taxation shows the initially quite evident and later more subtle similarity of the master-slave and king-subject relationships. Enslavement was a structural given in the monarchies, where it was commonly called *takhawul*. "They recognized his royal authority and proved of good counsel when he took possession of them,"[157] says Jâhiz.

What is most striking, however, is the meaning of *mamlaka*, that is, individuals or populations enslaved through force, a word that today still has the sense of "kingdom"! The word designates at the same time the power of the king and his slaves.[158] The royal hold, or *mulk*, is moreover synonymous with violent control over men and their property: *tamallaka* is applied to people illegally reduced to slavery through force.[159]

One understands that spaces of freedom existed only on the margins of royal territories, escaping their logic of servitude. This is conveyed by the language of the period, which establishes a clear difference between enslaved populations and those that escaped the authority of the kings. The chronicles mention groups that existed outside the royal authority and refused to acknowledge it. The *rawâfiḍ*, a name that would later be attributed to a Shiite faction, were those who kept their distance from

154 *Kachâf*, I, 631.

155 The land of conquest or of *fay'*, which etymologically means "return," that is, what God gave to the Muslims of the infidels' goods, either because the latter abandoned their goods to the Muslims or because they asked for peace in return for payment of a tribute or the paying of a ransom to buy themselves back. Yâqût, *Muʿjam al-buldân*, I, 58–59.

156 Al-Haroui, *Gharîbu al-ḥadîth*, I, 394–395.

157 *Bayân*, 592.

158 *Lissân*, X, 491.

159 Ibid.

their masters, like the herd sent to graze without a shepherd.[160] The *fawḍâ* populations, a term that today is rendered as "people of disorder," were egalitarian groups without a master, where decisions were made collectively.[161] In general, such autonomy was found in areas that were not easily accessible, far from the centers of power.[162]

To emphasize the degree to which servitude and royalty were connected, the free were defined as never having submitted to the authority of a king or paid a tribute to a foreign king.[163] Thus the members of such tribes "were people with the most noble souls and with the highest aims; they have never paid a tribute to any king."[164] *Adakala* was a group of that type, derived from *dakala* or "to walk on something," which made them people on top, nobles resistant to all submission. The word refers also to clayish water, which escapes the hold of authority.[165] The *allaqâḥ* were those who had never obeyed a king or been the property of anyone, a pure vein of liberty in some sense.[166] Obviously, in the struggle for power that would erupt following the advent of Islam, these classifications were of the greatest importance; they proved to be decisive in the competition that immediately eliminated the groups showing even a hint of servility. Mecca was thus a *laqâḥ* land.[167] One also spoke of *khula'â'*, or tribes that resisted royal authority.[168] Such attitudes were not just those of groups or tribes that were more or less powerful, but also those of rebellious individuals who lived in the margins of society. Thus a reckless black poet, who earned his living through robbery, exclaimed: "If I weren't strong, I would have been a slave; if I were a woman I would have been a slave. Oh, God, keep me from failure; as for the *hayba* [the aura, an allusion here to authority], no *hayba*! I fear no one!"[169]

Servitude revealed the profound nature of the bond of authority and particularly that of the relationship between the king and his subjects. The passage from the pre-Islamic state to the Muslim state, despite the apparent ruptures, occurred seamlessly as former kings were stripped of their authority and the caliphal authority was strengthened. Nothing

[160] Ibid., VII, 157.
[161] Ibid., VII, 210.
[162] One speaks of lands or *bilâd châghira*; *Tâj al-'Arûss*, VII, 39.
[163] *As-Sîra*, I, 70, note 4.
[164] *'Iqd*, III, 334.
[165] *Tâj al-'Arûss*, XIV, 239.
[166] *Al-Kâmil*, II, 724–725.
[167] *Tâj al-'Arûss*, IV, 190; Jâhiz, *Rasâ'il*, I, 187.
[168] *Aghâni*, V, 27.
[169] *Majma 'al-amthâl*, II, 13.

fundamentally revolutionary that might have established a new logic of power intervened in the social relationships; slavery was not questioned either up close or from afar, and it continued to intervene as a referent in the relationship of authority. What occurred instead was a reorganization of the authoritarian space that reshuffled the division of power between the king and the divine authority, in other words, between the master of earth and the master of heaven.

4

The Master of Heaven and the Master of Earth

Freedom in Arab society was perceived only in opposition to servitude, not as being founded on its negation, but, on the contrary, by objecting to its heavy presence, by asserting itself in strict coexistence with it. Servitude was the essence of the relationship of authority and the most extreme expression of that form of domination. Even if its manifestations differed as a function of the specific relationship, it formed the common core of the various relationships of authority. The status of *mawlâ*, which designated the close one, is an illustration of this. The word covers all relationships of authority; it expresses both poles of the relationship, that is, the two sides of the coin: it designates God, but also the king as well as the slave master, the relative and the companion, the father and the husband, but also the slave and the freed man.

The question of the relationship between heaven and earth, between the religious and the political, becomes weightier when it is raised from the perspective of proximity and more precisely of servitude. In other words, what parallels can we establish between the relationship of the faithful to God, that of the subject to the king, and that of the slave to the master? The bond of servitude traverses these three relationships and supports them to varying degrees. It is useful to point out the bridges that connect them in light of this bond, and to point out the role of the latter in the construction and demarcation of the different fields of authority. The master-slave relationship occupied a place of honor in the definition of the other relationships of authority, the essential lexicon of which is drawn from the language of servitude.

THE UNAVOIDABLE MIRROR: THE MASTER AND THE SLAVE

According to respected opinions, the most appropriate bonds for exploring the content of divine authority are the master-slave and king-subject relationships. "His is what the heavens and the earth contain."[1] says the sacred text. God is thus the absolute master with undivided power, like a slave's master, "because the slave," notes the jurisconsult Tabari, "is at the disposition of his master and cannot serve anyone else without his permission."[2] The jurisconsult comments on this verse: "Everything that is on earth is my property and my handiwork, and none of my creatures should adore anyone but me as long as they belong to me, for the slave must adore only his owner and must obey only his master."[3]

But though this relationship is an effective point of reference to illustrate the foundations of divine authority, there are, however, many notable differences that bear on the intervening transactions of each relationship.

Masters lived off the labor of their slaves, regardless of the type of work they did, for masters collected the fruit of the work. If the slaves were meant for domestic work, they spared the masters the expense of relying on a salaried worker. Thus masters had a material interest in their slaves, whereas God expected nothing from his faithful: "I demand no livelihood of them, nor do I ask that they should feed Me. God alone is the Munificent Giver."[4]

The very nature of mastery is the question here. The slave master was not infallible in his natural and social milieu; he could not live as an isolated being. Hence, unlike God, he was not a perfect master who could suffice unto himself. Despite the fact that his mastery over his slaves was the result of his seizing control, it had many limits. The slave could change masters by being sold or bequeathed, just as he could also be freed from slavery, which accentuates the imperfect nature of the mastery.[5] God's

[1] The Koran, 2:255. The mention of slavery in reference to notably divine authority is abundant. In Râzi we can point out the following instances: IV, Part I, 45–46, 115, 178, and Part II, 34; V, Part I, 38; VI, Part II, 169; VIII, Part II, 151; IX, Part II, 93; X, Part II, 38, 178; XI, Part I, 161, and Part II, 111; and many others.

[2] Tabari, *Tafsîr*, III, 10, and also X, 211: "the *mamlouk* owes obedience to his master and not to the one who has nothing."

[3] Ibid.

[4] The Koran, 51:57 and 52:257; *Kachâf*, IV, 396.

[5] Râzi, XIII, Part I, 104.

ownership, on the other hand, was fixed: he was "the Mighty One, the Invincible,"[6] and the only one who could be so. A man might escape enslavement to his fellow man, but his service to God was eternal: "There is no escape from adoration [*'ibâda*] or enslavement [*'ubûdiyya*] for creatures."[7]

The master and the slave were of the same species[8]; they shared the same nature. "In what He has provided, God has favoured some among you above others."[9] In other words, servitude, in the master-slave relationship, benefited the master, who directly or indirectly had an interest in it. In the relationship with God, servitude benefited the servant: "[T]hey are the winners in their adoration-servitude [*'ibâda*]."[10]

The relationship to God was in fact the bond of servitude tied as tightly as possible, rid of any material concerns or any contingency; it was the pure relationship of servitude in which the supreme master called for the exclusive recognition of his mastery. And it was total because the master of the heavens possessed not only the body of the slave, as did the master, but also his soul.[11] In perfect servitude, the servant did not seek to derive any material benefit or to be granted a pardon. Thus, in paradise, young servants, put at the disposal of the guests of the place, labored not out of self-interest, "as do servants on earth," but "with no other goal than to serve the well-being [of the guests]."[12]

Râzi notes a similarity between the relationship to God and that between the king and his close slaves – not the *mukallafûn*, from *kulfa*, from which comes the word for "duty" in Arabic, who had precise responsibilities. Speaking of the treatment reserved for believers in paradise, he states that "it happens according to the customs of the kings on earth." The author then alludes to the gifts of foodstuffs and monetary concessions that the kings heaped upon their favorites each time they increased their rank.[13] The parallel conveys the same logic, the transaction in both cases having no goal for the master except adoration. Thus, when a slave close to the king died before his master, "he goes before God in the condition of a brown slave," for the latter and the heretic were of the same

[6] The Koran, 51:57.
[7] Râzi, XIII, Part I, 105.
[8] *Kachâf*, II, 595–596.
[9] The Koran, 16:71.
[10] Râzi, XIV, Part II, 200.
[11] Râzi, XV, Part I, 137.
[12] Râzi, XIV, Part II, 218.
[13] Râzi, XIV, Part II, 217.

order in the popular imagination.[14] In any case, he would be subject to the worst difficulties in the beyond due to his adoration of someone other than God on earth.[15] In the relationship in question, the king effectively incarnated a divinity for those close to him.

The definition of the relationship of divine authority drew its content as much from the relationship of the king with his subjects as from that of the master with his slaves. The terms *malik* (king) and *mâlik* (owner) have the same root; their synthesis defined absolute authority.

The king's relationship with his subjects was different from the one that linked the master and the slave. "The king is king of his subjects, whereas the master is the owner of his slaves. The slave's status is inferior to that of the subject. It follows that the constraints of ownership are stronger than those [exercised] by royalty. From this perspective, the slave master is more powerful than the king."[16] The king's subjects could remove themselves from his command, which was impossible for a slave to do. Every king had to take the condition of his subjects into consideration, whereas the subjects were not obliged to obey his orders unconditionally; the slave, however, was obliged to carry out his master's orders. Thus mastery was stronger in relation to slavery; the *mâlik* (master) was more perfect than the *malik* (king).

We might, however, consider things differently. Owning slaves was common. Many were able to acquire slaves and to become their master, but to become king of a land was not easy. In fact, only "the most considerable and the most illustrious" were able to achieve that status. The king then was more noble than the slave master.[17] The sacred text seems to lean in this direction when it commands: "Say: 'I seek refuge in the Lord [*rabb*] of men, the King [*malik*] of men, the God of men....'"[18] The title of king appeared as one of the strategic attributes of God. Let us add that the king was more powerful than all the owners combined and that he legally had the prerogatives of justice; he was the one who administered punishments.

Nevertheless, these advantages were tempered by considerations of another kind. Even though he was rich, the king expected rewards from his subjects, who also expected them from him; there was a reciprocal greediness in the relationship. "The king has an aura and politics; the master, compassion and mercy"; the master was therefore good, unlike

[14] Râzi, II, Part II, 184.
[15] Râzi, XV, Part I, 93.
[16] Râzi, I, Part I, 192 and 193.
[17] Râzi, I, Part I, 193.
[18] The Koran, 114:1–2.

the king.[19] It was in the extreme relationship of servitude, that of slavery, that one finds a component as determinant as mercy, the corollary of total power. A reference to the relationship between father and son, which constituted an aspect of the master-slave relationship, intervenes here; it gives that mercy more consistency and a natural foundation.[20]

In fact, the place of servitude in monarchical authority was essential, as much in its formation as in its exercise, a fact that considerably decreased the difference between king and master. The master-slave relationship was thus the pivot of the relationship of authority, to which all other relationships were connected: they mirrored it and measured their worth by it. It is a prerequisite for an objective understanding of the relationships to God and to the king; the outcome of a relationship of force, it clearly exhibits what the other relationships stifled and masked: the absolute control over the subject.

Although slavery did not completely account for the relationship of authority, which covered a wide range of relationships, it was nonetheless the primary foundation of power; it was a layer onto which others were added, with varying tones but nonetheless connected to an original common source. Henceforth, one can better understand the play of mirrors in which the various relationships of authority participated. In the Koranic exegesis, the description of the relationship to the king is revealed to be an effective representation of divine authority.

THE ROYAL GOD AND THE DIVINE KING

The teachings that address the relationship to the all-powerful Lord draw their material from the power relationships that were familiar to Arab populations. In discussing divine anger, Zamakhchari presents an image of the king's wrath: "[T]hat is, vengeance and punishment are the procedures of the king when he is angry at one of his subjects."[21] The most highly charged popular representation of power and fear was that which was experienced in the relationship to the king. Thus it was used as an example to incite people to fear God and avoid his punishment.

To fully assess the imposing presence of the Lord on the day of resurrection, when he "comes down with the angels, in their ranks,"[22] one

[19] Râzi, I, Part I, 192 and 195.
[20] Râzi, XIII, Part I, 129.
[21] *Kachâf*, I, 27.
[22] The Koran, 89:22.

must look to the royal example. Each time the king "attends [a ceremony] in person, signs of consideration and authority are manifest and owing to his presence, whereas nothing similar is perceptible when only his soldiers, his ministers and those close to him, whoever they may be, are present."[23]

Far from limiting himself to the effectiveness of a pedagogy destined for a popular audience, the jurisconsult was, in fact, when faced with the question of the modes of exercising authority, driven to describe the workings of heaven in terms of the royal codes of conduct. The similarities in the language used to describe the two authorities are striking: one said of God that "His are the keys [*maqâlid*] of the heavens and the earth."[24] The word is still used today upon the enthronement of kings.[25]

Recourse to the royal model was not dictated by superficial considerations only. The nature of the bond between the king and his subjects, founded on servitude, was what attracted the jurisconsult's attention. The supreme Being, creator of the universe, was master of his creatures, who were his property; they consequently owed him absolute submission. "The creator is first an owner [*mâlik*], and the one who is his property [his *mamlouk*] owes him consideration and praise."[26] The powerful kings offered a concrete example of such submission; in this regard, they could serve as models in order to better instruct the general public as to the nature of the coveted submission.

Nonetheless, all these parallels ultimately entailed a conflict of jurisdiction, which did not escape the commentators. God is described as the king of the *mulk*, the royalty.[27] "Lord, Sovereign of all sovereignty, You bestow sovereignty on whom You will and take it away from whom You please,"[28] or even "He created you from a single soul.... Such is God, your Lord. His is the sovereignty. There is no god but Him."[29] The king shared with God the message of ownership and thus of servitude inherent in royalty; texts recognize this shared power of the king as a lieutenancy. God had absolute sovereignty, whereas the kings of the earth had only fragments of it.[30] The recognition of all sovereignty in God, in his quality

[23] *Kachâf*, IV, 739.
[24] The Koran, 39:63.
[25] *Kachâf*, IV, 135, and III, 88.
[26] Râzi, XIII, Part II, 50 and 11.
[27] Tabari, *Târîkh*, III, 221.
[28] The Koran, 3:26.
[29] The Koran, 39:6.
[30] Tabari, *Tafsîr*, X, 66.

as the single god, is explained by the fact that the Arab kings were the objects of an adoration equal to that of the gods.[31] But even recognized as fragmentary, the earthly sovereignty nonetheless contained, by that very fact, a share of the divine, as seen in the Koranic discourse. God, king of kings, not only recognized in the kings an authority by virtue of delegation, but by delegating his authority to the royalty bestowed a divine essence upon it. Thus royalty was the bearer of the divine secret of authority.

The modalities of granting lieutenancy refer to those that occurred between kings. Zamakhchari comments in this sense on the verse "David, we have made you [lieutenant] in the land"[32] when he notes: "That is, we have named you our lieutenant to reign on earth just as kings designate their lieutenants in a territory and thus make them kings."[33] Let us stress that David was traditionally considered to be the founder of royalty, which reinforces the argument even further: the problem was thus solved from the very beginning of the institution, which was secondary to the divine institution. Further, the lieutenancy, as practiced by kings, did not reach absolute power. "The earth is God's, said [the king]; I am his lieutenant. What I take is mine and what I give to others is a reward from me."[34]

However, the conflict of jurisdiction was far from settled, despite the limits assigned to "earthly" authority. The prophetic tradition reported that God would say on the day of the Last Judgment: "I am King; where are the kings of the earth?"[35] Only then would God take his revenge in his capacity as the single acting king.

THE AURA OF THE KING IN THE SERVICE OF GOD

The modalities of getting closer to God were similar to those that involved kings. To convert was only the beginning; in some sense that act constituted the first step after which the believer acquired his rank as a Muslim. Other steps remained to be taken, just as remained for the servants of the king, who were in fact divided into several categories: some, who were particularly active and showed devotion to their tasks,

[31] Tabari, *Tafsîr*, XI, 193.
[32] The Koran, 38:26. Translator's note: The English-language edition uses "master" instead of "lieutenant."
[33] *Kachâf*, IV, 86.
[34] Baladhuri, 20.
[35] Ibn Mâja, *Saḥîḥ*, I, 82.

therefore quickly climbed the steps and reached high ranks; others, who were less zealous, thus experienced no change in their status and could even find themselves demoted if not stricken entirely from the list of servants. The same was true for servants of God as for servants of the king. The Muslim who exerted himself in his adoration of God climbed the echelons and thus passed from the rank of believer to that of the faithful belonging to the inner circle. On the other hand, the Muslim who exhibited a lack of submission and indulged in bad behavior fell to the rank of the disobedient.[36]

Royal imagery abounds with teachings of submission and fear. Beyond the courtly rituals of protocol and pomp, it was used widely to express the profound nature of the relationship with the king and how one could become close to him. In prayer, which was the strongest expression of intimacy in the relationship with God, the all-powerful king was presented as an example to follow. "When the faithful puts on the attire of piety because he is before God, his right hand resting on his left hand, [he is] in the posture of one who is before a powerful king."[37] The aura of the sultan was called upon in the practice of devotion because of the fearful submission it inspired. Although he was to have thoughts only for the supreme God, a man in prayer recalled the king's authority in the solitude of devotion in order to increase his fervor. Prayer was thus advocated as in a court ceremonial. God, although invisible, had a *hayba*, an aura, that one was to keep in mind while worshiping, as was the case for the servant who reached the palace and hoped to be received there, the apogee being "prostration before God, just as the one who is honored by being invited to take a place in the palace prostrates himself before the king."[38] The king's visibility, a significant obstacle in the management of his relationships with his subjects, proved to be very valuable in conveying the authority of the invisible.

PROSTRATION: GREETING THE KING

Prostration was, however, the subject of much disagreement. A perfect and ostentatious symbol of submission, the posture, inspired by the position of the camel that lowers itself to enable the rider to mount, was common for kings. One prostrated oneself before the king; one kissed his rug

[36] Râzi, XIII, Part I, 26.
[37] Râzi, XIII, Part I, 64.
[38] Râzi, XIII, Part I, 66.

and his clothing. To touch his fingers was a considerable honor that was granted to powerful figures whom he thus distinguished. Al-Mutannabi, in his praise of the great king, elevated him to the extent that the steps of his throne were accessible only to kings dependent on his authority.[39] On the day of the Last Judgment, only the faithful believers would be able to prostrate themselves, whereas the disbelieving would find their bodies stricken with rigidity, unable to bend, and they would thus be deprived of the divine blessing.[40] Prostration was a privilege of proximity.

The king's aura brought his guests unconsciously to their knees, as if they feared a force ready to be unleashed over them. Prostration then became the posture in which, huddled over themselves, they showed proof of their surrender and waited to be assured of the safety of the premises. The visitor in fact experienced an impression of his imminent demise and feared it. "I heard," testified a visitor, "a voice so loud that no one could raise their voice any further in consideration for the king. I then understood that no one but he could raise his voice here. I then knelt down and prostrated myself in veneration of him."[41] The situation was thus the same among the people and as reported in the chronicle. Joseph received his family in the same way: "He helped his parents to a couch, and they all fell on their knees and prostrated themselves before him."[42]

Prostration was a greeting of kings. One of the Prophet's captains, having returned from Yemen, prostrated himself at his feet, saying that "Jews prostrated themselves before their great men and their scholars, and assuring that he had seen the Christians do the same before their priests."[43]

Prostration was the sign of indisputable submission. In a negotiation with the Prophet, the representatives of a tribe demanded "not to pay the tithe, not to be dislodged from their territory, and not to prostrate themselves." The term used is *al-jibâya*, which today designates taxation, thus suggesting that paying the tax was accompanied by prostration (let us not forget that the word was also applied, in one of its variations, to the act of castration, which symbolized feminization linked to servitude and the beatitude of the servant kissing the feet of his master).[44] The supreme

[39] Al-Mutanabbi, I, 165.
[40] *Fâ'iq*, III, 16.
[41] *Aghâni*, XIII, 230.
[42] The Koran, 12:100.
[43] Râzi, I, Part II, 194–195.
[44] "Chaste and timid, shaken by this sublime contact and by so much goodness, his mind in delicious disarray, Adrien Deume was on his way to the chief's side; he trembled in fear of making a misstep or misjudging the approach to his august superior. Sentimental and

gesture of submission to which the tribe refused to bend was conveyed, according to the commentators, either by *ruku'*, which meant standing prostration, or by kneeling with one's face on the ground.[45] The Prophet agreed to the first two demands of the tribe but rejected the third: the new authority could not in fact make a concession in matters concerning such a demonstrative symbol of power.

Prostration was a subject of friction between the divine and royal authorities. It poses a problem that goes as far back as Creation when one must interpret what God said to the angels: "I am creating man from clay. When I have fashioned him and breathed My spirit into him, kneel down and prostrate yourselves before him."[46] Such a paradox of man treated as God created a dilemma for the commentators. Some argued that prostration, here, was not intended as adoration, but simply as consideration; others saw it as prostration destined for God, with Adam, in this situation, being there only to indicate the direction of prostration. According to Ibn Kathîr, for most of the jurisconsults, the order to prostrate themselves was addressed to the angels of Satan and not to all of the angels.[47] The goal of all these commentaries was to rid the posture in question of its meaning.[48] As for Râzi, he specifies that "the objective of prostration was the exaltation and the recognition of servitude."[49] Thus it was denounced as an act of heresy. The one who prostrated himself before kings was a heretic: the posture, in that case, was called *kaffâra*.[50]

Regarding kings, the Prophet recommended in his teachings: "If they submit, then take from them their three staffs, precisely those that they have in their hands when the public prostrates itself before them."[51]

There was a great deal of suspicion regarding the insignia of royalty, symbols of an absolute authority that left to the divine authority only a

confused, smiling and perspiring, overwhelmed by the touch of a royal hand, too anxious to truly feel the sweetness of such contact, he walked with a smooth and distinguished step, listening with all his soul and understanding nothing. Seduced and feminine, shivering and light, spiritualized, a shaken virgin and timid bride led to the altar, he went to the arm of the superior, and his youthful smile was deliciously sexual. Intimate, he was intimate with a superior; he finally had a personal relationship! Oh the happiness of his tapped arm! It was the most wonderful hour of his life." Albert Cohen, *Belle du Seigneur*, Gallimard, Folio, 115.

[45] *Kachâf*, II, 657, and *Tâj al-'Arûss*, XIX, 266–268.

[46] The Koran, 38:71–72.

[47] Tha'labi, *Qasas*, 30.

[48] *Kachâf*, IV, 91.

[49] Râzi, X, Part I, 25.

[50] *Jamhara*, 787.

[51] *Nihâya*, II, 36.

weak margin for maneuver. The stripping off of every show of strength, even symbolic, was an obligation in prayer. A man must not keep his stick in his hand to support him; it would be a sign evoking royalty in the face of a divine power that wills itself to be undivided.[52]

The jurisconsults' efforts to signify the unique dimension of that power can be seen in the form of allusions to the magnificence and the extraordinary nature of royal authority, and in the unveiling of the essence of the king-subject relationship, of the relationship of subordination pushed to the extreme – of enslavement. According to Râzi, "the relationship of the Prophet to other men is equivalent to the relationship of masters to slaves, for he is closer to them than they to themselves, and the same is true of wives who are the mothers of believers.... Wives of others are thus to the wives of the Prophet as the slave is to the free woman."[53] It is precisely the strong proximity and the adoration inherent in servitude that created the supreme bond.

The chronicle reports that Arabs "called every subject of the king his slave [*ʿabd*, pl. *ʿabîd*, *ʿibâd*] or adorer," using the word recognized as having this meaning and softened by reason of its consecration in relation to God. Before the hegemony of monotheism and the formation of the Muslim state, such language was inscribed in everyday life.[54]

Thus God, explained the exegetes, spoke their language to them and took into account their ways and customs:

> All-Powerful God, speaking of his Being and of his qualities, spoke to the men in the way that was common to them while speaking of their kings and their chiefs. Thus, he made *Ka'ba* his house around which people moved as they do for the houses of their kings. He ordered them to go there to visit as they would visit the homes of their kings. He also said that the black stone was his right hand on earth and that he made it a place that people could kiss as they would kiss the hand of their king. In the same way and in the same spirit, He instituted a judgment and the day of the resurrection in presence of the angels, the prophets and the martyrs ... and granted himself a throne.[55]

This recourse to royal authority and to its modes of manifestation was accompanied, however, by a frequent warning that recalled the uniqueness of God; a line of demarcation was drawn between heaven and earth, even if it did not solve all problems. God was the king of kings, the

[52] Ibid.
[53] Râzi, XIII, Part I, 179–180.
[54] Râzi, XII, Part I, 89.
[55] According to Râzi, IV, Part I, 12; the Koran, 11:7, 20:5, 38:75, 69:71.

master of authority. He thus appropriated the space of royalty for himself; he was the king of all creatures and reduced the kings to the rank of lieutenant.[56]

ON THE DIVINE INHERENT IN THE MONARCHY

In reality, the power of kings was absolute.[57] Well after the advent of Islam, Mo'âwiyya was pleased to assert: "We are like time; the one whom we raise rises in dignity and the one whom we lower falls into debasement and scorn."[58] The very logic of the monarchical reign made the king one who, on many levels, bordered on the divine. An Omayyad prince once said: "No Quraysh before me has been installed on this *minbar* without having claimed to have a paradise and a hell, and to cause those who obey him to enter paradise and those who rebel against his authority to enter hell."[59] The divinization of the king by those close to him was a relatively common phenomenon. Speaking of Abû Muslim al-Khurâsânî and his followers, Tabari reports that "some of them adored him and saw him as God."[60]

For the people, the Omayyads were all-powerful kings whose power was unlimited. "They saw them as masters on the order of gods [*arbâb*]. They had power in their hands and exercised it as absolute masters like God: *rubûbiya*. Powerful oppressors, they governed on whim, killed out of anger, arrested people on suspicion only, pardoned by interceding and scorning the laws, protected traitors, and shunned good people."[61] Let us note that the word *ad-dîne*, which today commonly designates religion, also means submission, obedience, the authority of the king, and the payment of a tribute in recognition.[62] The king-god was thus not simply a fantasy of the king alone; he was part of the popular imaginary, alongside other divinities. The *miḥrâb*, the place reserved for princes in mosques, a sacred space where the commander of the believers, the lieutenant of God, sat, was also one of the names of the palace.[63] A certain caliph installed his throne in the *miḥrâb* in order to assert his position,

[56] Râzi, IV, Part II, 5.
[57] *Jamharat rasâ'il al-'Arab*, IV, 158.
[58] Ibid., II, 492.
[59] Tabari, *Târîkh*, VII, 165.
[60] Tabari, *Târîkh*, 71.
[61] *Aghâni*, XXIII, 255.
[62] *Al-Kâmil*, I, 223.
[63] *Tâj al-'Arûss*, I, 412.

thereby showing no humility during prayers.[64] Royalty thus became an essential relay in the relationship between believers and the divinity. In a place where God was assumed to capture all the attention of the faithful, the visible and palpable authority was always that of the king.

That the king was assuredly in a class of his own is confirmed by most written descriptions of him. "The caliph whom God has honored and whom he has elevated to a rank above men" is but a single example.[65] With the advent of Islam and the respect that was shown toward the divine authority, to honor the status of the king in the beginning created serious difficulties in epistolary exchanges. The art of political correspondence was particularly delicate; it required a great mastery of the language. Furthermore, it called for a honed knowledge of relationships of power and, when kings were involved, the art and skill of negotiating a space for the divine while at the same time preserving the exceptional status of the king.

Among the formulas that served to wish the king a long life, the scribes had to show great vigilance in their choice. It was preferable, despite a striking similarity, to use the words "May God make you last a long time" rather than "May God prolong your duration."[66] This verbal subtlety, while it marked a distance with the common mortal, maintained signs of the divinity of the king. Even in praise, it was the exception that remained the rule. The king was not praised for his normal and regulative actions but for his supererogatory works[67]; he was unique and his strength resided in his extraordinariness.

The modalities of praising and greeting the king have inevitably raised questions within the framework of the marking of spaces meant for the divine. Certain formulas were questioned; indeed their usage was forbidden. When prophetic tradition used the expression *at-taḥiyâte lillâh*, it was dedicated to God and to him alone. But it was in fact commonly used to greet the king. *At-taḥiya* has the same root as *al-ḥayat*, or "life." The chronicle reports that this greeting meant "royalty and immortality"; it was the appropriate homage to render to kings. It was then decreed for Muslims: "Say: the greeting [*at-taḥiya*] is for God." All of the terms that were part of the royal lexicon and served to talk about peace, sovereignty, and immortality were thus reserved for God, the king of kings.[68]

[64] Tabari, *Târîkh*, VII, 168.
[65] *Jamharat rasâ'il al-'Arab*, IV, 179.
[66] *Jamharat rasâ'il al-'Arab*, IV, 180.
[67] *Jamharat rasâ'il al-'Arab*, IV, 182.
[68] *Nihâya*, I, 18; *Tâj al-'Arûss*, XIX, 360–361.

Even today, this formula, used several times daily by the faithful who are completely unaware of its genesis, is the striking proof of a balance between heaven and earth, between divine authority and royal authority. It bears witness to the extraordinary presence of the king in the popular memory.

The will to henceforth reserve for God a greeting that was previously destined for the king is explained by the imperceptible shifts between divine and royal statuses. There was a logic unique to royalty that led to the divinization of the king, not only from the point of view of the subjects, but also in the representation of himself that the king encouraged, convinced of his celestial position.

Tabari reports the edifying story of a young king questioning his condition:

"I find royalty delicious. I don't know if I am the only one to have such an impression or if everyone shares it!"

He was answered: "Royalty is indeed so."

And so he asked: "What will keep it for me?"

And he was answered: "Your obedience to God."

After four hundred years of rule, Satan paid him a visit and the following dialogue took place between them:

"Who are you?"

"Have no fear, but tell me who you are."

"I am a human descended from Adam."

"If you were one of Adam's descendants, you would already be dead as they are all dead. Haven't you seen how people have died and how many centuries have passed! If you were one of them, you would be dead like they are, but you are a god, so summon the people to adore you!"[69]

THE DEATH OF THE KING

In post-Islamic discourse such an attitude, in fact inherent to the monarchy, was logically perceived as a downfall, of Satanic origin; or at the very least it was foreign to the original institution of royalty. Previously, the gods could have been implicated in it.

An-Nu'mânn, amazed by his work, looked at his palace, that is, at the fortress that was supposed to protect him, and he became worried at the idea of death. Legend has it that he dressed humbly and wandered the earth to persuade himself of his immortality. It had been predicted that

[69] Tabari, *Târîkh*, I, 114–115.

his faith in God and his renunciation of earthly goods would render him immortal.[70]

God therefore did not upset the immortality of the kings! Without drawing from legends, let us look at the case of the caliph Moʿâwiyya, who was alert to the earthly modes of access to maintenance of power. A former secretary of the Prophet, he had allowed himself to be seduced by the heights that he had reached. An intoxication with royalty pushed him to question a scholar: "Am I mentioned in one of the books of God?"[71] It was already from somewhere else that he looked at the human world that surrounded him!

This obsession with immortality in any case remained lively. A certain caliph concerned with this question, like so many of his predecessors, wearing his most magnificent robes and surrounded by his armed guards, looked at himself in a mirror; surprised at his allure and his beauty, he exclaimed: "I am the young king!"[72] The poet Abû Nuwâss, a great connoisseur of kings, said to al-Amîn:

O confident of God, live forever
  Death is for us, and you will remain
  And when we will no longer be, then be eternal![73]

There are countless such examples. It is reported that al-Hajjâj, the emir of Baghdad, asked an astrologer at the hour of extreme unction: "Do you really think that a king can die?"[74] Seeing such insistence, we can understand the continual advice of the jurisconsults who warned kings about death. Along with the summoning to justice, it was the subject to which they turned most often in their writings. The presence and inevitability of death were constantly recalled and emphasized to kings. Hassan al-Basri, the famous jurisconsult, stressed to the nonetheless very pious ʿOmar Ibn ʿAbdelʾaziz: "Even if you were the age of Noah and had the kingdom of Solomon, the faith of Abraham, and the wisdom of Luqmân, the terror of death is before you!"[75] Without even realizing it, the jurisconsult, strong in his warnings, still conveyed through his speech the legend of the immortality of kings. This shows the extent to which immortality still at that point remained connected to royalty.

[70] Jâhiz, *Sirâj*, I, 23–24.
[71] *Al-Kâmil*, II, 618.
[72] *Aghâni*, X, 234.
[73] *Aghâni*, XXV, 91.
[74] *Ichtiqâq*, 307.
[75] *Jamharat rasâʾil al-ʿArab*, II, 332.

The belief in the immortality of kings was scarcely surprising, since Arabs even believed in the immortality of those close to them. It was thus that some tribes thought of their soldiers as immortal.[76]

It may be useful to emphasize, given the opportunity, that the king's relationship with death was dual: it was his relationship with his own death, but also his relationship with the deaths of his subjects, over which he indisputably had control – a relationship that indirectly influenced his feeling of immortality, or his difference. No doubt because of the power of their kingdom, the Arabs believed that the Persians did not die.[77] In any case, the king never died like other people. His situation was not like that of common mortals, who, "when they die, they die!"[78] Even when he was assassinated, his death was appreciated and experienced differently. *Al-muchâ'ara* was the name given to assassins of the king.[79] People found it inappropriate to announce a regicide and the murder of a common man in the same way. Rather than proclaiming "the king has been killed," they preferred to say "the king has been marked by sacrifice," as was the case in rituals of divine offering: the animal to be sacrificed was first marked with a cut or stabbed on its side to make the blood flow. Henceforth, it had the status of offering, *al-cha'îra*, the plural form of which, *cha'âir*, designated rituals, notably those of pilgrimage.[80] The chronicle reports that the caliph 'Omar had a premonition: he dreamed that he was pecked twice by a red rooster and that he reported it publicly during Friday prayers. A few days later, he was stabbed.[81]

Death struck the powerful and the poor unequally. The death by starvation of many of the latter must have been at the origin of a feeling of inequality; the spectacle of abundance spread before their naked poverty assuredly played a role. The powerful lineages held on to their familial memory; they were present in the annals for a long time and thus immortal in that way, whereas poor families more frequently fell victim to extinction. The poor were more familiar with death, which threatened them in their everyday lives.

A number of titles and names attributed to the great men make explicit reference to an old age and a long life.[82] One need only read the tales

76 *Jamharat al-amthâl*, I, 388.
77 *Jamharat al-lugha*, I, 22.
78 Baladhuri, 38.
79 One speaks of diyat al-muchâ'ara or diyat Bayt al-mâl; Al-Kâmil, I, 101; *Tâj al-'Arûss*, V, 37.
80 *Tâj al-'Arûss*, VII, 33.
81 Ahmad Ibn Hanbal, *Musnad*, I, 20.
82 Al-Mutanabbi, I, 388.

of the prophets to see this. The caliph al-Mâmûn had a palace called *al-khulûd*, or "immortality," an explicit reference to paradise, the seat of eternal delight. The name given to this palace designated the man who, despite an advanced age, still had a dark beard and dark hair and had not lost his teeth.[83] The chronicle moreover endows kings with ages of several hundred years.[84]

In fact, the deaths of important people took on singular characteristics. When a chief died, people said: "The heavens and the earth cry for him, the wind cries for him, and the sun is darkened for him."[85] The superhuman nature of chiefs was strongly connected to such beliefs. Their deaths struck the imagination. The announcement was brought by horse: a rider went among the populations and invited them to mourn the one who was dead.[86] A certain chief's death was mourned from the summit of the mountains, a sign of the supernatural and of elevated status.[87]

THE HIGH PLACE IN PLACE OF HEAVEN

Elevation was in fact a prerogative of kings. Even sick, the king was carried by his servants on his litter.[88] He could not be laid on the ground; in the circumstances height seemed a denial of death.[89] The king was never to depart. In one of his processions, Moʿâwiyya had one of those accompanying him get down from the very tall camel he had been riding since he was higher than the king's litter.[90] When one addressed the sultan, one raised something toward him, for he was seated above, in a "high place." Elevation was a sign of nobility. One brought something up high for the king like a slave addressing his master, literally saying, according to the accepted formula: "I brought my request up high to him."[91]

Al-musba', which referred to the abandoned individual who became wild like an animal, escaped every social tie, and was dehumanized, also designated the slave descended from seven generations of ancestors stuck in servitude. Such a rooting in servitude, the lowest degree of debasement, paralleled the seven heavens that were the lot of the divinities

83 *Tâj al-ʿArûss*, IV, 438.
84 *Tâj al-ʿArûss*, IV, 449.
85 *Kachâf*, IV, 269.
86 *Islâḥ al-Mantiq*, 179.
87 *Majma ʿal-amthâl*, II, 172.
88 Ibn Chajari, 312.
89 *Aghâni*, XI, 32.
90 Baladhuri, 34.
91 Râzi, XII, Part I, 113.

and the object to which kings laid claim. *'Illiyûn*, a word derived from height, was a place in the seventh heaven to which the souls of the faithful ascended.[92] This play of mirrors, which on the one hand blackened the human condition by relegating it underground, only served to further brighten the other pole, which it carried to the summits. It was like the black night in the face of the sparkling heavens.[93]

In San'a, the capital of the kings of Yemen, there was a very famous palace by the name of Ghomdâne, which, according to legend, was built by Solomon. The palace showed its four facades: red, white, yellow, and green; within its walls were seven roofs separated from each other by forty cubits, or even by one hundred, according to some.[94]

The royal palace was in reality a fortress that was not easily taken by attackers. A closed space, hidden from view, it was a place of "somewhere else" that fascinated men and filled them with fear. In representations, the palace stood out from the landscape by its height and size; it climbed high into the sky. Its construction was attributed to the great kings,[95] like the tower leading to heaven that was built by the legendary king Nimrod.[96]

When the queen of Sheba came to Solomon, she ordered that her throne be protected "in the last of the seven rooms arranged like Russian dolls in the last of the seven palaces."[97] The door to each room was locked.[98]

The theme of the seven heavens contributed to the legend of the kings. Alexander the Great was called the Two-Horned One by the Arabs because he was believed to have touched one of the sides of the sun in a dream.[99] The fantasy of heaven was another obsession of the notables, that is, kings in power. The Arabs called those kings the "height of necks" or simply "the necks"[100] – by contrast, debasement was signified by the shortening and sagging of the neck.[101] The chronicle thus speaks of an Arab chief with a considerable fortune: "He was one of the most noble among the notables in sight of his tribe and had a huge house with a door

92 Plural of *'iliyi*; *Tâj al-'Arûss*, XIX, 696.
93 *Tâj al-'Arûss*, XI, 200.
94 *Tâj al-'Arûss*, V, 153.
95 *Tâj al-'Arûss*, IV, 118.
96 Tabari, *Târîkh*, I, 179.
97 *Kachâf*, III, 355.
98 *Kachâf*, III, 349.
99 *Nihâya*, IV, 52.
100 *Nihâya*, III, 173.
101 *Ichtiqâq*, 559. Note that being freed was related, from a certain point of view, to the liberation of the neck, as if it were a question of freeing it from its bending!

to heaven."[102] Heaven, in this case, was whatever provided shadows from above. Thus the roof of a house was called heaven, as were the clouds and the rain.[103] Heaven in this society had quite earthly resonance. The royal court and the mystery that surrounded it indeed evoked the heights of heaven. The veil here was meant to simulate the invisible.

THE VEILED KING, OR THE CONSTRUCTION OF THE INVISIBLE

Jâhiz imagined the following dialogue:

> The king said to his keeper of the veil: "You are my eye, thanks to which I see, and a protector alongside whom I seek peace. I have conferred upon you responsibility for my door, so then how will you act with my subjects?"
>
> The veil keeper responded: "I will watch them with your eyes, I will take them into consideration according to their rank with you, I will lower them before you by making them wait before your door, ... and will keep you informed about them just as I will inform them of your intentions."[104]

The king was divided in two. The choice of his veil keeper, or *ḥâjib*, occupied all his attention. Al-Mansûr taught his son that the *ḥâjib* should be neither ignorant or naïve. He was to demonstrate an inexhaustible energy, the doors of kings always being open. He was to be concerned only with deciding which visitors should enter, without giving the impression of viewing people from above. The *ḥâjib* was the "very face" of his master, said al-Hajjâj.[105] He made a distinction among the arrivals according to their status. Dignitaries enjoyed favored treatment; the commoner was shown no special consideration. It was mentioned that the one who was responsible for the people at the palace gates "must be an obedient slave, constantly looking out for the security of the king, of great strength and rough language inspiring fear, but using violence only when justified. He must act neither familiar nor friendly, but dour before any doubtful individual."[106]

The language used at the palace was thus chosen according to social categories. Following an unjustified killing of a virtuous man on the order of a caliph, a slave spoke out to one of the caliph's sons, showing

[102] *Al-Hutay'a, Diwân*, ed. Ibn Sikkite, 266. This concerns a certain ʿUtayba Ibn al-Naḥass al-ʿIjliyi.

[103] Ibn Qutayba Abî ʿAbdallah ibn Muslim, *Adab al-kâtib*, Muassassat ar-Rissâla, 1999, 85.

[104] Jâhiz, *Rasâ'il*, I, 33.

[105] Jâhiz, *Rasâ'il*, I, 40.

[106] Ibid.

his indignation in the face of such an injustice: "He is the commander of believers; he does what he wants and does so knowingly!" The son responded: "I speak to you in the language of nobles and you speak that of a commoner."[107]

One took care to assure that established rules were followed. It was customary to acknowledge notables and not to shame them in front of others, waiting until after they had crossed the threshold into the palace.[108] Hârûn ar-Rachîd had a doorkeeper for the upper classes[109] and others in *Bâb al-ʿâmma* to receive the general public.[110] These doorkeepers, called *aḍ-ḍalit*, were responsible for using force to shove and push undesirables from the king's threshold.[111]

When one considers the benefits that access to the sultan could procure, that is, the social prestige that could result directly or indirectly from it, one can understand the power held by the *ḥâjib*, whose latitude in dealing with visitors was considerable, in spite of the demands and recommendations of his master. Granted, a hierarchy of visitors was established. Indeed, one encountered the *ahl al-ʾidhn*, persons who were permanently authorized to enter the palace and who were themselves classified into categories. There were those who needed no authorization, such as the muezzin, nocturnal messengers, people from the border regions, and cooks.[112] Someone close to the king stated: "I went to the palace of Muhammad [a caliph] in the middle of the night. I was one of his entourage, and I had access to him that not even his slaves or kin could have."[113]

However, beyond and in spite of established protocol, the corruption of the veil keepers, who were very susceptible to bribes, opened the door to special favors.[114]

One of the distinctive signs of kings was the veil, for which the *ḥâjib* or the chamberlain of the royal house[115] was responsible. The veil was one of the symbols of authority: "It is not vouchsafed to any mortal that God should speak to him except by revelation, or from behind a veil."[116] It was

[107] Tabari, *Târîkh*, IX, 289.
[108] Baladhuri, 215.
[109] Tabari, *Târîkh*, X, 94.
[110] Ibid., XI, 84.
[111] *Tâj al-ʿArûss*, XII, 503; see also X, 470.
[112] *ʿIqd*, I, 90.
[113] Ibid., I, 155.
[114] Baladhuri, 30 and 48.
[115] Ibn Kathîr, *Tafsîr*, II, 52.
[116] The Koran, 42:51.

thus that God spoke to Moses; it was thus that he spoke to the angels, "as the king speaks to some of those who are close to him from behind the veil," noted Zamakhchari.[117] The *ḥijâb* allowed the king to keep his distance from the masses, to escape the ordinary, hierarchical human norms by recourse to invisibility, which provided the foundation for the goodwill established by his uniqueness. "Cause them to wait" was the king's way of enforcing the proper order of things: it foretold the possibility – or not – of being received; it directed the establishment of the high place. Waiting created an intense moment that inserted a certain distance into requesters' and visitors' relationships with the king. Fear had time to be instilled in the most resilient of souls, who found themselves isolated and diminished in a place that scarcely lent itself to relaxation. The one who was placed in waiting was subjected to the spectacle of the keepers of the veil, the continual comings and goings of a multitude of servants whose demeanor and constantly repeated expressions conveyed their fear of the master who housed them and the little concern they had for visitors; thus a feeling of impotence, a sense of being reduced to a passive submission, was heightened in the one who was waiting. The veil proclaimed the gulf that separated one from authority.

The great Abû Sofiyâne, head of the most powerful family of Mecca, was forced to wait at the door of the Prophet; the great lord, feared and respected, powerlessly watched the parade of people whose condition was quite different from his status; in this act of waiting, he was emptied of his substance.[118] Access to the Prophet was not automatic; only those closest to him could enjoy it.[119]

The veil asserted the established authority, which assigned to its competitors the rank of a simple subject.[120]

In the early years of Islam, in that initial phase of struggle against the existing powers, it was necessary to desacralize the royal authority and capture its aura to establish the nascent authority. The veil was thus called into question, for the mystery that it cultivated around the king, the closed space that it created, a clear evocation of the *ghayb*, the divine mystery, which was considered to be God's alone. In fact, the *ghayb* was the unknown, that which was hidden from sight: "I heard a voice from behind the *ghayb*, that is, from a place that one cannot see."[121] The use of

[117] *Kachâf*, IV, 226.
[118] *Nihâya*, I, 290.
[119] Ibn Mâja, *Saḥîḥ*, I, 69.
[120] *Nihâya*, III, 422.
[121] Tâj al-ʿArûss, II, 295.

the veil was thus denounced. The caliph ʿOmar, "each time that he named a governor, would require four things of him: not to ride a horse, not to have a veil keeper, not to wear linen cloth, and not to eat white bread." He was particularly insistent with his local agents about the veil: "Beware of using the veil; carry out your affairs in plain sight."[122]

The veil removed the king from the mass of mortals and freed him from his human shell. It released him from the bonds of friendship and kinship, made him an exceptional being, superhuman simply by virtue of his invisible and inaccessible position. Joseph, in receiving his brothers, "ordered his veil keepers to keep them at a distance. He spoke to them only through an intermediary. Thus we understand that they were not in a position to recognize him, without forgetting that the aura of the king and the pressing need causing great fear prevented them from staring at the king in a way that would have enabled them to recognize him."[123] The veil was the most efficacious way to make the image of the king an abstraction. Taken out of sight, the king was idealized; paradoxically, he thus became accessible to the popular imagination.

The place where people waited before being granted access to the king, the space that was the object of so much envy, was also a space of doubt and agony. It was like the place where captives were kept while awaiting their verdict. Veils multiplied with increasing power; only trustworthy men could pass through the succession of veils that protected the king.[124] The veils were crossed successively before reaching the one who was being solicited. According to the prophetic tradition, seventy veils surrounded the throne of God, and each one of them was burning to the extreme.[125] In fact, the strict protocol that accompanied access to the king constituted an entire ritual of repeated precautions, displays of power, and judging stares that put nerves on edge; its effectiveness was such that, even unveiled at the end of the journey, the king remained inaccessible. Court decorum further prohibited anyone from looking at the king directly. The king remained veiled by his very authority and by the aura that surrounded him.

When he went out in public, his sumptuous robes made him "the standard that the nobles and the white camels watch from behind the veil," as the poet sang.[126]

[122] Jâhiz, *kitâb al-ḥijâb*, 31, in Rasâʾil, I.
[123] Râzi, IX, Part II, 132.
[124] *Bayân*, 392.
[125] *Nihâya*, II, 332.
[126] Al-Akhtal, 74.

The veil cannot be summed up only as barriers erected around the king; the veil was intrinsic to him and caused him to border on the divine. He was the *sumdûr*: he dazzled those who raised their eyes to him, and their vision was weakened as a result.[127] A luminous halo protected him and blinded his subjects; it required a filter, just as the sun must be glimpsed through the clouds. It was unbearable to look at God directly, according to the prophetic tradition. The same was true for the king: the institution of the veil in return made him into a dazzling sight, like the gods.[128] In other words, it was the physical absence of the king that established his considerable presence. By keeping the king out of sight, the veil became the sign of his presence; veils "showed observers that they were there, behind it," a chronicler shrewdly noted.[129]

It was in servitude that kings found the most secure veil. *An-nassîf* was a cloth that a woman wore on top of her clothes, so named because it covered her body from probing looks. The term also designated the servant, the *khâdim*,[130] because he came between the master and others, thus forming a veil that was thickened and strengthened by the number of slaves.

Many kings never appeared in the company of their courtiers without a veil. No one ever saw Abû Jaafar al-Mansûr drink anything other than water. He showed his admiration for singing by a movement of the veil; the *ḥâjib* then appeared and blessed the singer in the name of the king.[131] But there were also many princes who spent their time uncovered. They were not without a veil, however, because they were veiled by the presence of their numerous servants. This is why the king was called the *ḥasîr*, that is, the veiled one, or to be precise, the surrounded one.[132]

The slave covered the master's nudity without the master being bothered by his presence, because one was not bothered by the presence of children and even less by merchandise that one possessed. Thus when Fatima, the Prophet's daughter, showed her discomfort at uncovering herself in front of a new slave that her father had given her, the latter said to her: "There is nothing wrong; we are your father and your slave," using the word *ghulâm*, which means "minor."[133]

127 Tâj al-'Arûss, VI, 546.
128 *Tâj al-'Arûss*, VII, 124.
129 *Fâ'iq*, III, 194.
130 *Tâj al-'Arûss*, XII, 503.
131 Jâhiz, *kitâb at-Tâj*, 31–32.
132 Kûrâ', 179.
133 Râzi, XIII, Part I, 180.

With the advent of Islam, free women, unlike slaves, had to be veiled in order to remove from the sight of men anything that could call attention to their femininity.[134] It was reported that when the caliph ʿOmar saw a veiled slave woman, he "beat her with his stick and said: 'Dog, you have the audacity to look like a free woman!'"[135] The veil (*ḥijâb*) was thus a border between servitude and freedom, between what was protected and what was not, between the pure and the impure. "The female slave threw her veil outside the house."[136] The slave lived uncovered; she was a possession, assured the jurisconsult, and the constraints of buying and selling necessitated that she be looked at and examined as one would a farm animal.[137] Slaves were intermediaries between the inside and the outside; they revolved around the kings and veiled them from the sight of the commoners. They accentuated the king's resemblance to the gods, who were like him in all but name.

NAMES OF GOD, NAMES OF KINGS

In the letter that a requester addressed to an Iraqi emir, the praise leaves no doubt about the status of the recipient: "O Khalid [the emir's name], I love you for ten qualities: God is benevolent and you are benevolent; God is generous and you are generous; God is merciful and you are merciful; God is lenient and you are lenient...."[138]

The competition that involved names intervened at every level of the social hierarchy. The king made no concessions on his qualities, which were not to be the cause of any confusion. During audiences, the greatest caution was exercised when announcing the names of people received by the king; in no case was the announced name of the visitor to coincide with a royal quality.

The king had the privilege, if he received a visitor and discovered upon asking that the visitor's name designated one of the royal qualities, of being endowed with that quality by the visitor, who then called himself by his father's name. This is what a certain Said, whose name means "the fortunate," son of Murra, said when the caliph asked him his name: "The

[134] *Kachâf*, III, 543.
[135] Al-Haroui, *Gharîbu al-ḥadîth*, I, 448.
[136] Ibid., II, 57.
[137] Râzi, XIII, Part I, 189.
[138] *Jamharat rasâʾil al-ʿArab*, II, 356.

commander of believers is the fortunate [Said]; as for me, I am only the son of Murra."[139]

We know how the uncle of the prophet Muhammad, al-ʿAbbâss, responded to the question "Who is the greatest [*al-akbar* means "the oldest" and is also one of the names of God], you or Muhammad?": "He is more considerable than I, and I was born before he."[140] (The word he used is connected to height[141] and in particular to royalty: *al-kibriyâ'*, meaning greatness, pride, and magnificence at the same time.[142]) The same was true of God.

It was said in the prophetic tradition that "the most contemptible name that a man can use for God is 'king of kings,'" because that title was already used to designate the most powerful kings and was found in the work of poets. "You are a sun, and the kings are the stars; when you appear, none of them can be seen," said an-Nâbigha, addressing an Arab king.[143]

God occupied the space of the king himself by having exclusive mastery over him. He was the king of kings; he possessed, the jurisconsult tells us, "the *mulk* [royalty] and used it in the way that an owner uses what he possesses."[144] The king of a land, or *malik*, is defined as he who possesses the inhabitants.[145] The hold of royalty was in reality stronger than that of ownership (*al-milk*): "Private property is less important than royalty. All royalty is ownership, but not all ownership is royalty." God is then quite simply the *malik*, the King.[146] He combined the *milk* and the *mulk*, the ownership over his creatures and kingship; he had *malakûte*, the supreme power.[147] Being a king necessarily entailed possession of all the preroyal qualities that were the attributes of nobility. The *mulk* presupposed many components, notably the abundance of goods of all kinds, land, animals, and slaves.

The names of God encompassed all the virtues that made a perfect chief[148]: the Merciful (*ar-Raḥmân*), the Irresistible (*al-Jabbâr*; *al-jabr*

[139] Jâhiz, *kitâb at-Tâj*, 85–86.
[140] *Tâj*, 86.
[141] Baladhuri, 451.
[142] Râzi, XV, Part I, 256; Ibn Hilâl, *al-furûq*, 201.
[143] A-Chi'ru wa chu'arâ', I, 165 ; Al-Haroui, *Gharîbu al-ḥadîth*, I, 219.
[144] *Kachâf*, I, 344.
[145] *Tâj al-ʿArûss*, XIII, 648.
[146] *Jamhara*, 981.
[147] Râzi, XII, Part I, 106.
[148] Râzi, II, Part II, 6.

designates royalty), the All-Powerful (*al-'Azîz*), and so forth.[149] All of his names made up God and his uniqueness. The divine gathered for its benefit all the qualities of supreme virtue and power recorded in the annals of nobility and chiefdom. Some of these names were decreed as being unique to Him and were forbidden to others. Such is the case with *ar-Raḥmân*: "Say: 'You may call on God or you may call on the Merciful [*ar-Raḥmân*]: by whatever name you call Him, His are the most gracious names.'"[150] According to some commentators, this name, given to one who went to the extremes of mercy, would have been unknown before Islam. The confirmed jurisconsults, however, reported its use, notably by priests; Musaylima, a claimant to the prophecy, was called *Raḥmân al-Yamâma*. It was also asserted that Arabs gave the name to their children.[151] Linguists mention its existence in ancient chronicles.[152]

Though the use of most of the names for people other than God was allowed, some were exclusively reserved for him: *Allâh*, *ar-Raḥmân*, *al-Khâliq* (the Creator), *ar-Râziq* (the Dispensor). The Koranic preamble (*al-Fâtiḥa*) establishes that exclusivity: "In the name of Allâh, *ar-Raḥmân ar-Raḥîm*: the All-Merciful, the Merciful." The association of these two names came from the need to distinguish the King from kings, the first being more specifically God, but the goal of adding a second term was to eliminate any ambiguity that could arise from the formerly recognized use of each of those terms before the advent of Islam.[153]

THE NAME OF *ALLÂH*

In any event, the use of such names was subsequently forbidden, as Tabari reports.[154] The restriction of the lexical space unique to divine authority is particularly obvious when one examines the name of *Allâh*, a name incontestably reserved for God. A name unique to God, it was, according to some, invariable. Its origin has been linked to *ilâh* or *al-ilâh*, if not to *walaha*, that is "to lose one's mind," or *alahtu*, in the sense of "to be attached to someone" or "to completely trust" him. It might also come from "to be veiled," "to hide," and thus "to come from the invisible," all meanings that convey the principle of divinity. Let us note that all these

[149] Al-Haroui, *Gharîbu al-ḥadîth*, I, 219.
[150] The Koran, 17:110.
[151] *Ichtiqâq*, 58.
[152] *Tâj al-'Arûss*, XVI, 278.
[153] Ibn Kathîr, *Tafsîr*, I, 33.
[154] Ibn Kathîr, *Tafsîr*, I, 34.

meanings come together in the strongest relationship of unrestricted attachment: the relationship of servitude. The great commentators, however, came to a common agreement that the name *Allâh* did not derive from other terms[155]; it was a sui generis name created for God and for him alone, even if Râzi mentions that it is of Hebraic origin.[156]

Let's look at what dictionaries say on the subject. In *Tâj al-'Arûss* it is found under the heading for *alaha* and *ilâha*, which mean "to adore." It is reported that *Allâh* was the most considerable name for God because it combined his most perfect qualities. *Ilâh*, that is, the adored one, is the root, which gave *al-ilâh*; at that time, the term "was applied to God, may He be praised, and to idols adored by the populations,"[157] including the sun.[158] In order to avoid any confusion with idols and out of the allegedly more technical concern of shortening the word intended for common usage, the word was contracted to *Allâh*.

This concern with abbreviation was, however, not considered a valid argument by all the authors; some argued that other words, no less common, should have also undergone the same treatment. Al-Jawâhiri notes that the word owed its fate "to the unique meaning that it contains and that is found in no other."[159] For other authors, the evolution of the form of the word was explained by the attribution of a majestic title to God.[160]

Some sources say little on the debate over the origin of the word, or they avoid it altogether.[161] However, earlier readings of the sacred text still carry a trace of it, notably those of the praise in the preamble (*al-Fâtiḥa*), which were reported to have included the base word *ilâh* instead of *Allâh*. That reading is attributed to Bedouin tribes, presented as being ignorant of the rules of the Koran, as still being attached to their ways, and, probably, as not having a true awareness of what was at stake.[162]

The new lexicon that took into account the new distribution of authority seems to have been imposed only gradually, as the changes that occurred in the interpellation of the divine lead us to believe. For some time, things were unclear, as is illustrated by a verse in which the chiefs

155 *Tâj al-'Arûss*, XIX, 7.
156 Ibn Kathîr, *Tafsîr*, I, 31. For the Hebraic origin, Jean Chevalier and Alain Cheerbrant, *Dictionnaire de la Bible*, Robert Laffont, 1989, 318.
157 Tâj al-'Arûss, XIX, 7.
158 Ibn Fâris, *Mu'jam maqâyis al-lugha*, I, 69.
159 *Siḥaḥ*, VI, 119.
160 *Lissân*, XIII, 469.
161 *Jamhara*, II, 1084.
162 *Lissân*, XIII, 478.

of Pharaoh's people say to him: "Will you allow Moses and his people to perpetrate corruption in the land and to forsake you and your gods?"[163] "Gods" is rendered here by *âlihataka*, which lowers Pharaoh to the rank of a mere king, but Ibn 'Abbâss, starting with the fact that he was considered to be a god, reads it as *ilâhataka*, or "your adoration."[164] We can indeed see the desire to deny that king the status of god, even if it is clearly seen in other verses of the sacred text. One can also see that the early compromise subsequently gave way to intransigence.

THE NAME OF THE MASTER

Another name, *ar-Rabb*, was the object of just as much attention. Its particular function was to combine all the attributes of authority; it described the lord and master. The word is tied to ownership: the *rabb* of something or of a living being was the person who owned it. It was also related to education and obedience.[165] It was commonly used to express various relationships of authority, but it had a particularly strong divine content. The Koran confirms its use vis-à-vis the divinity: "They make of their clerics and their monks, and of the Messiah, the son of Mary, Lords [*arbâb*] besides God."[166] The term was in fact used for priests and kings.[167] A priest addressed his flock in a way that left no doubt: "Oh, my adorers [*'ibâdi*]," and they responded: "We are here, our Lord [*rabbanâ*]."[168]

Here again, servitude is the central element. The term was used by slave masters and by kings; Joseph spoke thus to the wife of a king about her husband: "My lord [*rabbî*] has treated me with kindness."[169] *Ar-rabb* designates God, the master, the lord, the father, the husband, the educator, the benefactor.[170] It describes hierarchical relationships that combine ownership and education, as illustrated in these words exchanged between the prophet Abraham, when he was a child, and his mother:

[163] The Koran, 7:127.
[164] *Lissân*, XIII, 468. Also the reading by Mujâhid. However, divinities are unanimous; see Râzi, who, in this debate, advances very superficial arguments, *Tafsîr*, VII, Part II, 172, and Tabari, *Tafsîr*, VI, 27.
[165] Râzi, IV, Part II, 98.
[166] The Koran, 9:31.
[167] Gérard, Dictionnaire de la Bible, 1169.
[168] *A-Chi'ru wa chu'arâ'*, I, 106, and also *Aghâni*, IX, 101.
[169] The Koran, 12:24.
[170] *Nihâya*, II, 179, and *Kachâf*, I, 20.

"Who is my *rabbi*?" he asked.
"I am," answered the mother.
"And who is yours?" [he asked.]
She said, "Your father."
Then the child asked his father, "And who is *rabbuk*?"
The father replied, "The king of the land."[171]

Islam prescribed using the term outside of God only as a supplementary title.[172] It was, however, usual to use it for kings, as is seen in poetry and in the Koran itself.[173] The title was also used for certain figures who were highly regarded among the populations. In one tribe, the place of worship was called *al-rabba*.[174] Hichâm Ibn al-Mughîra, one of the great men of Mecca, who had distinguished himself as a giver of food, was thus evoked upon his death: "See the burial of your god [*rabbukum*]."[175] The father of Khâlid Ibn al-Walîd, one of the most famous warriors of Islam, a renowned arbiter before Islam, bore the name of "Just" and even *al-waḥîd* in the sense of unique, singular, and incomparable, a meaning that the word would later lose in *al-waḥîd* and *al-aḥad*, which were devoted to God.[176]

The tradition decreed to no longer use the term *ar-rabb* notably in the relationship between master and slave, whereas it had commonly served to express ownership. Applied to goods, it posed no problem, because those were neither susceptible "to enslavement nor speaking subjects." But even in the latter case, it was tolerated only as a supplementary phrase.

There was thus a great deal of competition surrounding the terms for the divine. The development of a space unique to God drew from the lexicon of chiefdom and royalty before it was strictly limited, at least in part, to be used for Allah. The competition also extended to different attributes of the monarchy, and first of all to one of its major symbols: the throne.

THE KING'S THRONE AND THE AMBASSADOR'S CHAIR

A diplomatic incident that occurred at the end of the nineteenth century at the court of a sultan from Morocco, Hassan I, illustrates how attached

[171] Râzi, *Tafsîr*, VII, Part I, 39.
[172] Ibn Kathîr, *Tafsîr*, I, 36.
[173] *Labîd*, 26.
[174] *Fâ'iq*, I, 316.
[175] *Ichtiqâq*, 101–102.
[176] *Aghâni*, VI, 15, note 1.

the "master," whether god or king, was to the exclusivity of his authority. Considered insignificant and thus unworthy of historiographic literature, the incident occurred during the mission of Charles Euan Smith, the plenipotentiary ambassador of the United Kingdom to Morocco, when the latter came to present his credentials to the king.

Charles Euan Smith, accompanied by members of the British consulate from Tangiers and by a military delegation, arrived on May 12, 1892, in Fez after a two-week journey. An exceptional reception was planned for the mission that day, both by the population and by officials. The minister of war, the chamberlain, the caid of the *Mechouar*, the governor of the city, notables, and representatives of all the professions were present.[177]

A very specific point in the tale of the mission deserves our attention. It concerns a marginal incident relating to protocol. Devoid of importance for historians preoccupied by the tenor of the negotiations, it is extremely revealing when viewed at a distance, from the perspective of the monarchical power mechanisms. An American journalist who was accompanying the mission as a special envoy of two newspapers, the *Central News* and the *Daily Graphic*, reported the incident. He notes that the sultan was seated comfortably during the first audience that he granted to the ambassador Charles Euan Smith, whereas only a chair without a back or arms, a simple stool, had been offered to the ambassador. The ambassador apparently had one of his attachés say that at the next audience, if he would not be offered a seat in which he could sit comfortably, in the best conditions to carry out his mission, he would bring one himself. According to the sultan's close entourage, never before had an envoy of a foreign nation dared to ask such a thing! Everyone, according to the source, sat on the same stool without complaining to anyone! But the response was not long in coming. At the next audience a choice of chairs was offered to the ambassador, thus bringing the incident to a close.[178]

Beyond the anecdote, a question deserves to be asked: Was this just a simple incident of little interest, or was it, on the contrary, a fact that revealed a logic of power?

[177] For the details concerning this event, see Khalid ben Sghir, *al-Maghrib wa Britania al-ʿudhma 1886–1904*, state doctoral thesis, Department of Literature and Social Sciences, University Mohammed V, Rabat, I, 54 et seq.

[178] Stephen Bonsal, *Morocco as It Is, with an Account of Sir Charles Euan-Smith's Recent Mission to Fez*, London, 1894, 78–79, in Khalid ben Sghir, *al-Maghrib wa Britania al-ʿudhma 1886–1904*, 56, note 85.

The throne was the symbol of all-powerfulness. The Koran teaches us: "It was God who in six days created the heavens and the earth and all that lies between them, and then ascended the throne."[179] The image of God in the fullness of his power is shown the same way, in the sacred text, on the day of the Last Judgment:

> When the Trumpet sounds a single blast; when earth with all its mountains is raised high and with one mighty crash is flattened into dust – on that day the Dread Event will come to pass.
>
> Frail and tottering, the sky will be rent asunder on that day, and the angels will stand on all its sides with eight of them carrying the throne of your Lord above their heads.[180]

While everything is collapsing, God asserts his authority and his supremacy more than ever. He is "the King of Judgment Day,"[181] the only king when no one else can claim such a title. The throne of God then appears carried by eight angels the size of the universe, singing God's praises and having a human appearance or appearing similar to lions or other animals that symbolize strength, comments a jurisconsult. The image evokes that of kings at the height of their grandeur, having their armies march before them[182]; it was borrowed from their rituals. The throne was thus the symbol of power where it was supreme.

The prophet Muhammad, at the beginnings of the revelation, when the angel Gabriel presented himself to him, said: "I then raised my head and there he was in the air, seated on his throne."[183]

The Queen of Sheba, according to a servant of King Solomon, "has a splendid throne."[184] Her father reigned over all of Yemen. According to the chroniclers, she descended from forty kings, a long lineage that certainly confirmed her royal legitimacy. The exegesis reports the description of her throne: it measured eighty cubits in length, width, and height, or according to some chronicles, thirty cubits instead of eighty. It was made of gold and silver encrusted with all sorts of gems; its pillars were of red and green precious stones, with pearls and emeralds. It was guarded within seven rooms, each with its door locked.[185] The image recalls the sequencing of the heavens.

179 The Koran, 32:4; Tabari, *Târîkh*, I, 32.
180 The Koran, 69:13–17.
181 The Koran, 1:4.
182 *Kachâf*, IV, 590.
183 *Nihâya*, III, 207–208.
184 The Koran, 27:23.
185 *Kachâf*, III, 349.

According to Zamakhchari:

> [T]he throne was what expressed royalty the best. One says that the king sits on the throne of a certain land even if he never went there in person.... Kings differ as to their ranks. For the one who possesses [*yamliku*] a small town or a small territory, custom has it that he sits on a *sarîr*, one of the terms that usually designates the throne. The one who rules over a vast territory and who has kings under his authority has a *sarîr* for himself; his vizier has a chair [*kurssi*]. The throne and the chair are usually found only in large kingdoms. Thus the King of the heavens and the earth, by reason of His all-powerfulness, mentioned this as that was the custom.[186]

which we are to understand as meaning in the royal courts.

The meanings of the term *al-kurssi*, "chair" in Arabic, are broached in the commentary on the well-known verse of the chair that celebrates divine power: "His Throne is as vast as the heavens and the earth."[187] Interpretations vary. According to some jurisconsults, the term designated a huge body, on the scale of the heavens, the earth, and the universe. According to others, it was the Throne itself, because the *sarîr* is mentioned in the literature as a throne as well as a chair. Others differentiate between chair and Throne; the first would be above the seventh heaven or under the earth. The most common explanation makes it a huge body under the Throne. For some, the term would designate the placement of the feet under the throne,[188] precisely where the servants placed themselves prostrated, venerating their king. We shall return to this.

According to other commentators, the chair in the Koranic verse was a metaphor for authority and royalty. Arabs call the origin of all things *al-kurssi*. The word can designate the very person of the king by the fact that it is his seat: the name for the place of the king was ultimately applied to the king himself.[189] For others, the chair meant knowledge and also the scholar, that is, the academic chair, for the scholar's place is in knowledge; the chair was then used to designate both the scholar and his knowledge, because both were supports and foundations.

Finally, the goal of using such a word was to illustrate divine power, to give it a concrete representation from a didactic perspective. This also explains the vocabulary used in the usual relationships of authority, with royal authority naturally being the most established and the most striking

[186] Râzi, XIII, Part I, 148.
[187] The Koran, 2:255.
[188] On this point see Tabari, *Tafsîr*, III, 11.
[189] Râzi, IV, Part I, 11.

earthly model of power. Thus, the exegesis teaches, God erected the *Ka'ba* in the image of royal houses, the black stone as the divine hand that people kissed as they kiss the hand of their king; thus he presents the final Judgment Day and its ritual in the image of the courts of royal justice.

It was in this logic that God was granted a throne: "The Merciful ... sits enthroned on high,"[190] and He described it as "[t]hroned above the waters,"[191] as He described the rituals that were connected to him: "You shall see the angels circling about the Throne, giving glory to their Lord"[192] or carrying the Throne. And it was in this logic that He spoke of the chair.[193]

The throne thus ultimately symbolized the reign, that is, pure, unique, and uncontested authority. To designate the throne of the kings, the term *sarîr* was used most often, with *al-kurssi*, or "chair," being used much less often. The throne took over any material forms that were too narrow for it and thus stripped it of its aura. Its status exceeded that of a simple object; it was a grandiose and unobtainable object. The divine throne was the perfect illustration of that extraordinariness. A chair that was not only bigger and taller than the others, it was outside the realm of the comparable, the material, the human. From that, we get that to speak of the throne when discussing kings was to speak of their dignity and their reign more than the object on which they sat.

This explains the consequences of this conception; it explains the conflict between the throne of the king and the chair of the ambassador: the throne of the king possessed refined majesty only as a concept. The word released representations, turning the throne into an outsized object; however, the Arabic word did not originally designate a piece of furniture: *Al-'arch*, the throne, says the dictionary, "is the throne of God and it is incommensurable.... Men know it only through the name."[194] The throne of God comes from the invisible; it has no materiality that would lead to confusion. The throne of the king, on the other hand, oscillated between the visible and the invisible: it welcomed the unveiled king, facing the public that he had to dazzle. Ideally immaterial, the throne saw its brilliance tarnished by the irremediable metamorphosis into a real object. For when reduced in reality to the form of a chair, even one that was situated on high, overseeing the audience, as tall and wide as possible, and

[190] The Koran, 20:5.
[191] The Koran, 11:7.
[192] The Koran, 39:75.
[193] For this debate see Râzi, IV, Part I, 11–12.
[194] *Tâj al-'Arûss*, IX, 137.

glistening with pearls and brilliantly colored gems, the throne lost its magic; it suffered precisely from its materialization.

Even in the terminology unique to God, the chair could lead to confusion, as can be seen in the various commentaries cited above. Thus a number of exegetes explicitly subordinate the *kurssi* to the *'arch*, that is, the chair to the throne. The term *kurssi* then designated the placement of the feet. God having neither son nor *radîf*, or second, the supremacy of his throne thus left no room for confusion; the mention of the chair can only be understood as a negation of the *ridâfa*, the substitute, which brings us back to kings: In the divine setting, the chair denoted its irreducible difference from the throne, troubling kings with its lack of throne-ness. The chair in heaven, it was said, is beside the Throne, in God's hands. But the chair and the throne were incomparable.[195] Ibn Kathîr is adamant on this subject: "It was reported that Hassan al-Basri said that the chair is the throne, but the truth is that the chair is different from the throne and the throne is larger."[196] According to the prophetic tradition, the dimensions of the throne were incredible, unlike those of the chair.[197]

In fact, it is the transposition of monarchical terminology into the divine setting that caused confusion in the divine space, which excluded any shared authority. But even on earth, the genesis of the royal throne explains the king's reticence to allow a chair in his presence.

The throne was an element that rested in the heights and not on solid ground. It was incontestably, by its very origins, above human beings. It covered them with its blessing, protecting them from the torrid heat of the inhospitable Arabian deserts. It promised survival to the isolated individual who lacked protection from the implacable sun. All of these traits were attributed to the royal person and came from afar.

Etymology supports this representation. The *'arch* or throne is indeed the roof – *al-'arich* encompasses everything that can provide shadow,[198] – or that which protects: at the moment when dates were picked, the family members took shelter from the sun in huts called *'arch*, made out of reeds and palm leaves. One also speaks of *'urûch*, or houses of Mecca; through metonymy, the word *'arch* was applied to the city itself.[199] In that word, the reference to a paternal authority who watched over his children from on high is explicit.

195 Ibn Kathir, *Tafsîr*, I, 404–405.
196 Ibid.
197 Ibid., 405.
198 *Jambara*, II, 728.
199 Kûrâ', 105.

ʿArch also designated the chief. Because it served to name the Bedouin tent or house, if not the palace, it is very probable that the word was first applied to powerful chiefdoms that dominated the oases and provided food and drink to populations in difficulty. Providers of shade, that is, of sustenance and protection, they thus acceded to chiefdom. The origin of their authority, their redistributive function, earned them the name of *ʿarch*, which came to designate authority alone, and more specifically supreme authority, that of kings and later that of God. Thus *ʿarch*, the roof, the throne, preserved its aerial allure and its immensity, which have pervaded representations of it since its origins.

The veil, the royal *ḥijâb*, through the mystery that it created, was precisely aimed at feeding the popular imagination in that direction. During public audiences, the chamberlain used the magic of protocol to safeguard the impression of immensity. He established the decorum crucial to the materialization of the throne, its return to earth. The room where the audience took place had to be transformed into a miniature universe where the heaven and the earth came together. Through that crucial staging, the king could be simultaneously present and distant, earthly and heavenly. And to prevent any possibility of confusion, the king's seat differed radically from those of his guests.

The king took his place upon the *sarîr*, consecrated by usage as the throne of kings. Unlike those in front of him, he was free to lie down or to take a seated position. Among all who were present, only he was free to choose his movements and his position; he assigned his guests theirs and dictated their attitude. The *sarîr* was not an actual chair. A huge bed converted to a sofa, it represented well-being, power, and glory. The term came from *as-surûr*, which meant an uncommon degree of interior happiness, which was hidden by the kings' serene expression.[200] Beyond that meaning, as we have seen, the throne was wherever the king sat, even if it was merely a simple rug like that on which the caliph ʿOmar Ibn al-Khattâb appeared.

The King's council was never left to chance; it was the object of meticulous care. The majesty of the audiences was intentionally organized to the smallest detail. Tabari reports the beatific exclamation of a king's companion when he saw the king leave his *sarîr*: "He descended from his throne onto the earth."[201] The throne was otherworldly; it put the king

[200] *Tâj al-ʿArûss*, VI, 511–519.
[201] Tabari, *Târîkh*, IX, 266.

beyond human reach. And it served to mark his difference, his nobility, his centrality.

Receiving one of his provincial governors, a potential competitor, the caliph Abdelmalik invited the governor to sit beside him on his throne before speaking at length with him. Then "he told a young slave to take his sword. The governor said then: 'We are God's, O commander of believers!' The caliph responded: 'Do you expect to sit beside me with your sword on you?' And he took the sword."[202] The threat of disgrace could lead a guest to death. One approached the king in a weakened state, naked and disarmed; the vertigo induced by the king's high place did the rest. This was one of the procedures that compensated for the materiality of the throne.

Returning to the opening diplomatic incident, to invite the British ambassador to sit on a low stool certainly constituted a strategy that was part of the management of royal audiences and that assigned an undeniably inferior status to the sultan's guest; it forced him to raise his eyes to the master of the place, to look at him with consideration and fear. Obviously, the ambassador of the empire on which the sun never set could not agree to be placed in a beggar's posture; such a thing was unacceptable to him, an insult to the representative of the world's most powerful nation, that of the industrial revolution. He knew what he was doing when he demanded a chair. The ambassador's stool was a chair reduced to its simplest expression, one that would not overshadow the majesty of the throne. Like in heaven, the royal throne intentionally maintained the placement of the chair at its feet.

THE KING SITS ALONE ON HIS THRONE

The elevation of the throne was closely linked to the establishment of the monarchy and to the degree of royal power. With the consolidation of the reigning powers and the loosening of tribal bonds, the strongest vertical hierarchies established themselves to the exclusion of others, and the person of the king gained in strength and brilliance. The distance between the monarch and his entourage widened.

In the early days of the Muslim empire, when competition was in full force, the borders between the throne and the chair were still fluid and could be crossed. The unstable balance of power at the time necessitated

[202] Tabari, *Târîkh*, VII, 167.

compromise. The caliph ʿOthmân made a place on his *sarîr* for al-ʿAbbâss, the uncle of the Prophet; for Abû Sofiyâne, the chief of the Omayyad clan; for al-Ḥakam Ibn al-ʿAss; and for al-Walîd Ibn ʿOqba.[203] Before him, ʿOmar had already seated al-ʿAbbâss and Abû Sofiyâne beside him, arguing that "the former [was] the uncle of the Envoy of God and the latter, the lord of Quraysh." In other words, the throne of ʿOmar welcomed the ancestors of the two imminent dynasties, the Omayyad and the Abbasid, anticipating the events to come.

Under the Omayyads, the usage evolved. Only the notables of the clan in power could sit with the caliph on his couch, whereas the descendants of the Prophet, the Banû Hâchem, sat on chairs. The chair gradually became the throne's foil, a function that came into full force during the rise of the Abbasids: Abû al-ʿAbbâs as-Saffâḥ sat alone on his throne. The Banû Hâchem sat on chairs, and the Omayyads, on cushions.[204]

Certainly, the chair and the cushion were obvious signs of distinction for the guests who received them among the crowd present at the audience. The Prophet always offered tribal chieftains a cushion, saying: "When you receive the lord of a people, honor him."[205] The cushion certainly was not the bare ground, but despite the consideration it reflected, it still conveyed a lowered status.

Al-minbadha, or cushion, was called that because it touched the ground, upon which it was thrown. *Al-anbadh*, the people it was thus supposed to welcome, were those who no longer had any power in reserve or were in the process of losing any remaining advantage[206]: the cushion served as a public message announcing that they were going to be demoted from the rank of lords to that of simple subjects. Then, the mechanics of servitude would take over and gradually strip the king's servants of any attributes formerly granted them by virtue of their ranks. The king henceforth had only subjects before him.

[203] *Aghâni*, V, 135.
[204] *Aghâni*, IV, 338.
[205] *Fâʾiq*, III, 400.
[206] *Tâj al-ʿArûss*, V, 401.

5

The King and His Subjects

God's entourage certainly resembled that of kings in many ways, and servitude seems to be the bond that controlled God's relationship to the faithful just as it did the kings' relationships to their subjects. The jurisconsults' repeated mention of the rituals of the royal courts to clarify the relationship to God originated from concerns that were more than strictly didactic.

The king was not, however, just an abstract concept; his disadvantage was his being made of flesh and blood. Thus he owed it to himself, in his relationship with his subjects, to remedy the carnal reality that he could not shed; he had to find a solution to his encumbering presence. Of course, as we have seen, the royal veil, or *ḥijâb*, by decisively contributing to the construction of the king's elevated place and to the establishment of levels similar to the seven heavens that kept his subjects at a sufficient distance, constituted an essential element in the divinization of the king. But the regulation of the king's relationships with his subjects was equally important for the mechanisms that it put into operation. The modes of regulation had the aim, in practice, of attending to the king's image in order to solidly establish the place of servitude. Already as he came into being, the king, having just emerged from his cocoon as tribal chief, appeared surrounded by mystery. The qualities attributed to him with the intent of establishing his authority strangely recall, at least in part, the beautiful names of the God to come.

THE MIRACLE OF ROYALTY

The *sayyid*, or lord, was first and foremost the owner, the one who was endowed with great wealth, the sharif of noble extraction, the generous and the magnanimous, the warlord, the primus inter pares.[1] More than the first, he was the beginning and the origin: he was the foundation and the essence of the group.[2] The hierarchy left no room for confusion; the second position was clearly assigned: the *sayyid* had a lieutenant, the *ʿâqib*, meaning "the one who comes after."[3] The king was distinguished by his clothing: the turban was the sign of chiefdom, its saffron color being reserved for great dignitaries.[4] In processions and on all other occasions, he walked before his people with the lofty gait that befitted his rank. A common man, it was said, revealed his status in the way he walked, by turning his head too often, gesticulating, and occasionally glancing behind himself at inopportune times.[5]

The chief was powerful. His power emanated from his strong physical presence. He was corpulent, had a long stride, and spoke with a loud voice: "It was pleasing to see and hear him."[6]

He was strength and wealth, the *Ṣindîd*, the one with considerable wealth, the dispenser of all gifts, the *bahlûl*.[7] He was the recourse and the unshakable support; like the nourishing tree, he was the one to whom people appealed in the inherent difficulty of desert life. He was the protector to whom one confided one's weakness in desolation and solitude, in the face of the adversity that came from enemies as well as the elements. The chief supported his tribe and interceded on their behalf with kings and the powerful; he was the captain who courageously faced trials and resolved difficulties.[8] He granted shelter and food to the traveler in need. It was reported that the public crier of a certain ʿAmer Ibn Toffayl shouted at the top of his lungs on the esplanade of Souk ʿOkaz, singing his master's praises: "If there is a traveler, then I carry him! A hungry man, then I feed him! A man who is fearful, then I reassure him!"[9] The divine accents of such an offer established a chiefdom with solid foundations that were inscribed in the subconscious of the population.

Wealth was thus the precondition for belonging to the chiefdom. It inaugurated the phase during which the pretender, the insistently self-proclaimed giver, attempted to establish his tribe's recognition of his

[1] *Nihâya*, III, 173.
[2] *Tâj al-ʿArûss*, I, 3, this concerns *al-badʾ*.
[3] *Nihâya*, III, 268; Ibn Hilâl, *Al-Furûq*, I, 39.
[4] *Majma ʿal-amthâl*, II, 104.
[5] *Majma ʿal-amthâl*, II, 71; Baladhuri, 213.
[6] *Tâj al-ʿArûss*, XV, 507; *Al-Kâmil*, II, 571.
[7] *Tâj al-ʿArûss*, V, 68–69, and *Al-Kâmil*, II, 725.
[8] *Al-Hutayʾa*, 29, note 3; *Tâj al-ʿArûss*, VI, 465–466.
[9] *Majma ʿal-amthâl*, II, 104.

redistributive activity, before acceding to the position of the one who would establish supplication as the unique mode of benefitting from his generosity, that is, before becoming king.

The generosity that the pretender demonstrated had resounding and staggering repercussions from the moment he entered the chiefdom. In Arabia, the warlord derived a considerable benefit from the campaigns that were led under his command. First, he received one-fourth of the spoils of war, *al-mirba'* – or one-fifth after the advent of Islam – and the *nachiṭa*, that is, all the fruits of the rapine that preceded the battle, but also *aṣ-ṣafâya*, that which the chief claimed for himself even before proceeding to split the rest – a privilege that eloquently marked the degree of absolute power even at the first moments of its birth – as well as every contested object during the division, or *ḥukmuhu*, and, finally, the *fuḍûl*, or "indivisible surplus," in other words, that which remained because it could not be divided up.[10] War and rapine thus constituted a source of considerable wealth and enabled the accumulation of huge fortunes. The chiefs of large tribes became petty kings thanks to the considerable concentration of goods in their hands and the absolute power they assumed over their followers.[11] Their nobility, with the evidence to prove it, left the doors of royalty wide open for them.

The nobility of the chiefs was the clay that kings were made of. Mo'âwiyya tells us that a noble man was "one who is feared in his presence but lamented in his absence,"[12] or in other words, a pillar on which a system rested. It was a nobility that was acquired through perseverance in war as well as in peace and that most often was the fruit of generations, for nobility increased with the age of a chiefdom. In typical descriptions, it was necessary to descend from at least three generations of chiefs to have a claim to royalty.[13] Chiefs also had to be free persons, a precondition for nobility, with a pure freedom that no vice had sullied; their ancestry could include no captive as far as memory went back.[14]

The chief, the dominant pole in a system of servitude, was the procreator, the stallion who never showed weakness, who never gave in to base professions.[15] The origin was determinant in access to royalty: to be in a position one day to claim the throne, one had to belong to dominant

[10] Chajarat ad-dur, 131; Al-Haroui, *Gharîbu al-ḥadîth*, I, 417; *Ichtiqâq*, 103 and 334.
[11] Râzi, II, Part I, 188.
[12] Jâhiz, *Rasâ'il*, I, 164.
[13] *Aghâni*, XIX, 196.
[14] *Ruqayât*, 186.
[15] *Jambara*, 1145; Al-Haroui, *Gharîbu al-ḥadîth*, I, 152.

clans, to masters of caravans and of money, to officials responsible for watching over the holy places, to great dispensers of largesse.[16] The reference to the noble stallion, *al-fanîq*, indeed recalls how the selection that took place to designate the elect was no less than the natural order of things, as just as the best animals stood out within a herd. Thus, the insignia of royalty did not arise from any artifice or from stories made up of wars, ruse, and rapine. The throne fit like a glove on the king who fully deserved it. The crown rested on "a head that one believed to be made of gold."[17]

The Omayyads were called "the ore of royalty," and their chiefs were the stars that shone in the sky.[18] In general, the king was associated with a light that illuminated the earth. In the Arabic language, the king was the *sultâne*, that is, the proof. He was so because no naysayer was ever supposed to confront him, because he was the grandiose symbol of the divine on earth. The word derives from *salite*, which means oil among the Yemenites and elsewhere designates a sesame pomade that was used in oil lamps.[19] The king was the guide who led his servants and lighted their way.

Crowned, he was the *michwadh*, a sumptuous and tragic image borrowed from the sun, when, haloed by a ribbon of clouds, the star seemed to be wearing a turban. This solar spectacle occurred during years of drought, when the dust gave a thin cloud a pale color verging on yellow that gave the sun a halo.[20] A sun breaking through the darkness of difficult times, the king incarnated here a divinity whose majesty no crisis could harm. He resided in the inaccessible heights above men who were at the lowest point of their weakness. He also lighted their nights, being the *badr*, or full moon. He was the fire, *al-waḥa*, as is asserted by Ibn ʿArabi.[21]

The king's ring had a specific name that symbolized fortune.[22] The kings had many virtues and performed many miracles: they were reputed to heal rabies, a gift that was transmitted from father to son[23]; their medical virtues, extended thanks to the nobility of their blood, covered

[16] *Aghâni*, XXIV, 99 and notes.
[17] *Ruqayât*, 175.
[18] *Ruqayât*, 64 and 36.
[19] Tabari, *Tafsîr*, XI, 595; Râzi, IX, Part II, 43.
[20] *Tâj al-ʿArûss*, V, 378.
[21] *Fiqh al-lugha*, 325.
[22] *Islâḥ al-Mantiq*, 12.
[23] *Ichtiqâq*, 225; *Majma ʿal-amthâl*, I, 345–346; Jâhiz, *Kitâb al-ḥayawânn*, II, 10–11; *Aghâni*, XV, 308.

madness and illnesses of the body tied to the loss of an organ.[24] In general, the king's ability to confront difficulties of all sorts was deeply established in representations; he was the *mundhir*, the one who warned his servants of danger.[25] He had a relationship with the otherworldly.

A true divinity, he was endowed with superhuman powers, like Solomon. Magic was certainly one of his talents, establishing his bonds with the invisible.[26] In Muslim tradition, King David, the first king of the sons of Israel, was all-powerful and wise, mastering the fundamental professions that assured life, speaking to birds and animals.[27] The first kings, according to Tabari, were magicians; they drew their power from the supernatural. They were true gods, masters of the visible and invisible worlds. Thus they were the initiators of everything that facilitated material life: they expanded the use of wool and skins, the weaving of cloth, the manufacture of weapons, the expansion of textiles and silk-making; they promoted the domestication and raising of animals, masonry, the use of stones and marble, the construction of baths, mineral work, and the use of pharmacopoeia. And they reminded their servants of the relationship that bound them together: "They assured them that the king was their master, their owner and the one who protected them from the ills of old age and death."[28] Kings were free men in the face of servants. They enjoyed this immanent freedom that shone brightly, which no vicissitude could extinguish. The king, they were assured, was a god.[29]

Pure, unsullied freedom was their privilege. The *ʿâhil*, or great king, a word still commonly used today to designate sovereigns, was the free man without restrictions, left to himself; he was the absolute master of himself.[30] From this position, the kings could not cross over to the other side. Even in captivity, their status protected them from any attempt that could cause a blow to their condition, so great were the mystery and the fear that surrounded them. Thus it was that one did not cut the *nâsiya* of kings, the tuft of hair that was shaved when a captive was freed to symbolize the hold over him.[31] The ransom to be paid in the case of captivity was very high, on the order of a thousand camels at least, no doubt for

[24] *Naqâʾid*, I, 104.
[25] *Tâj al-ʿArûss*, VII, 518.
[26] *Islâḥ al-Mantiq*, 32 and 70.
[27] *Kachâf*, I, 296, and III, 343.
[28] Tabari, *Târîkh*, I, 111–114.
[29] Ibid., 126.
[30] *Tâj al-ʿArûss*, VII, 432–433.
[31] *Naqâʾid*, I, 55.

small-scale petty kings.[32] Just as there was a closed field of servitude that locked slaves in by marking them indelibly, there was also, on the opposite extreme, a space reserved for royal lineages, whose sacred nobility was untouchable.

Social conventions protected them from any decline; a barrier was solidly erected between the two poles. Accession to royalty was on the order of a miracle. When the Israelites fled from slavery by the Copts, the Koran has Moses say: "Remember, my people, the favour which God has bestowed upon you. He has raised up prophets among you, made you kings."[33]

To be king was to cross a barrier that put one beyond the reach of the common man, a barrier that made one the master. According to a jurisconsult, "the king is the one nobody approaches without being authorized": the mystery was already there, on the cusp of investiture. Slavery and royalty were thus connected and went together: "Their houses were spacious, with fountains. They had goods and slaves at their disposal. And the one who had such a situation was king."[34]

At the very origin of royalty, then, was slavery, without which an incorruptible freedom could not be manifest; on the other hand, the slave had the protection of his master and lived in his shadow. He was a privileged witness of the king's mystery and his complexity; he was aware of his human and superhuman qualities.

HUMAN AND SUPERHUMAN

A young slave who worked in the service of the king told this story:

I and another slave who was the same age as I worked in the service of Abû Jaafar al-Mansûr, in his private chambers. He isolated himself in a room that he used as a sort of refuge, consisting of a small space with a tent made of thick cotton cloth, a rug, and a blanket. When he did not come out for an audience, he was in an excellent mood and cheerfully tolerated the chattering of the children.

When he put on his official robes, his color changed, his face became dark, and his eyes became red. He then left the room, with all that might occur. When his audience was finished, he came back. We greeted him when he entered, pushing the joke to the point of reproaching him![35]

[32] *Aghâni*, II, 117; *'Iqd*, V, 144.

[33] The Koran, 5:20.

[34] Râzi, VI, Part I, 154–155.

[35] Tabari, *Târîkh*, IX, 265.

Thus there was a public king and a private king! What relationships did his private personality have with his successive incarnations? His daily metamorphoses were inscribed in the life of the palace, with its scenes and its setting, but it was far from a production: the metamorphosis of the king, as reported here through the eyes of a child, seems indeed to have been a natural occurrence. This is a precious account of the double life of the king.

The same witness reported that al-Mansûr confided in him one day: "O my child, when you see me dressed for an audience or back from my council, let none of you approach me for fear that I may hurt you."[36] Thus the human king warned against the outbursts of the superhuman king, as if the repercussions of the latter completely escaped the control of the former! He informed his people behind the veil, those who circulated within the universe of his mystery, in his secret space. In that other place, beyond the royal veil, the monster seemed to be calmed. His isolation protected him from himself, from his human body, and from his shortcomings due to the weakness of his human personality. When Ja'far the Barmecide, disgraced and incarcerated, wrote to the caliph Hârûn ar-Rachîd imploring him to receive him, the caliph categorically refused. Masrûr, the slave in whom he most closely confided, reported: "I informed ar-Rachîd that Ja'far begged him to look at him with his own eyes. Ar-Rachîd said: 'No, he knows that if my eyes see him I will not kill him!'"[37]

The human is thus there, lurking within him, with his fears and his remorse, and the king was wary of his own humanity. Should the veil be torn, the mystery escaped. The broken king was then banished from the heavens; the king was naked. A caliph lost his throne and pitifully traversed the streets of Baghdad: "I am the commander of believers; fight for your caliph!"[38] he called out to passersby. He went to the prison and had the prisoners freed so they could join his cause, but they all fled without coming to his aid.

Without the bond of servitude, authority lost its foundation. Born of that bond, it was extinguished when the bond was broken. Without it, sovereignty was stripped of its aura, deprived of support, and thus disarmed. The king, formerly a brilliant head of the army, became ugly and fearful; his humanity, reduced to its miserable expression, took over. His

[36] Tabari, *Târîkh*, IX, 265.
[37] Tabari, *Târîkh*, X, 94.
[38] Tabari, *Târîkh*, XII, 74.

solitude and his misery were unveiled. Rid of the sham of the pomp, he was pitiably metamorphosed.

The man/king, having taken refuge in his nook, beyond the reach of the spectacular, was under the secure protection of his servile entourage; the only ones to have access to him were his most trusted slaves, those who were at the extreme of servitude, those for whom he was simultaneously a god, a king, and a master. His excesses and his weaknesses were stifled and hidden by the thick silence from inside. Surrounded by women, eunuchs, and young servants, the king no longer needed a veil before that crowd of legal minors without virility.

The Omayyad caliph al-Walîd Ibn Yazîd was bathing in a vat of wine while the illustrious Ma'bad was singing. He heaped gifts upon the musician and begged him to stay silent about his bacchic baths. When he got out of the tub, a swarm of concubines surrounded and covered him in order to keep the secret of the king's body.[39]

It was reported that another caliph, Yazîd Ibn ʿAbdelmalîk, was so delighted by a performance of song that he began to dance frenetically, followed by his concubines, until he lost consciousness and fell to the ground with them in a faint.[40] In another scene, he went as far as to strip completely, throwing down all the barriers that protected the king, without the help of his close servants.[41] From door to door, from threshold to crossed threshold, from veil to raised veil, one reached the ultimate veil, the one that was on the king's body itself; it was made not of stone walls but of the chain of servants on the front line, whose task was to maintain order. They formed his shield against disorder, against the disorder of showing a face that revealed his emotions, against his own fragilities. A Yemenite king was called Dou al-Ad'âr because he had reportedly brought from the Maghreb slaves whose gaze was always downcast; he thereby guaranteed a diabolical entourage that nothing could get through.[42] He also reinforced the king's superhuman quality, a completely closed field beyond the reach of any human contact.

The belt formed by servility thus enabled the king to do away with his human shortcomings. Here the master-slave relationship, in the most extreme sense of the term, that of the *ʿubûdiyya*, which was used for circles close to God, played the role of buffer and of regulator of the servile relationship, taken in its broadest sense, connecting the king to his subjects.

[39] *Aghâni*, I, 61–62.
[40] *Aghâni*, I, 78.
[41] *Aghâni*, II, 219.
[42] *Tâj al-ʿArûss*, VI, 438.

The king's relationship with his closest slaves was in fact the school of his formative years, where his authority was shaped[43]; against it he measured the bonds of dependency, of varying intensity, that he would subsequently have to maintain and manage. A benefactor offering a young slave to one of his friends wrote to him: "I am sending you this young slave so that you can use him to practice controlling your anger!"[44]

The slaves who formed the king's hermetic seal had a view of aspects of his personality that were erased from the image that was delivered to the public. For the king indulged in distractions, expressed his feelings, and sometimes gave free rein to his fantasies. Hichâm Ibn ʿAbdelmâlik confided in one who was close to him that the only pleasure in which he could not indulge as often as he liked was to free himself from the observance of the strict rules of royal conduct.[45] Moʿâwiyya asked someone near him about the meaning of pleasure. The person said to him: "You must order the youth of Quraysh to leave us," and then he continued: "Pleasure is the banishment of good manners."[46]

One must be careful, however, not to form too hasty an idea of the king as a person based on these anecdotes. The king was in reality one and only one, despite the contradictory expressions of his public and private personae. Absolute power was the common denominator of his two faces. He was both sides of that power at the same time. The following was said of an Omayyad caliph: "When he became angry at someone, he gave the order to whip him in his presence; then he conversed without paying any attention to him until he died under the whip."[47] This was the tough, pitiless exterior of the king whose entourage trembled at the mention of his name, yet who was reputed among his clan to be a refined poet and one of its most intelligent members.

The servile veil thus freed the king, who then gave free rein to his humanity. He could assume the role of tender father and attentive lover. The caliph ʿOmar, notoriously "severe and harsh," admitted: "As soon as we kings retire, we are like every one of you."[48] The cruel despot al-Hajjâj, despite his "evilness, tyranny, insolence, and unilateral power," recognized, speaking of his wives: "By God, I am like a demon when I appear before you! But, by God, if you saw me kissing the feet of one of

[43] M. Ennaji, *Soldats, domestiques et concubines*, 157 et seq.
[44] *Jamharat rasâ'il*, II, 344.
[45] Jâhiz, *Rasâ'il*, I, 146.
[46] Ibid.
[47] *Aghâni*, XII, 271.
[48] *Aghâni*, III, 96.

them!"[49] And Yazîd was astonished when, entering the chambers of his father, the caliph Moʿâwiyya, he found him on the floor while one of his concubines sat like royalty upon the bed. However, the interior space was politically out of bounds. The relationships that were maintained there did not affect the king's lofty role. The rule, in fact, was that the responsibility of servitude increased with proximity to the king and had the function of a veil. The words of the caliph to his son are enlightening: "Go back where you came from! Concubines are playthings, and the man at home with his family is like a child."[50]

Granted, the bursts of tenderness that the king showed in private supported the idea of his human frailty, but the king did not abandon his body. Those of his close entourage were aware of the illusion of that state of things. They knew how to read, under the flow of affection, signs of the presence of the harsh and intractable master, which could awaken and leap out at any moment onto his prey. They did not trust the royal expression, which they knew was limited. Everything could change. Anger, suspicion, envy, badly handled drunkenness could follow the tender caress of the hand and be expressed with the sharp edge of the sword.

Thus having proximity to the king was not without danger! How, in that cage without a door, in that unknown interior space, could one tell what was grace and what was disgrace? What was life and what was death in the dangerous game of being close to the king? The king that Moʿâwiyya described as being similar to a child was prone to unpredictable rages; his infantilism would suddenly turn him into a lion that would rip his detractors to shreds.[51]

More than unpredictable, the royal ire was unjustified, and its inexplicability contributed to the mystery of the king. It erupted when one least expected it, and pardon could just as quickly follow in its wake, without definitively calming it. Hârûn ar-Rachîd, familiar with those outbursts, said: "When we kings become angry against one who is close to us and then we later pardon him, there remain in us traces of that anger, which nothing can calm."[52] His son and worthy heir, al-Mâmûn, added: "The king is like a lion or a fire, so do not expose yourself to his wrath."[53]

When angry, he was like raging floodwaters. *At-tâghiya*, the tyrant at the height of his strength, also designated the river that overflowed

[49] *Aghâni*, III, 97.
[50] Baladhuri, 75.
[51] *ʿIqd*, V, 69.
[52] Jâhiz, *Tâj*, 92.
[53] *Aghâni*, XI, 342.

its banks and carried away everything that stood in its path.[54] Memory thus classified the king's mortal anger on the same level as the raging elements![55] Jâhiz strongly calls attention to this point, emphasizing that kings are not to be understood using the same criteria as humans. No parallels of that order can be drawn; no norms can be established.[56]

The courtier who allowed himself to go too far in his familiarity with the king ran a great risk. The poet Abû Nuâss, a familiar at court, was greatly troubled when the caliph called for him and had him sit "so close that they were knee to knee." His stays in prison had taught him to beware of such proximity.[57] The caliph Mûsa al-Hâdi, who entertained without a veil in the company of his evening companions and musicians, was "of a rough nature and a bad temper." He quickly took umbrage with courtiers who had not been warned of his abrupt mood changes.[58]

The rules of the game dictated that such situations be avoided. The king had to maintain a balance between the interior and the exterior so as to preserve the magic of the reign. The example of the caliph al-Ouâthiq, a wine lover who gathered his companions early in the morning to drink, was not to be followed: "I have decided to drink early in the morning. I will not sit on the throne. I will sit with you and we shall be as one. And so, form a circle."[59]

The musician Brâhim al-Mûsili, who was introduced before Hârûn ar-Rachîd in one of his new homes, reported:

> He was settled in the center of the courtyard with only one slave, who was serving him a drink. He was wearing his summer robes, a delicate tunic covered with a red cloak stamped with his insignia. From what I could see, he seemed to be affable and welcoming.... Then he called for his servants, and one hundred appeared.... That was the end of the appearance of a man at home like anyone else. Then Masrûr the Great arrived and gestured to the caliph that he had some news to tell him. Ar-Rachîd listened to him. He then exploded with anger; his eyes became red and his veins popped out.[60]

However, among the qualities of the royal person that were praised, self-mastery appeared high on the list. The king showed neither excessive joy upon hearing good news nor any sign of distress when misfortune

[54] Râzi, VII, Part II, 135.
[55] Râzi, X, Part I, 14.
[56] Jâhiz, *Tâj*, 59.
[57] *Aghâni*, XXV, 213.
[58] *Aghâni*, V, 199.
[59] *Aghâni*, IX, 340.
[60] *Aghâni*, V, 237.

struck.[61] But, seen from both sides of the veil, he appeared better in the totality that revealed the truth of his nature. The interior space abounded with affection; it also abounded with anger when contact with the public space imposed the constraints of his aura on the king.

His close and proven servants knew what to expect. They remained on their guard even when the master showed the greatest satisfaction with them. They knew the lava that could rise and overflow without pretext. Wariness was second nature to them. They endured reprimands and punishments without flinching. They never strayed from the obligations connected to their status as slaves, whatever their merits might have been.[62] They used language of absolute servitude to respond to the king's commands. Their unwavering motto was: "The minds of the kings are the kings of minds."[63] Their lowly status, which they demonstrated on every occasion, was the best tool they could use to aggrandize their master. It was they who turned a fragile being into a god inaccessible to the common man.[64] They were an essential component of his feared and adored Majesty. They participated in his brilliance and his *hayba*, or aura.

THE KING'S *HAYBA*, OR HIS AURA

Fear and admiration. That was *hayba*, which expressed the mixed feeling that took hold of people at the mere thought of the king. Fear was blended with the ecstasy produced by the spectacle of the extraordinary, to which were added respect, veneration, and fear, as in the *ijlâl*, or the attitude of the individual before God. *Al-ijlâl* – this cannot be emphasized strongly enough – gives us one of the major expressions of royal grandeur: "His Majesty the King" was expressed by *jalâlate al-malik*.

The *hayba*, a fear that took hold of people upon the mention of authority, was the fruit of the very real threat represented by that authority, the fruit of the public demonstration of violence. Granted, that fear was only one aspect of *hayba*, but it was important.[65] The mystery that surrounded the king in representations, and the protocol of the court to which the visitor was subjected, participated in the inoculation of *hayba* in people's minds.

[61] *Ruqayât*, 186.
[62] *'Iqd*, I, 24–25.
[63] M. Ennaji, *Le Makhzen al-Aqsa, la correspondance d'Iligh*, II, unpublished.
[64] *'Iqd*, I, 31.
[65] Tabari, *Târîkh*, VI, 107.

A caliph expecting to receive a delegation from Egypt gave instructions to his chamberlain: "See to the entrance of the members of the delegation. Shake them up! Upset them as much as you can! Each one of them, upon arriving before me, should feel that he is lost."[66] The orders were so well executed that the first one to enter called the master of the place the envoy of God!

This anecdote leads us to the early days of the state as an institution in the Muslim world. Authority cynically put into place the necessary protocol to bedazzle its onlookers. With the Omayyads, rituals intended to destabilize those who sought an audience with the king were put into place; panic was to take hold simply at the thought of crossing the palace threshold. A man approached the king "with his chest filled with fear and his heart racing, even when he is received in order to be honored, ennobled, heaped with goodwill, and intended for a high office."[67]

The fear of the one who entered into an audience was so great that Ibn ʿAbbâss, himself a man of the court, advised that one should recite a prayer to forearm himself against the wrath of the tyrant: "God is great and more noble than what I fear and what I am wary of. Oh God! Lord of the seven heavens and Master of the immense Throne, support me against your slave, his soldiers, his allies, and his followers. Blessed be Your Name and great Your Praise and great be the one who comes to Your aid; there is no other God but you."[68]

Pomp reinforced *hayba*. The caliph Moʿâwiyya was attentive to his appearance, and during an audience, he wore "his turban the colors of fire [and] wore kohl." "He was very handsome."[69] The people visiting the sultans also had to dress in a way that paid homage to them and conformed to the rituals imposed. "That gives more solemnity to the occasion," stressed one who was in charge of clothing, "and shows more consideration and respect."[70] Under the Abbasids, the king's entourage and servants wore different costumes depending on their rank. As for the master himself, his dress during audiences was meant to accentuate the feeling of surrender and submission that never failed to take hold of his visitors. Everything combined to incite fear:

[66] Tabari, *Târîkh*, VI, 169.
[67] *Kachâf*, III, 375.
[68] *ʿIqd*, III, 222.
[69] Tabari, *Târîkh*, VI, 169.
[70] *Bayân*, 481.

> How can one show one's enemies, frighten the hearts of the disobedient, engrave the most extraordinary trouble in the bosoms of the common folk, if not by elevating the sultan to the highest rank? And how can one increase power, if not by impressive displays? [The people] can be remedied only with threats and will follow the right path only if you frighten them. They will submit to what is useful and beneficial to them only through a policy that combines love and *mahâba*.[71]

We will later examine what the love and friendship of the kings consisted of.

Spectacle and stagecraft determined the public image of the king. Close by during audiences or public processions, he had to appear distant, elevated, extraordinary, and untouchable. Hârûn ar-Rachîd, animated by the legend of the great kings, had his procession preceded by very young slaves called "ants," who dissuaded the public from getting too close by throwing projectiles at them.[72] This technique recalled the legend of King Solomon served by men, animals, and demons: wasn't that legendary king accompanied by birds of prey?[73] From the procession of ar-Rachîd, the popular imagination retained the vision of a lion king riding atop the clouds, before whom men sang his praises. In many respects, this portrait also evokes angels in heaven celebrating the Master of the Universe.

One king's squadron was called *al-Malḥâ'* because of its remarkably brilliant steel gray color.[74] Anything that gave off light and increased the *hayba* was very prized. This caliph "set off in his warship to shine [*ḥarrâqa*], like a lion. Never had the people seen a spectacle to rival such magnificence, nor a sovereign more handsome than this king."[75]

To impress, shock, and frighten went hand in hand. The strength and violence deployed in the processions enveloped the king in *hayba*. Ibn Ziyâd, one of Mo'âwiyya's governors, was, according to the chronicle, the first to affirm the authority of the state. He fortified the royalty for his caliph. "He forced the people to obey, pushed the limits of sanctions, brandished his sword, made arrests on the basis of suspicion, and punished in spite of any doubt. And so the people became afraid … and feared him like no other *wali* before him, and he spared no force in his blows."[76]

71 *Bayân*, 471–472.
72 *Aghâni*, XXIV, 227.
73 Al-Mutanabbi, I, 168.
74 *Tâj al-'Arûss*, IV, 217.
75 *Aghâni*, XXIV, 86.
76 Tabari, *Târîkh*, VI, 107.

The use of weapons was only part of the production of fear; the king also fascinated the people with his majestic comportment. Having come in pilgrimage to Mecca, Moʿâwiyya "entered Medina followed by fifteen yellow mares bearing magenta saddles, with concubines in flowing robes astride them … such that the people who beheld it were discomfited."[77] Governor of the region under the caliphate of ʿOmar, he had had to justify to his chief the necessity of such magnificent retinues. A lord, the son of a lord, and used to commanding authority, he knew that such actions were necessary to establish a respected and feared state; ʿOmar could not continue in his austere ways.

The sumptuousness and magnificence of the royal residence contributed to reinforcing the *hayba*. Among the Omayyads the court was already luxurious. An individual thus describes his entry into the home of the caliph Hichâm:

> I entered a spacious home covered in marble, the slabs of which were separated by golden bars. The walls were the same. Hichâm was seated on a red rug and was dressed in silk of the same color. He was scented with musk and amber, and before him were golden vessels full of musk that he stirred with his hand, thereby emitting the perfume. I paid him my respects, he gestured for me to approach him, and then I kissed his feet.[78]

A familiar admitted to the company of Sulaymân Ibn ʿAbdelmalek Ibn Marwân "found him seated on a bench covered with green silk cushions atop red marble, in a garden of crisscrossing branches [which is one of the descriptions of paradise] and ripe fruit. And … in an area of flowers and grass … were concubines, one more beautiful than the next."[79] The visitors, whether courtiers or not, who sometimes had to wait a long time before being introduced, were seized with ecstasy and awe before the display of such wealth.

Al-Asmaʾi, in the home of Hârûn ar-Rachîd, was aware of the beauty, the light, and the ordered servitude:

> When I entered, ar-Rachîd was seated facing the hall, as if the moon had haloed him with brilliance.… Candles surrounded him, affixed to the supports of the podium; servants stood at attention on the rugs. A slave had risen to hear me pay my respects. He said to me: "Salute!" Which I did.[80]

[77] *ʿIqd*, IV, 383.
[78] *Aghâni*, VI, 85.
[79] *ʿIqd*, IV, 68.
[80] *ʿIqd*, V, 297–298.

In the council of ar-Rachîd, servants carrying lances stood in two rows at his sides.[81]

This arrangement of slaves immediately created a veil between the master, whether he was a king or not, and the rest of the world, and it created a *hayba*. The chronicle reports that a certain wealthy notable thus entered a Turkish bath: "He has a *hayba* and is accompanied by his slaves."[82] Hassan, the son of Hassan son of the imam ʿAli, appeared in public on horseback, preceded by two black slaves who were "remarkably tall, imposing like pillars."[83]

Whether armed guards, everyday servants, friendly companions, or concubines, slaves were an indispensable part of the *hayba* mechanism. Upon the death of one of his musicians, the Abbasid caliph al-Mutawakil lamented the disappearance "of one of the shining jewels of royalty that increased its beauty."[84]

The king's person also had to radiate an air of majesty intended to cast a spell over the public. He was not to appear arrogant but rather to inspire familiarity tempered with an inaccessible loftiness. Fear and dread were not enough to describe the complexity of the royal air. We learn that "there was a difference between *mahâba* and pride. *Mahâba* in fact flows from a heart filled with veneration, fear, and love for God. Then the heart is invested with light and is covered with the cloak of *hayba*, and the face shows the sweetness and *mahâba* that softens hearts and brings peace."[85] More prosaically, the king's assurance in his vocation and his mission established the brilliance of his natural majesty. Pride and arrogance, born out of ignorance and affectation, did not mislead the public: they were the province of petty kings of narrow rule; they were the traits of those who set themselves up as monarchs without a true vocation for it. The boastful and proud chief was the one who affected a haughty air while holding his head up in a ridiculous way, like a horse being led by the bridle.[86]

The great man never turned to look behind him. He was the *asyad*, the one who looked neither to his right or to his left. This term comes from an illness, attributed to a vein at the top of the head, that strikes camels and makes it impossible for the animal to turn its head. For the king as

[81] *Aghâni*, XVIII, 220.
[82] *Aghâni*, I, 63.
[83] *ʿIqd*, VI, 38.
[84] *Aghâni*, XXIV, 5.
[85] *Tâj al-ʿArûss*, II, 499.
[86] *Tâj al-ʿArûss*, IV, 306; one then speaks of the *kaymakh* king.

for the lion, the word designates the noble and naturally haughty stance of the master who struts before his court.[87]

These manners were not limited to the king himself. His entourage and the greats of the kingdom were advised to speak to people only through gestures and not to look at them directly. Through their attitude, the royal *hayba* would indirectly fill their hearts.[88] The Koran, as part of the global approach that delimited the domain of the divine authority, condemns the use of these manners if adopted by a tyrant. It calls upon the prophet in this regard: "Do not treat men with scorn, nor walk proudly on the earth."[89] The *hayba* of the king, on the other hand, was natural, tightly connected to light and beauty.

A great king was the one who radiated light, even if he did not wear a crown, as his turban took its place.[90] The light gave him the brilliance that made him celestial.

The oft-praised beauty of the kings, a central element of their *hayba*, drew all eyes toward them; all the magnificence of their entourage was reflected on them. Brusquely addressing some kings, the prophet Muhammad called them *arwâ'*, that is, Adonises, before whom the crowd was seized with admiration for their splendor and that of their spectacles.[91] "O noble kings, powerful and handsome," the Prophet wrote about them!

The king had a brilliant beauty that left its mark on one's mind; he seemed to burn with the ardent fire of youth, which fed his desire to appear immortal.[92] The kings of the Banû al-Mundhir lineage were renowned for their beauty to the point that Arabs called them "stars" and compared them to flames.[93] Among them, the king an-Nu'mânn was preserved in legend: paradise was said to contain "a tree that wore the dress of its inhabitants, redder than the anemones of an-Nu'mânn," an allusion to the bright red flowers that the king was said to have discovered, during one of his outings, in the crevice of a dune, which he immediately ordered to be protected. The flower's name was also attributed to its color and to its resemblance to a flash of lightning, which recalled the brilliant light of the king.[94]

87 *Tâj al-'Arûss*, V, 72, and also VII, 91; al-Mutanabbi, I, 284.
88 *'Iqd*, V, 438.
89 The Koran, 31:18.
90 Al-Mutanabbi, I, 165.
91 *Tâj al-'Arûss*, XI, 182.
92 *Nihâya*, II, 438, and III, 281 and 419.
93 *Ichtiqâq*, 188.
94 *Nihâya*, XIII, 492–493; *Tâj al-'Arûss*, XIII, 249–250. An-Nu'mânn reigned between 582 and 602 CE.

But the king's beauty was most often inspired by his spectacle and the fear it incited, or in other words, the *rahba* of the prince.[95] Strength, as a habitué of the royal courts pointed out, was indeed the best clothing, the attire of the conqueror.[96] It was, however, celebrated in discourse as natural and immanent. The public nevertheless perceived it as supernatural and extraordinary. The king's features were called *subuḥât*; they emitted a divine light that exalted his servants. They paid tribute to him: "Glory to the king! Praised be the king!" Incidentally, to pay tribute to God and sing his praises daily (*subḥân allâh*),[97] one used the same terms that designated the traits attributed to the king. Beauty made submission into a reflex performed without hesitation, or in short, a completely natural attitude. Its deadly force wiped out any desire for resistance.

The *hayba* produced an invincible fear and stripped the subject of personality. Recognized servants were to be completely invested by it. Thus, "when the slave approaches the fearsome sultan, he forgets his own self, and, with all his heart, all his mind, and all his feelings, he turns toward him, concerning himself only with the sultan and forgetting the rest of the world." He was subject to an extreme fascination that made him a devout servant in body and soul. He delighted in serving and approaching his king. The hypnosis of power took possession of him. The king was his god: "The slave entered a state of death regarding himself and his own fate."[98]

For the servants closest to the king, seeing him as a god was understandably neither a theory nor a flight of fancy. They, more than other subjects, were inclined to adhere to that concept. The Koran stresses that in the face of the all-powerful divine, the fear of majesty reduces man to solitude: "But the face of your Lord will abide for ever, in all its majesty and glory."[99]

The *hayba* belonged exclusively to authority; it was the manifestation of mastery. The example of the caliph ʿOmar illustrates its power even though he never relied on the artificiality of pomp as he moved about.

ʿOMAR THE KING AND THE CALIPH!

Without question, the royal *hayba* instilled fascination as much in the popular milieu as in high places, among Islamic authorities. Disparaged in

[95] *Aghâni*, XXIII, 194.
[96] Al-Mutanabbi, I, 165.
[97] *Tâj al-ʿArûss*, IV, 77.
[98] Râzi, II, Part II, 142.
[99] The Koran, 55:27; see also 55:78.

discourse and explicitly denounced, the royal model nonetheless inspired the admiration of the most orthodox caliphs. By their own admission, they delighted in tales that described the pomp of royal courts in the greatest detail.

The company of a certain Abû Zubayd al-Tâ'î, a Christian, familiar in Persian courts and noble residences to which he was invited during celebrations, was very sought after. His shrewd knowledge of protocol and monarchical rituals made him a well-appreciated guest of the caliphs. The caliph ʿOthmân called him near and liked to listen to his tales.[100] Among the facts that were said to have undermined ʿOthmân's position with the public, let us note, according to Tabari, his very conciliatory attitude toward the kings of Kufa and the largesse he showed toward them.[101]

The legend of the kings was very much alive, constantly renewed. People recalled Jadima al-Abrach, king of Ḥirâ, who, legend has it, was the first to have worn sandals, to have had servants carry candles, and above all to have traveled at night![102] In other words, he was credited with having transformed a chiefdom into a kingdom, having given the king his brilliance, and having conquered the power of the night. This tale was firmly inscribed in the tradition of extraordinary kings who, like King David, were initiators and innovators. It was, in fact, a fascination with absolute authority, more than a fascination with the kings themselves, that promoted the exceptional nature of the monarchy.

The caliph ʿOmar liked those stories; he plied the poet and knight Zayd Ibn Muhalhal Ibn Yazîd, whose visits even the prophet Muhammad appreciated, with questions.[103] However, the caliphal model of ʿOmar, as recorded in Arab memory, was light years away from the royal model. He was situated, in truth, at the very origins of the Muslim state; structures were just beginning to be put into place, and authority was not yet solidly established. (The royal model would have also begun with the advent of prestigious chiefs, warlords of proven nobility, and demagogues whose skills were recognized by their community.) The caliph's prestige was at its peak and would pave the way for the institution of hereditary dynasties. To enlarge the empire and obtain the resources that were indispensable for a viable state structure necessitated a union that

[100] *Aghâni*, XII, 151.
[101] Tabari, *Târîkh*, V, 106.
[102] *Aghâni*, XV, 302.
[103] *Aghâni*, XVII, 247–272.

only the caliphate, still encircled by the holy aura of the Prophet, was in a position to ensure.

Without being a king, 'Omar had an aura that was found only in very powerful emperors. However, he was assuredly the chief least concerned with pomp, having pushed the removal of it to the extreme. The *hayba* due to the qualities of a chief or king was found in its most pure state in 'Omar, whose personal ascension was the determining factor.

People feared him to the point of not daring to speak to him. They preferred to speak to 'Abderrahmân Ibn 'Aouf or 'Othmân, who were his appointed intermediaries.[104] 'Omar's roughness was legendary. The descriptions that the chronicles offer of him confirm the image of a coarse man. He was seen distributing food, "standing, leaning on a cane, wrapped in a knee-length cloak. He was a tall man who looked like a shepherd."[105] His power, absolute and unshared, already bore the seed of legitimate violence. "I strike the disobedient,"[106] he said, waving his stick before him like a shepherd designating a camel who has wandered from the herd and must be led firmly back to the right path.

He demonstrated a power that arose from his natural charisma; the *hayba* of the prince was in him, in the halo that surrounded him; it had no need for the magic of artifice and in fact profited from the renunciation of it. The caliph did not have guards to protect him; no veil kept him from public view. He could still appear in public as a man similar to others, at least in appearance.[107]

'Omar's model quickly faded, however, with his successor 'Othmân, on one hand because of 'Othmân's personality and his inclination toward compromise, and on the other hand, more fundamentally, because of the exhaustion of the model itself, with authority calling upon auxiliaries in flesh and blood. The classic logic of the domination of the state apparatuses regained priority.

The strongest relationship of servitude was the one that connected man to the divinities, to the supernatural. Because he was in reality a prophet manqué, a thaumaturgist prince, 'Omar legitimately maintained a relationship of servitude with his subjects that continued their relationship of absolute servitude with God. In fact, without being king, 'Omar exercised an unshared power. A certain great notable, one of those whose

[104] Tabari, *Târîkh*, IV, 3.
[105] *Fâ'iq*, I, 261.
[106] *Nihâya*, III, 213 and 208.
[107] *Fâ'iq*, IV, 72.

support was bought in the early days of Islam,[108] clearly demonstrates that proximity and attachment to the king were by far stronger in the case of almost absolute servitude. Comparing his ties with the caliph and those with his successor, he wrote to ʿOthmân, full of reproach: "ʿOmar suited me much better than you. He frightened me and thereby made me pious, and heaped me with gifts and made me rich."[109]

ʿOmar inspired fear by his very nature. His conversion to Islam constituted a step forward and a considerable advantage by reason of his courage and determination as a leader. A steadfast Muslim whose advice was heeded, often unquestioningly, he drew from the wells of pure servitude in the name of a sacred cause. His command suffered no questioning.

The man was truly exceptional. ʿAisha said of him: "What excellent mother took care of him and fed him abundantly with her milk!" His mother made him, she specifies, an incomparable man, "unlike any other," a unique man![110] ʿOmar had a divine characteristic, "two right hands," an expression symbolizing the strength and power of a great tyrant.[111] In that expression, his extraordinary capacity for work, perfectly done, was praised, as was his great strength and great firmness[112]: he was *al-aḍbat*, gifted in both hands, thus like God, with an unsullied left hand. He was like the lion "gripping its prey in a powerful grasp and overcoming it so that it can no longer escape,"[113] as the poets sang, just as they did – not without merit, to be sure – to the glory of another prince, al-Mâmûn the Abbasid: "Neither of your hands are left; you have two right hands."[114]

The grip of the caliph ʿOmar, described as *al-khidab*, or great and rough,[115] was strong. Even if the caliph said that power was "a matter of suppleness without weakness and strength without violence,"[116] ʿAisha complained of his tyrannical exercise of power by using expressions typically applied to royalty to describe him: "By God, the muzzle was not put on our noses!"[117] – that is, that we are not held by tight reins! Or even explicitly evoking servitude: "ʿOmar has pressed the earth and it has borne its fruit," meaning, according to the commentary of Ibn al-Athîr,

[108] Al-mu'allafati qulûbuhum.
[109] *Jamharat rasâ'il*, IV, 44.
[110] *Nihâya*, III, 160.
[111] *Jamharat rasâ'il*, III, 403.
[112] *Nihâya*, IV, 297.
[113] *Tâj al-ʿArûss*, X, 322.
[114] *Aghâni*, XXIII, 48.
[115] *Nihâya*, II, 12.
[116] *Fâ'iq*, IV, 276.
[117] *Fâ'iq*, I, 384.

that he "has oppressed its inhabitants and has made them his servants," leaving them no respite.[118] No doubt ʿAisha had her own motivations, notably reacting to ʿOmar's misogyny, but she also was aware of the practices of chiefs who were more political and less intransigent than he. By reason of his status, she could be critical. Her words, in any case, emphasized the despotic traits of the caliph and the royal content of his power: "Chosroes and Caesar ruled as they saw fit, and you are like them."[119]

We can understand that those who approached ʿOmar experienced great fear and that his *hayba* was imposing, like that of the greatest kings. It was so because of the huge symbolic capital he had in a society still largely marked by the Bedouin values of courage and generosity, one that still bore the living memory of its most worthy kings. But it was so also by virtue of the strong impression ʿOmar left in his wake. During one of his visits to the prophet Muhammad, ʿAisha was struck by "the diadem of his face shining with light."[120] The proverbial beauty of the king is there, natural and existing prior to his reign. The diadem was indeed the monarchical insignia of antiquity!

The intractable poet al-Ḥotayʾa, whom he imprisoned, or, more precisely, threw into a dungeon, for a supposed outrage that he had committed toward a notable, thus sized up the absolute power of the caliph, calling him by the title of *malik*: "O king who today commands as far as the plains and plateaus of Basra and Gaza."[121] He was pardoned thanks to supplication invoking the logic of the king's pardon, the very logic that earlier had landed him in the dungeon.

Granted, ʿOmar had banished all the luxurious symbols of royalty. Having received the sword of an-Nuʿmânn, the legendary Arab king, he gave it to one of his captains without a concern for the symbolic weight of such a relic[122]; he drew his own reliquary from another register.

ʿOmar went about alone, according to the chronicle.[123] His own slave stood at the door as chamberlain.[124] Unlike a king, he was magic enough that his private being and his public existence were confused in the eyes of all. He did not need thick palace walls or protocol to bring

118 *Nihâya*, I, 102.

119 *Nihâya*, III, 327.

120 *Fâʾiq*, III, 273.

121 M. Ennaji, "Le diable et le bon Dieu," in *L'amitié du prince*, 105–124.

122 *Fâʾiq*, II, 193.

123 Jâhiz, *Sirâj*, I, 214.

124 *Fâʾiq*, III, 429.

his visitors to their knees. Despite this apparent simplicity, and without recourse to the indispensable strategies employed by his successors, a heavy veil nonetheless separated him from his subjects. At his death, his son ʿAbdallah performed the mortuary duties and covered him with his shroud. His slave Suhayb led the funerary prayer.[125] His austerity and his strong presence made him, in the Muslim memory, a model of the anti-king.

The caliph ʿOmar was indeed a man of his time who had a keen awareness of the constraints and alliances dictated by the dynamics of the social structure. He was, regardless of the myth, quite concerned with respect for the social hierarchy.[126] He was not part of the group that went so far as to ask the Prophet to abolish slavery in a concern for equality claimed by a nascent religion mismanaged by notables. Although ʿOmar undertook to free the slaves of Arab origin, he nonetheless encouraged slavery: "Buy slaves in great numbers; it often happens that the slave earns more than his master."[127]

The caliph existed in a world defined by servitude. He could conceive of freedom only by its antonym: slavery.

ʿOmar was an intermediary with heaven. The Koran confirmed his wisdom on many points. He was the sword and the scales of justice, and his words held the weight of law. This was not a new phenomenon. Kings in Arabia had long held the extraordinary privilege of imperative speech. The king was the *Qayl.*

IMPERATIVE SPEECH

In one of his letters the prophet Muhammad calls upon the "*Al-aqyâl al-ʿabâhila*,"[128] thus using names that denoted the kings. "People of perfect and complete freedom," he called them, "whom no one commands and who are accountable to no one." The dictionary defines them as "kings of Yemen, solidly established in their royalty, from which they cannot be removed."[129]

[125] Tâj al-ʿArûss, I, 24.

[126] *Nihâya*, III, 327.

[127] Al-qurtubî abî Yûsuf ibn ʿAbdillah, *Bahjat al-majâliss wa unss al-mujâliss, Dâr al-kutub al-ʿilmiyya*, I, 789.

[128] Letter to Wâ'il Ibn Ḥujr and the people of Ḥadramout; *Aqyâl* is the plural of *qayl. Jamharat rasâ'il*, I, 60–61. The verb *ʿabhala* applied to the camel designates the one left free to itself, which no shepherd can order to return. *Tâj al-ʿArûss*, XV, 461.

[129] *Siḥaḥ*, V, 18–19.

The term *qayl* derives from the verb "to say," literally, "the one who says"; here it means not a charlatan or an eccentric but, on the contrary, one who speaks his orders with assurance and certainty.[130]

The meaning assigned to the word *qayl* is far from unambiguous. Some authors use it as a synonym for viceroy, chamberlain, or petty king with limited command over a tribe and other subjects in the region.[131] Others use it as a name unique to the king who wields imperative speech.[132] The *qayl* was also "the one who speaks to the king, who is heard by him, and who speaks to no one but him."[133] The word itself refers both to the mastery of language that directly or indirectly plays a decisive role in the formation of royal power, and to the mastery of the language of command, which the king monopolized in the exercise of his authority. According to Ibn Sidah, *qayl* described the king from Ḥimyar, who ordered what he wanted.[134]

Imperative speech belonged to the king. The privilege of speaking was granted to him, and this confined his entourage to silence. For the great poet al-Farazdaq, who saw Arab society as consisting of two very distinct poles, the powerful and the servile, the king was "he in whose presence one did not speak."[135] We can see, then, how much the poet, whose words were his raison d'être, had a keen awareness of the mortal silence to which those who approached the king were reduced.

In the presence of a certain prestigious chief, "one of the signs of power was that no one uttered a word in his council."[136] Even where it was not a question of royalty, the *majliss*, or council, of the prophet Muhammad scrupulously respected the order: "When he started to speak, the people present lowered their eyes and fell silent as if birds were circling over their heads."[137]

The king was the indisputable one "whose words and orders were to be carried out," confirmed a certain jurisconsult.[138] For everything that had to do with decision making, with considerable business matters, and with the realm of the sacred, in which humans were incapable of decreeing anything, his words were law.

[130] *Fâ'iq*, I, 14–15.
[131] Al-Haroui, *Gharîbu al-ḥadîth*, I, 130. See also *Ichtiqâq*, 480, and Ibn Chajari, 253.
[132] *Lissân*, XI, 575–576.
[133] *'Iqd*, III, 373.
[134] Tâj al-'Arûss, XV, 238.
[135] *Naqâ'id*, II, 21.
[136] *Majma 'al-amthâl*, II, 50.
[137] *Majma 'al-amthâl*, II, 376.
[138] *Nihâya*, IV, 122.

In ancient Arabia, the irregular dating system imposed by the lunar calendar posed a problem in the organization of group activities. Serious harm thus resulted for the community that had to lower its weapons at the beginning of the holy months and put an end to profitable war operations. The voice of the *qayl*, whose prerogatives knew no limits, could overcome the constraints of the calendar and thereby slow the approach of a holy month.

Since the king had supernatural qualities in the form of relationships with the invisible world, whose unforeseen events he could master,[139] his speech was filled with mystery. He was the holder of imperative speech who uttered authoritative sentences allowing no hesitation.[140] According to one king, "I am above any vice or sin, and my word cannot be disputed."[141]

The king of Ḥimyar, Ḥaddâd Ibn Ḥammâl, a figure who was shrouded in legends, including that of his union with the queen of Sheba, was called the "Deafening, thunderous din," which indicates the resounding echo of his commands.[142] The king's words were decisive. Their power was inextricably intertwined with the specter of death that surrounded him. To live in his proximity was to live in constant fear of incurring his wrath. This is why memory retains the thunderous voice of the kings.

The king was the *saffâḥ*, as the first Abbasid caliph was called, that is, the generous one who had the means to give, but also the one who was in the position to speak, by which we mean to order. The word refers, in its broadest meaning, to the power to cause bloodshed.[143] That these three qualities are united in a single word and that, moreover, the word names a king whose reign had inaugurated one of the most prestigious Arab dynasties is a strong indicator of the intense perspicacity of the royal speech. The tongue of Ḥassâne Ibn Thâbith, the designated poet of the Prophet, fortified with the respect and authority of the master's speech, became a decisive organ that asked only to put his word into action: "O Messenger of God, it seems to me that if I put it on a stone, it would break it, or if I put it atop a head, it would shave it."[144]

Thus one might say that the king was the word itself, for his speech carried an exclusive meaning; it left room for no other. The servants who

[139] Tabari, *Târîkh*, I, 113.
[140] *As-Sîra*, I, 43.
[141] *Tâj al-ʿArûss*, I, 261.
[142] *Jamhara*, 1006.
[143] *Tâj al-ʿArûss*, IV, 91.
[144] *A-Chiʾru wa chuʾarâʾ*, I, 305.

were obliged to speak, even if only to execute his orders, were expected to do so in silence, concealing their voices from his earshot. Regardless of the circumstances of their service to the king, they were like the living dead: they spoke with the voice of the dying and the starving, who no longer even had the strength to make their pleas heard. Such was the speech of servitude, dictated by the fear that the master inspired, by their lowly status, and by the desire to show that status. In the relationship of authority, the king's utterances had an outsized echo, while the voices of subalterns were reduced to silence.

One attributes to ʿAisha, the wife of the Prophet, the following statement, which she pronounced upon seeing someone reciting the Koran: "I have seen a man who gave the impression of being on the verge of death, so inaudible was his voice."[145] It was, however, recommended in prayer and in submission to the Supreme Master not to go so far as to assume such a posture: "Pray neither with too loud a voice nor in silence, but, between these extremes, seek a middle course."[146] In reality, however, the inaudible voice, which conveyed the insignificance of the adorer before his master, became entrenched in usage.

It is reported in prophetic tradition that, as his death drew near, the Prophet lost the use of his speech. His companions, who were beside him at that difficult time, described that day as the "day of silence." On this day of silence, the Prophet was present for no one but God, to whom he was completely devoted.[147] Servitude allowed no speech except that of the master!

Thus we can understand better the reticence or whispering before the king, the *takhâfut*, which was in fact a quasi-silence, the negation of the servant's own person and his surrender to the power of the master. The servant spoke when the master of speech ordered him to do so, for the king liked to be praised for his power, in the image of God, "who hears only the one who praises him."[148]

The speech of the king had no equivalent; it was unlike that of anyone else. The voice of the solicitor had to be feeble, a necessary quality for a voice directed toward the heights of the king.

A notable came to pay his respects to the king an-Nu'mânn. With a nonchalance touching on unawareness, he demonstrated a remarkable

[145] *Tâj al-ʿArûss*, III, 47.
[146] The Koran, 17:110.
[147] *Tâj al-ʿArûss*, III, 87.
[148] *Tâj al-ʿArûss*, XI, 227.

eloquence tinted with arrogance to the point that he enraged the king, who said to him:

"If you want, I can ask you questions that you will not know how to answer." . . .

And so the king gestured to one of his slaves to slap him in the hope that he could be put to death if he crossed the line in his response. The king then said to him: "What do you say to that?"

He answered: "An insolent servant."

Once again the king had him slapped and asked for his response. He answered: "If he had been scolded for the first slap, he wouldn't have committed the second!"

And again the king had him slapped and waited for his response.

He said: "A king who educates his slave!"

Another slap was given, to which he responded: "You are the king. I appeal to your mercy."[149]

Silence was the rule; legitimate speech belonged to the king. The construction of the Muslim authoritarian model reinforced this royal privilege by subjecting the king's subjects to his undisputed speech. In the prophetic model, this consecration was obvious. No one was ever to raise his voice in front of the Prophet. The hierarchy of speech here was the cornerstone of a system. The prophetic speech was a light that dispersed the darkness and called for an attentive and submissive listening. The master-slave model was thus at its highest point. Though it happened, the jurisconsults stressed, that the slave would raise his voice in the presence of his master, no such thing could be accepted in the relationship with the Prophet, in which forgetting the self was obligatory.[150]

As for the caliphal model, it was supported by this example and by its reference to heaven as the final arbiter, with the intent of disallowing any questioning of its orders. It thus reinforced the ancestral experience of royal power in terms of submission. The caliph was then also a *qayl*, one who occupied a higher level because he wielded a definitively superior speech. A rationalization of the relationships of power occurred to the detriment of egalitarian tribal relationships and reinforced authoritarian modes of power. Heaven aided in establishing a hierarchy that society could not produce on its own. Initiative and decision-making power were seized for the benefit of the chief who, through speech, was henceforth endowed with all the extraordinary attributes that his command presupposed.

[149] *Aghâni*, XXIV, 249.
[150] Râzi, XIV, Part II, 98.

This evolution is evident from the beginning, as the Koran shows: "Those who call out to you while you are in your chambers are for the most part foolish men. If they waited until you went out to them, it would be better for them. But God is forgiving and merciful."[151] Prayer was the royal path to divine mercy. It reinforced the monopoly of the master's command and endowed his speech with a benefactory ability that expected only supplication. This was true of the king, whose subjects had to solicit him with passion to receive a pardon or to be granted a favor.

THE BEGGARS OF SERVITUDE

A certain king is said to have stated: "The doors of kings are for beggars, sojourners, and countrymen."[152] Thus the solicitor waiting at the palace gates was always in conquered territory, and no one objected to that. Beggars, followers of all types, solicitors of all kinds, and the merely curious had long since accompanied the processions of the kings. Taking into consideration the flood of people at their doors was a common and everyday task to which kings were strongly attached.

A considerable crowd surrounding the royal residences was indeed the obvious mark of great renown and esteem among the population. Rumors of a court's largesse or parsimony circulated rapidly by word of mouth. Thus great attention was paid to groups that formed, distinguishing, among the starving hordes begging for a pittance, between local folk and strangers who had come from distant lands, and between those who had been there for a long time and those who had recently passed through the gates of the city. Above all, one took careful note of their condition and attempted to determine their rank. The underlying movements of the society were manifested in the bustle of these variegated crowds. One alerted the king; he responded through his solicitude.[153]

The solicitor par excellence was the *assâ'il*, or beggar. Driven by hunger and urgently holding out his hand, he was the one whose requests were aimed at satisfying his needs, beginning with sustenance. *Al-mustat'im*, a term derived from the realm of food, designated the man without means who begged to be fed.[154] "You people, it is you who stand in need of God."[155] Their condition obligated them to turn to him and adore

151 The Koran, 49:4–5.
152 *Jamharat rasâ'il*, III, 364.
153 Ibid.
154 *Kachâf*, I, 217.
155 The Koran, 35:15.

him. Beyond material poverty, moral need also put one on the path to solicitation.

One of the fundamental aspects of servitude consisted of putting the individual in the position of chronic solicitor, lowering him, making him admit and recognize his need for the master, and then making him express it. From there, and often without really being aware of the mechanisms at work, he found himself forced to follow the standard procedure: turn to the king, publicly in most cases; the elite usually solicited him in writing. That procedure, which recorded the requests, was an act heavy with significance for the upper classes of society. Whether expressed in writing or aloud, by appearing at the door to the palace in front of everyone, the specific request was a preamble to royal favors, just as prayer preceded the bestowing of divine blessing and favors. Like prayer, the act of requesting had its rules and rituals. And without it, the walls of the palace remained closed and unresponsive.

Waiting at the doors was part of the solicitation process. The solicitor frequently had to resign himself to a prolonged wait that was indicative of the entire process. It made solicitation a supplication that was intensified by its duration. The proof was shown when the individual finally crossed the threshold of servitude with determination and, most of the time, with delectation. The royal reception – warm, cold, or glacial – was proportionate to the person, to his place in society, and to the degree of subjugation intimated in the encounter.

This situation was good business for the slaves who were stationed at the doors, who took advantage of it for their own profit. The notables who had come to ask favors of the king worked their influence and their contacts within the palace to avoid the discomfort of a prolonged wait outside. In a message that a notable wrote to the caliph al-Mâmûn following a prolonged wait at the caliph's door, his recognition of his servile status could not be more obvious: "If the Commander of the believers thinks it good to free his promise from the captivity of the chains of postponement by responding favorably to his slave and by authorizing him to go back to his land, it would be very good."[156]

The symbolic chains of captivity, evoked to obtain the expected favor, ensnared no other than the solicitor himself! To solicit, in the lexicon of royalty, meant to enter, willingly or driven by the vicissitudes of fate, into a condition of captivity that, it appeared, could only be lifted by royal consent. The ultimate goal of all solicitation was indeed that gradual

[156] *Jamharat rasâ'il*, III, 430.

enchainment that came out of the logic of enslavement by the royal authority, the keys of which in large part were beyond the reach of the solicitor.

The king's benevolent acts, or his pardon, were granted neither by chance nor according to a strict concern for charity; they arose from an implacable logic that slowly and methodically wove the ensnaring net of servitude. The king was in a position to disregard the solicitor entirely or to prolong his wait; the reason for this was neither negligence nor an unconcerned indifference, nor even his temperament, but instead an intentional act that was intended to further intensify the request and increase the debasing effects of the solicitation. Here is the response given in a high place to an individual who was disappointed that his request had not been satisfied: "To forget someone does not mean to neglect him, just as making him wait is not the same as abandoning him.... It was your right before us to remind us of your person!"[157] One thus had to endlessly solicit without showing a hint of weariness, constantly maintain hope, and always be ready to begin again, insofar as that resuming, judged legitimate by the king, was inscribed as a completely normal phase in the process of solicitation.

One thus discovers varying degrees of solicitation that are illustrated in everyday life by the approaches of professional solicitors struck down by poverty. The *faqîr*, or poor person, maintained a reserved attitude despite his difficult living conditions. The *miskîne*, whose obvious poverty and servility betrayed his true condition, was the typical model of the classic beggar[158] or *as-sâ'il*, literally "the one who asks." Canonical alms were recommended for these two categories of solicitors.[159] *Qunû'*, the attitude also recommended in prayer, was servile solicitation. It was the practice of the beggar who held out his hand to passersby, bowed as a sign of submission, and showed the most humble attention to his benefactor.[160] It is said that the term also referred to an itinerant beggar who traveled far and wide.[161] The *mu'tarr*, on the other hand, accosted people without holding out his hand, not going so far as to openly express his request for food, money, or anything else.[162]

157 *Jamharat rasâ'il*, IV, 283.
158 Ibn Hilâl, *Al-Furûq*, 194.
159 The Koran, 9:60.
160 The Koran, 22:36.
161 Ibn Hilâl, *Al-Furûq*, 198.
162 *Tâj al-'Arûss*, XI, 428–429.

A certain king argued that the one who deserved his gift was the one who solicited it and insisted until it was given.[163] This is because authority wanted above all to be formally recognized. According to the prophetic tradition, God loved *al-milḥâh*, the slave who persevered in his supplication. But insistence was fruitful only if the implored authority expected it. In the opposite case, it could prove to be detrimental and, consequently, ill-advised.[164] In any event, solicitations that remained in vain were abundant. *Al-moḥâssar* was the individual stuck at the palace doors, receiving no response despite his prolonged and obvious presence.[165] And the solicitation of one whose debasement touched the deepest abyss of servitude was carefully ignored. Such was the fate of people in disgrace and those on the fringes of society, who had neither money nor patronage.

Here we are far from the *joud*, or disinterested generosity, offered without solicitation and with nothing expected in return, that was so highly cherished by pre-Islamic Arab society, in which giving was done without calculation. The *sakhâ'*, or classic generosity, rarely intervened without a duly formulated request.[166] The centralization of power that occurred with the advent of Islam and the extension of the Muslim empire favored the spread of this practice, which was central to the monarchic system.

Soliciting the king required a proven know-how to derive great benefit from it, and was never without the risk of failure. To make use of servility was the surest means to reach the king, to get information to him, to have a request heard, to move him, to beg his pardon, or to carve out a place for oneself in his entourage. His intermediaries, the slaves outside of the *ḥijâb* (royal veil), regardless of their status and their area of intervention, knew the royal habits. They were aware of the comings and goings of the king. The echoes of his fury shook them from morning to night. They watched for his hours of favor and disfavor. They guessed the right moment to slip him a note. They knew how to wait for the moment when the king would allow and grant requests. The way the request was transmitted was essential: a tender poem, sung with the voice of an angel, could be a decisive weapon. The intimate moments when the king "gave up" his royalty, when liquor softened his soul, or when seasoned poets sang his praises just so were also opportune. Interior slaves were, in this regard, formidable intermediaries.[167]

163 *'Iqd*, II, 122.
164 *'Iqd*, I, 224.
165 *Tâj al-'Arûss*, VI, 274.
166 Ibn Hilâl, *Al-Furûq*, 190.
167 *Aghâni*, XXII, 22–23.

The king ignored those who rested on their laurels, hesitating to risk soliciting his generosity: "We are generous for the one who solicits us. We leave to his own devices the one who does not need us, but we love the solicitor among you."[168]

Caught in the model of servitude, the solicitor became involved in a mechanism that led him, step by step, into a situation that was fundamentally unenviable. Part of the elite often paid the price of this process. Pressed from all sides to solicit and seemingly aggrandized by so much attention, they soon found themselves right in the middle of the list of anonymous requestors, their fate as yet unknown. The king could raise hopes by dispensing, and then deprive to the point of despair. In both cases, dishonor was clear and debasement certain. In the event that those who belonged to the circle of habitués among the social and intellectual elite fell into disgrace, they found themselves brutally deprived of what they had judged to be definitively theirs. Thus, a great poet who saw his life threatened and then was reassured of his fate, but who was deprived of any largesse, wrote to one who was close to the caliph ʿAbdelmalik Ibn Marwân: "What does my survival mean if they leave me alive, but in fact dead, no longer having the right to largesse as the others do?"[169] The bond of servitude continually returned to the power over life and death, symbolic or otherwise, that the king had over his servants, either in fact or through his largesse.

The elite, whose avowed agreement and submission mattered to the king, ultimately allowed themselves to be won over through need or fascination. At the least murmur of solicitation, its members were welcomed with open arms and extreme benevolence. A great jurisconsult, al-Waqidi, finally came out of hiding and sent a modest request in writing. The caliph's response is enlightening: "I have instructed that you be given twice what you asked for. And so, hold out your hand no longer, for the treasuries of God are open and His hand is generous with his bounty."[170] The reminder of God's benevolence was intended to highlight the modalities of access to bounty on earth.

Solicitors, prey to real problems or concerned with climbing the echelons, were very particular in the formulation of their requests, which left no doubt about the divine status of the king. Such was the case for this solicitor, whose request was reported to a master: "He has addressed his prayer to you alone and places all his hopes in you."[171]

[168] Baladhuri, I, 91.
[169] *Ruqayât*, 36.
[170] *Jamharat rasâʾil*, IV, 380.
[171] *Jamharat rasâʾil*, IV, 310.

As in prayer, the supplication was addressed to the king alone. Perfect adoration left no room for infidelity. This parallel reveals the profound significance of solicitation: a submission that was only the beginning of servitude. Indeed, people asked the prophet Muhammad about the most highly recommended and most profitable moment for prayer, when one's proximity to the Creator was greatest:

"O Messenger of God! What part of the night is the most propitious for praying to God?"

He responded, "The most distant heart of the night."[172]

A jurisconsult commented that this was the last third of the night, or to be even more precise, the penultimate sixth. That is, the time of night marked by complete inertia, when there is no light, when life and movement are hidden from view and when the forlorn and crushed servant implores the Unique One. ʿAisha, the wife of the Prophet, reports that the Prophet slept the first half of the night and stayed awake the second half to pray. Abû Horayra explains that God came down to earth during the final third of every night and said: "Whoever solicits Me, I will give to him. Whoever calls upon Me, I will answer. Whoever asks My pardon, I will grant it." And so forth until dawn.[173] Thus, the moment to make requests was the one when fear was the greatest, precisely the fear that was inspired by the darkest of night in a universe still populated with superstitions and ghosts. In order to be heard, one had to demonstrate unwavering loyalty to the master and had to solicit no other authority.

The modalities of solicitation, the nature and content of what was granted, and the mode of giving took into account the nature of the relationship between the solicitor and the one who was solicited. The competition between the notables of the Hashemite clan and the Omayyads illustrates a particular aspect of this relationship, and one of its initial phases, when the king did not yet have a full mastery of the logic leading from solicitation to servitude. A letter from Moʿâwiyya to them is revealing:

I swear before God that you are assured my benevolence and that my door is wide open to you. There is no pretext that could suspend my benevolence toward you or any problem that would close my door to you. However, upon examining our relationship, I have noted something else. You think that what I have in my

[172] *Nihâya*, I, 311. See also Ibn Mâja, *Saḥîḥ*, I, 406.

[173] Ibn Mâja, *Saḥîḥ*, I, 407.

hands is more rightfully yours than mine. When I grant you a gift that takes into account what is due to you, you say: he has given us less than our due and has shown us little consideration. So I find myself in the deprived state of the one who merits no grace even if he does justice to the one who calls upon him and helps the one who solicits his aid.[174]

The king, master of abundant wealth – he uses the word *al-khayr* in this sense, that is, boundless abundance normally attributed to God – generously granted benefits to those who solicited him, even if he also recognized their right to revenue from the public treasury. The Hashemite clan, descendants of the Prophet, considered what they received as their due and not as charity granted as alms! The two lineages of kings were in competition, even though the very powerful Hashemite clan was temporarily out of power.

Solicitation took the form of distinction bestowed upon the solicitor when he was notified with diligence and sympathy of the king's endorsement. The solicitor cultivated the illusion of a particular status due to his personal merits and the regard that was bestowed upon him from above. Thus one person wrote to the caliph: "If asking others means lowering and debasing oneself, coming to you is by the grace of God a considerable honor. Never, in fact, do You become aware of a free man in difficulty without your donation preceding his solicitation, thus sparing him from asking and debasing himself."[175]

The distinction made here between the free man and the slave is pure illusion. The king, unlike the slave master, had no need to buy his slaves. The black slave, assigned to domestic tasks, represented the prototype of the servile person and attracted representations of servitude. The solicitor, unlike the black slave, believed he was untouched by any stain that could call into question his prerogatives as a free man that might arise from his solicitation. Royal servitude was a concept broader than private slavery. To be the king's man, within the framework of a servile relationship, did not mean to have come into his possession through a commercial transaction, but the absence of such a transaction in no way diminished the servile nature of the relationship between the king and his servants. *Mamlouk* slaves, that is, the legal property of the master and other servants legally free in service to the king, all fit within the model of royal servitude. That servitude had its rules and its mechanisms. The

[174] *'Iqd*, IV, 11.
[175] *'Iqd*, IV, 219.

relationship that connected the king to his servants was less strict than commercial slavery in certain aspects but stronger in others.

To solicit a royal pardon was one of the most eloquent chapters of solicitation. The act immediately put the solicitor on his knees. A king's pardon carried a particular significance by the fact that it seemed to arise only from the king's goodwill, a manifestation of the kingly mystery.

THE PARDON OF KINGS

Having come to implore King Richard III to pardon her son, the Duchess of York delivered these poignant words:

> Nay, do not say, 'stand up';
> Say, 'pardon' first, and afterwards 'stand up.'
> And if I were thy nurse, thy tongue to teach,
> 'Pardon' should be the first word of thy speech.
> I never long'd to hear a word till now;
> Say 'pardon,' king; let pity teach thee how:
> The word is short, but not so short as sweet;
> No word like 'pardon' for kings' mouths so meet.[176]

Maternal distress brings mothers of all kinds to their knees to save a beloved child. A prince's mother who came to solicit the same pardon as the Duchess of York but in a different climate, Zobeida, the stepmother of al-Mâmûn, begged him to have mercy on her brother al-Amîn:

> All sins, O Commander of believers, however great they may be, are small compared to your pardon. Every failure, however serious it may be, is minuscule compared to your grace. It is thus that God has constantly inspired you. May He extend your reign and render your fortune perfect! May He perpetuate good through you and chase away evil!
>
> This is the letter of a soul in pain who places in you her hopes in life when facing the vicissitudes of time and in death to be remembered well. If you deem it fitting to have compassion for my weakness, for my humble submission, for my lowly position, and for the ties of blood, may God respond favorably to your expectations, then do so, and remember the one who, alive [his father, the caliph Hârûn ar-Rachîd], was my intercessor with you.[177]

The caliph executed her brother, giving the order from the throne.

The king pardoned when he reigned as absolute and uncontested master. In the exercise of authority, perfect mastery and command entailed a

[176] Shakespeare, *Richard III*, Act V, Scene III.
[177] *Jamharat rasâ'il*, III, 315.

wise and cynical application of the pardon. A pardon was meant to support the king's power and not reveal a weakness. To preserve obedience in the future, the master had to punish when necessary.[178] It was the policy of divine conduct: "If We showed them mercy and relieved their misfortunes, they would persist in sin, ever straying from the right path."[179]

The pardon was an attribute of power. The power of the King of kings was absolute by virtue not only of his inexhaustible benevolence but also of his mercy (*raḥma*). In the opinion of the jurisconsults, mercy required nothing from the beneficiary in return, unlike the pardon, as it was applied in other hierarchical relationships, whether between father and son, husband and wife, or master and slave: the jurisconsults felt that it was granted out of fear of punishment, out of a concern for mercy, or quite simply because of human weakness,[180] which was not the case with God, the ultimate source of all command (father, husband, master, king).[181]

Ḥilm, or clemency, was one of the most respected qualities in ancient Arabia. The three pillars of chiefdom were in fact bravery, charity, and clemency.[182] Most of the great lords had demonstrated this, such as the "man of pardon," so named for his reputation in that domain.[183] Far from softness, which signified weakness and a lack of judgment, clemency served as a mark of nobility and a sure sign of a virile and steadfast command. Yazîd, the brother of the Omayyad caliph Moʿâwiyya, having refused a request by Hassan, the nephew of the Prophet, was taken to task by his brother, who attributed his lack of perspicacity and wisdom to the influence of his mother, that is, to the inconsequence of female judgment.[184] Moʿâwiyya wrote to him on the subject: "I understood that you had two judgments. One of them came to you from Abû Sofiyâne,[185] the other from Someyya. Regarding the one from Abû Sofiyâne, it was made with both goodwill and resolution; as for that of Someyya, it is similar to the judgment of her kind."

Moʿâwiyya rejected his brother's decision and thus acceded to Hassan's request, adding "as for the fact that you did not welcome his intercession

178 Tabari, *Tafsîr*, IX, 235.
179 The Koran, 23:75.
180 Râzi, XII, Part II, 126.
181 Râzi, XIII, Part I, 10.
182 *Fâʾiq*, II, 206.
183 *Aghâni*, XVIII, 280.
184 The filiation of Yazîd was the subject of discussion; see *Jamharat rasâʾil*, II, 37, note 5.
185 Abû Sofiyâne was the father of Moʿâwiyya and chief of the Omayyad clan; he was the great lord of the tribe of Quraysh at the advent of Islam.

with you, you have rejected this opportunity to the benefit of the one who is more worthy of it than you."[186]

Moʿâwiyya is often cited as an example of a magnanimous king. This quality apparently earned him recognition for having a superior political sense. Some considered him to be the most seignorial chief after the prophet Muhammad, even more accomplished in this regard than the caliph ʿOmar.[187] But looking closely, his striking goodwill was only a front, despite the truth of the recorded facts. The pitiless and bloody sword of the king was always unsheathed and placed in other hands that did not have the leisure to be merciful. The king in fact punished people through his auxiliaries and his agents. When the time came for a pardon, however, he retained for himself the privilege and the merit of pronouncing it; his merciful gesture was to be the object of great publicity and thus had to take place in public.[188] The principle was the same as that of charity. God, the King of kings, the model of perfect authority, distributed gifts himself and delegated any work of death or destruction to the prophets or the angels.[189] Like God, the great kings did not have a left hand that was capable of sin.

To pardon, especially to pardon someone condemned to death, carried extreme importance; the act emphasized the all-powerfulness of the king. Such clemency amounted to giving life, that is, the fundamental act performed by none but the supreme authority. It is recorded in prophetic tradition that, upon creating Adam, "God created him with His own hand, then made him in his presence." Another version adds that God "spoke to him face to face," that is, directly, without a veil and without having one of his angels intervene as a representative or a spokesperson.[190]

The great kings did the same. Moʿâwiyya thus felt it necessary to explain to one of his governors:

> We should not govern people in the same way; we would then be perceived as one and the same. Let us not all be indulgent, for if we did, the people would be happy to disobey us; nor let us all be harsh, for we would push them to extremes. For you, it is more fitting that you impose harshness and severity, and for me, [that I practice] clemency and mercy.[191]

[186] *Jamharat rasâ'il*, II, 38.
[187] *Nihâya*, II, 418.
[188] *Jamharat rasâ'il*, II, 416.
[189] *Kachâf*, IV, 38 and 446.
[190] *Nihâya*, IV, 8.
[191] *Jamharat rasâ'il*, II, 39.

The king's pardon was the twin brother of his anger. One did not see the light of day without the other. Poets wrote about this anger that was tempered by clemency.[192] Thus al-Hajjâj, the famous tyrant of Baghdad, where he ruled as the Omayyad governor, found himself constrained by his masters to divorce an Alaouite descendant whom he had taken as his wife. He obeyed the orders of his masters: "Oh, descendants of Abû Sofiyâne! You love to pardon, and pardon presupposes wrath. And so we displease you now in the hope of your pardon to come!"[193]

Similarly, a woman whose imprisoned son risked death and obtained a royal pardon only by the will of the prince said "I don't want to know his sin or to see you prove his innocence. Take note of his release as the proof."[194] In this we hear echoes of another king with a nearly identical reply: "Pardon, pardon! And I, unjustly too, must grant it you."[195]

The king who recently took the throne or who had just emerged from his cocoon as warlord was obliged to make himself feared by the might of his sword. The accomplished king, however, demonstrated his clemency first and foremost. An adviser praising his master's power suggested the royal path to follow in the case of a man condemned for serious crimes: "If you kill him, kings before you have put to death others who committed lesser crimes than his. If you pardon him, you will be the first to pardon a man like him."[196]

The gift of life, *'istihya*, which we will examine below, thus arose from the king's magnificence. It was on the order of a miracle. The condemned man, darkened with sins, was condemned by the law. The legislating and ruling king struggled mightily with himself to make room for the magnanimous king who granted clemency. This bipolarity gave him the privilege both to condemn and to pardon. The king's ability to pardon came from his extraordinary nature. Ruled only by his own volition, he was the only one who could pardon. The logic of the pardon seemed to reside in his very person, which emphasized his distance from the world around him more than any veil possibly could. The king was indeed unique!

He moved from one extreme to another. Here we speak of the mystery of might and power. Uncertainty weighed upon the minds of his subjects. His succession of life-and-death edicts bound together the opposing

[192] *Ruqayât*, 46.
[193] *Al-Kâmil*, I, 239.
[194] *'Iqd*, II, 85.
[195] Shakespeare, *Richard III*, Act II, Scene I.
[196] *Aghâni*, X, 146.

poles that were the domain of the king alone; clemency was his favored weapon and the definitive proof of his absolute power.[197]

A condemned individual, facing death, begged the king to grant him *al-amân*, that is, safety: "'What do you expect to do with [my pardon] when you are on your way to death?' explained the king, firm in his decision. [The condemned prisoner] responded that thanks to the pardon, his children and property would be saved."[198]

The king was aware of the extent of the privilege granted to him. That is exactly what made the gesture so lofty and divine. In the preamble to the sacred text, God himself first claimed the power to grant mercy, to signify his all-powerfulness: He wanted to be first and foremost "the Forgiving, the Merciful."[199]

More than a way of flattering the competitor and winning him over (*musâna'a*) as one might believe it to be,[200] the *ḥilm* that supported the pardon was a sign of strength and domination. In the sacred prayer recited for the dead that they may rest in peace, "May God cover him with His mercy," the word used, *taghmmada*, derived from the sheath of a sword. The mercy of God was supposed to hide our sins and to erase them,[201] but a sheath can never hide the fundamental, bloody reality of the sword. The pardon was like a sheath: it hid the sword temporarily from sight but still reminded one of its presence. For grace could, without warning, be transformed into disgrace. Many former prisoners, those who were still lucid after having endured torture in the king's jails, received his pardon and took care to get away quickly before the royal anger returned and threatened the little life they had left.[202]

The royal pardon was thus the product of a bond of oppression, violence, and enslavement that publicly announced the dishonor of the subjected party. The words that designate submission and debasement describe three stages, or three cases: first, the lowering after violence and oppression (*ad-dhul*); second, after the dominated one has shown proof of resistance (*ad-dhal*); third, the debasement of mercy, which intervened in a situation of submission and complete enslavement (*ad-dhil*),[203] as

[197] Ibid.
[198] *Aghâni*, XIX, 135.
[199] The Koran, 1:3.
[200] Baladhuri, 107.
[201] *Tâj al-'Arûss*, V, 152.
[202] *Aghâni*, XVIII, 280.
[203] *Tâj al-'Arûss*, XIV, 253.

seen in the sacred text: "Treat them with humility and tenderness and say: 'Lord, be merciful to them. They nursed me when I was an infant.'"[204]

One image of the debasement that followed resistance is that of the crushed rebel throwing himself upon the king's footstool, kissing the king's feet and taking to his knees to beg the king's pardon. The gesture, both common and expressive at the time, gives us the word, derived from the word for "footstool" (*al-gharz*, or leather stool), that means a surrender and request for clemency after a revolt.[205] To ask for pardon on one's knees was the sacred image of the bond between clemency and servitude. The pardon of the all-powerful king had no other presupposition or outcome. It was inscribed in his mystery, in the secret of his reign.

THE SECRET OF THE KING

The following passage is attributed to the Abbasid caliph al-Mâmûn:

> People are not in a position to assess kings in their relationships with their viziers in the way that they are able to assess the contrasts between kings and their protégés, the people of their entourage, their creatures, and those close to them. As for the latter, in fact, people see only their respect, service, assiduity, and good advice, and they see the kings punish these individuals in a clearly unjust fashion, to the point that some say that the kings take such action to seize their property or other things that one does not easily give up.
>
> Perhaps envy, boredom, or the desire to change have something to do with the kings' motivations. There are, however, certain betrayals that touch the heart of royalty or sacred things. The king cannot allow himself, in these specific cases, to reveal to the common man [*'âmma*] the place where the weaknesses of royalty [*sa 'awra*] reside nor to offer proof showing that the punishment was commensurate with the sin that was committed. The king cannot refuse to punish so long as his grievances remain inaccessible to the general public and unknown to many of those close to him.[206]

Like the heavens, only the master and his men of the secret, that is, the closest of the close, possessed the knowledge, or were within the mystery of the *ghayb*. In order to legitimize his secret, in other words the raison d'être of his reign, which he would confer fully upon his heir only at the moment of his last rites, the monarch did not make use of the privileges naturally pertaining to the relationships of servitude connecting him to those close to him and to his great servants. He was not the slave

204 The Koran, 17:24.
205 *Tâj al-'Arûss*, VII, 115.
206 *Bayân*, 597.

master arguing, on the surface, for his legitimate prerogatives as owner. A refined, superior logic led to the indispensable retention of information, to the balance of the monarchical system, to the almost physical laws of equilibrium between the inside and the outside, and to the necessary enclosure of the royal universe.

The *ʿawra* could not be laid bare: a term used by the Abbasid caliph al-Mâmûn cited above, literally meaning the genital apparatus, it must be understood here as the openings of the royal body, and by extension those of the kingdom. If the *ʿawra* were to be revealed, the king's very being would be called into question; he would lose the mystery without which he could not exist. This indeed relates to the indiscretion of Adam and Eve, which laid bare their humanity and delivered them to the harshness of life on earth. Celestial beings, they were demoted to life on earth as simple, naked humans. The king claimed for himself an elevated status; he was in a high place and could not bring himself to renounce his status. His secret absolutely had to be preserved.

Defined as a fortress with an inaccessible secret,[207] the king constituted the pole around which the government was established. "Being in the secret of the king's own" meant to form the core of the government, the most noble part. The "secret" of each thing was the best part of it, without equivalent: the secret of a valley was its most fertile and fruitful land.[208] It referred to purity and essence.[209] An enviable quality in man, it was indispensable to kings.[210]

Raised in a universe hidden from exterior view, the king was trained in the secret from birth. One monarch wrote to his heir: "Choose your *bitâna* [those closest to you], your companions for retreat and those who are in your secret, from among people of knowledge and piety of the *khâssa*, among the people of your house and among those of your generals who have the wisdom that comes with age and experience." He added, after listing a number of details relating to perspicacity in making decisions and giving advice, that these individuals must be "interiorly acquired by [literally, bent toward] obedience."[211] "They must fear you and venerate you," the monarch added, emphasizing the royal gravity that his son should assume whenever circumstances demanded it. The *hayba* was indeed the mask of the royal secret!

[207] It is called *Ḥasir* in *Jamhara*, I, 514.
[208] *Jamhara*, I, 121.
[209] Kurâ', 225.
[210] Jâhiz, *Sirâj*, I, 413.
[211] *Jamharat rasâ'il*, II, 412.

To be feared and at the same time to show proof of affection for each member of the circle of the secret was precisely the difficulty that the king encountered when choosing who would belong to his inner circle. To be so distant and at the same time so close! The management of the relationship to the inner circle was crucial. Here servitude proved once again to be the appropriate model. The king allowed those close to him to accede to the intimate space of royalty, where his grandeur was constructed and his misery and fragility were revealed. The king was well advised to select counselors with proven intelligence and know-how. They had to demonstrate an upright character and a strong, resilient personality, but their function imposed upon them an effacement that came close to elimination: in the king's proximity they became the living dead. By having access to the king's secret, from which the mass of humanity was excluded, they were enclosed, nearly entombed. The relationship between the king and his servant in the secret brings us back to the paradigm of the divine entourage: God resolved the dilemma of the secret thanks to a unique entourage cut off from the outside, whose only reason for being was to adore Him, to venerate Him, and to serve Him to the letter. The fiction of angels was not of much help to the king, who had to deal with men in flesh and blood. This was a congenital weakness of the royal body for which servitude served as a screen. Giving his son a final piece of advice about how to select his *bitâna*, the king added, "Know that even if you remain alone with your secret, with the veil lowered and your doors closed, it will no doubt be revealed to the public."[212]

Keeping the secret was a problem not only for kings; it was one of the major concerns of authority at any level. God says in the Koran: "We have decked the heavens with constellations and made them lovely to behold. We have guarded them from every cursed devil. Eavesdroppers are pursued by fiery comets."[213] The chronicle cites Ibn ʿAbbâss as a commentary on that verse. According to him, demons were not initially banned from heaven. They were allowed to enter and took advantage of the privilege to listen to the news of the *ghayb*, the invisible or the secrets of God, which they transmitted to the seers on earth. Once Jesus came along, they were excluded from three heavens, and with the arrival of Muhammad, all of the heavens were closed to them. Despite that prohibition, they sought to get close to heaven to uncover the secret. Thus flames were

[212] Ibid.
[213] The Koran, 15:17–18.

thrown at them to burn them and punish them for their indiscretion.[214] Nowhere was the secret sufficiently guarded, not even in heaven!

An essential asset in the conquest and maintenance of power, the secret was the object of envy and ferocious competition. Boasting of his difference from the caliph ʿAli, Moʿâwiyya said: "He was a man who uncovered his secret when I kept mine,"[215] castigating the man as *dhuhara*, extrovert, who did everything out in the open.[216] The literature abounds with the strategic importance of this information.[217] To protect one's secret was to keep the advantage over the enemy; the king had to maintain the upper hand by controlling the secret. His *bitâna* served as a shield that padded his interior space and kept it relatively well sealed to prevent leaks that would inform the common folk, but its protection was never a given.

The king did not reveal himself to the view of the commoners, but he had eyes everywhere, inside the palace and outside it: a true organization that kept him updated on the facts and movements of his entourage, the dealings and plans of his enemies, and the state of mind of the populace. It formed a "secretariat of the Secret, of the Treasury, and of the Royal Seal," an infallible weapon of the monarchy.[218] Just as the actions of men on earth were recorded by angels assigned to that task, like scribes placed to the right and the left of each man who were supposed to scrupulously record, respectively, the good and bad actions, the royal keepers of the secret were divided into two orders: one, called *al-namûss*, was responsible for the sector of good, and the other, *al-jâsûss*, for the sector of evil.[219]

To seek information and find it: such was the profession of the *jâsûss*, "who inquired about hidden things, most often in the realm of evil"; that is, he was responsible for digging into the intimate affairs of people; he took note of their secret actions and their difficulties,[220] what they hid from others out of fear or modesty. His name was also associated with an imminent end; it had monstrous and demoniacal connotations that reflected on the person himself.[221] In the popular imagination, the *jâsûss* was associated with death and catastrophes.

[214] Râzi, X, Part I, 134.
[215] *Bayân*, 288.
[216] *Al-Kâmil*, I, 480–481.
[217] Baladhuri, 20–24.
[218] *Aghâni*, XXIII, 85.
[219] *Nihâya*, I, 272, and Al-Haroui, *Gharîbu al-ḥadîth*, I, 315.
[220] *Tâj al-ʿArûss*, VIII, 224.
[221] Ibid.

The king's secret keepers were not a good omen. They came from a distant and obscure world; their appearance on the scene was frightening and foretold disaster that would soon claim its victims. The *namûss*, or holder of the secret, himself evoked a universe of ruse, treachery, and traps. The term, moreover, designates the lookout where the hunter hides in wait for his prey. In this hierarchical universe of agents that unfolds in obscurity, *an-Nâmuss al-akbar* was the head of the organization of the secret, a figure who remained opaque even for the king's entourage.[222]

Beyond the confines of the palace, the king had no other secret space. The secret of the royalty could not be shared. Every secret place besides his own was reviled and denounced as pure subversion. *Waswâsa*, to speak without being heard, or to whisper from mouth to ear, gives us one of Satan's names (*al-waswâss*), the one whom the Koran denounces in the verse that closes the sacred book: "from the mischief of the slinking prompter who whispers in the hearts of men...."[223] To cultivate and protect secrets other than in the service of the king was ultimately to break the bonds of servitude.

We can understand that there was a *diwân* of the Secret and of the Treasury, bringing together two domains whose communication, most of the time, took place underground: the crime that fed on secret deliberations often arose from temptation and a desire for riches. The word *waswâss* also designated the rustling of jewels, a fascination for which led to trouble and rebellion. The term expresses a hint of female indiscretion, held up as planting a seed of discord in the relationship of authority: we are not far from original sin here.

Servitude proved to be the most efficacious way to control the royal secret. A secret is that which is kept silent, what the individual hides away from others, what is kept from others' knowledge. As soon as it is told to someone, a secret, in the strictest sense, is lifted. To tell something to one person without another person knowing what is being told, that is, to whisper softly, in a tone of confidence, belongs to a category other than the secret (*an-najwâ*), as is specified in the sacred text: "Do they think We cannot hear their secret talk and private converse?"[224] It was in this way that God spoke to his prophet Moses. It was also in this way that the pilgrims implored Allah, among them the caliph Hârûn ar-Rachîd, whose slave Masrûr said: "I was so close to ar-Rachîd that our clothes

[222] *Lissân*, VI, 243–244, and *Tâj al-ʿArûss*, XI, 31. He was also found among the auxiliaries of God, notably the angel Gabriel; see as-Salihi, *Subul al-hudâ*, in Ibn Sa'd, *Kitâb at-Ṭabaqât al-kabîr*, I, 165.

[223] The Koran, 114:4.

[224] The Koran, 43:80.

touched, while he was attached to the veil of the *Ka'ba* imploring [in a tone of confidence] his God."[225] Let us note in passing the firm unity of the king-slave pair.

The word designating a secret in Arabic, *as-sir*, also means coitus and gave its name to the concubine intended for carnal relations (*as-suriya*). The carnal bond was called thus by reason of its necessarily secret nature. The language makes a distinction, however, between coitus with a free woman (*sirriya*) and with a concubine, doubly preserved: from the public on the one hand because of the nature of the act, and from the spouse on the other, for the sake of domestic harmony. (This secret is in fact shared between two people but occurs within the framework of an intimate and secret relationship due to the constraints imposed by its very nature.[226])

The secret and its management could only be the product of a solidly established relationship between its guardians and the person of the king, who formed a single entity, the royal entity. His servants existed only as an extension of the king's own being, as his ears and his acting hands. The perfect hierarchical relationship spoke with one voice, that of the master. The revelation founded upon absolute confidence in the person of the messenger assumed the existence of a master on one side and his slave on the other.

The action of "sending a messenger in confidence to one of his trusted slaves"[227] was called *waḥy*, which means "revelation" in Arabic and refers to words passed secretly. In the chain of fidelity, servitude was incontrovertible.

On the subject of confidence, God says in the Koran: "Long before them, the people of Noah disbelieved. They disbelieved Our servant [*'abd*], and called him a madman."[228] The perfect mastery of fidelity and the complete assurance that one could place in it were seen only in servitude; God therefore called his messenger, in this case the prophet Noah, a slave. Râzi stresses that this comes from the fact that "a slave reports the words of the master more faithfully than a messenger does."[229]

The king of imperative speech watched over his words, which had the force of law, and conferred them only to those creatures who belonged to his closest entourage.

[225] Jâhiz, *Sirâj*, I, 223.
[226] *Siḥaḥ*, II, 356–359.
[227] *Tâj al-'Arûss*, XX, 280.
[228] The Koran, 54:9.
[229] Râzi, XV, Part I, 32.

6

The King and His Entourage

THE *MAJLISS*, OR THE KING IN AUDIENCE

A group of poets were getting ready to be received by the caliph Hârûn ar-Rachîd in one of his palaces in ar-Raqqa.[1] They came to praise the prince and sing of his wondrous deeds; they were many in number and waited patiently at the door. They anticipated a recompense that would be well worth their trouble; along the way they had heard tales of the prince's generosity.

The moment they had been waiting for finally came, and they were called to enter. But their first steps were unpleasant indeed. One of them later reported: "The caliph had just finished slitting some throats. We had to sidestep puddles of blood as we walked up to him!"[2]

Nevertheless, they immediately began to sing his praises. Such an entrance, in which the visitors had to step over the flowing blood, added to the king's *hayba* and to the legend of his all-powerfulness. Already, without anything else having occurred, the newly arrived guest entered the room intoxicated by the tales he had heard of the court's magnificence, its protocol, and the royal majesty, and his heart was filled with anxiety and fear. Tales of the grandeur and might of kings were abundant, spread by rumor and recounted by poets and chroniclers. Back from a long journey after having been received at the court of the legendary king Dhi Yazan, some Arab notables, including, according to the chronicle, the paternal grandfather of the prophet Muhammad, reported that they saw

[1] Yâqût, *Mu'jam*, III, 67.
[2] *Aghâni*, XVIII, 220–221.

the king "rubbed with amber to the point that he shone, his scalp brilliant with musk applied to the part of his hair, wearing two green cloaks, one of which covered his shoulders, and holding his sword in his hands, with kings as well as viceroys and the sons of kings seated to the left and to the right."[3]

The king thus was, and always had been, above everything and everyone. Those present were not in front of him, but "in his hands," that is, in his power, like Lilliputians delivered to the all-powerfulness of a giant. His serious and haughty gaze effortlessly took in everyone and examined the look on their faces with the haughty and unforgiving air of the master who seemed to know or guess everything. This earthly god automatically took inventory of who was present or absent and counted the faithful and the infidels.[4] Such was the king in audience.

Nothing was left to chance in the organization of the *majliss*. The place occupied by each individual indicated one's status and rank alongside the sultan. To the king's right was considered to be the best place.[5] That highly coveted spot was reserved for the powerful of the kingdom and to those of the king's creatures who were in his favor at the moment. The caliph ʿOmar allowed only the principals of the tribe of Quraysh to be near him. A poet praised a tribe whose noble principals held places in "the *majliss al-ayman*," which, translated literally, means "the right-hand council."[6] Moʿâwiyya had his son Yazîd on his right, his Omayyad clan surrounding him, and the noble families farther away in the *majliss*.[7] In other words, with so many groups together in one place considering themselves to be just as many councils, it became necessary to distinguish among this horde of personalities of various standings and diverse interests, and the competition was fierce. Priorities were signaled even within a single category. Each person sought to enter according to his rank and the prescribed order by emphasizing his distance from the others. Reinforced by the monarchical spirit, differences were evident even in the way people dressed.[8]

The king classified people according to his will. Upon the arrival of noteworthy figures, the master of the place himself took care to direct his obliging attention toward them. It was a great honor to be thus surrounded

[3] *ʿIqd*, II, 21.
[4] *Jamharat rasâʾil*, II, 420.
[5] *Jamharat rasâʾil*, III, 89.
[6] *Naqâʾid*, I, 217.
[7] *Aghâni*, XX, 227.
[8] *Aghâni*, V, 392–393 and 402.

by the king's consideration and to be summoned by him, directly, to take one's place. Certain newly arrived notables who approached the imam ʿAli were distinguished by the caliph as he tossed two cushions to them as a sign of distinction and consideration, insisting that they take their places in spite of the hesitation they showed.[9] As much as the distance to the king, the distinction conveyed by a cushion or a chair played a part in indicating one's degree of elevation and rank. It was a recognition of the individual's preeminence over the others who were present. Thus the king an-Nu'mânn gestured to one of his guests who already had a cushion, "had him approach, and gave him another one." Everything that came from the king was a pretext for classification; thus the aforementioned king ordered his slaves to "give ten mouthfuls on his plate [to one of his guests] before the others present had even begun to eat."[10]

The regulation of relationships with those in attendance was strictly governed by the mastery of the social rules and by the statuses and functions of the people present. But that regulation, even once the royalty was firmly established, in a certain way still recalled the successive stages of development of the monarchy. The same process was continually retraced with people of considerable social capital whom the powerful royalty sought to subjugate and gradually to enslave. ʿOmar Ibn ʿAbdel'aziz, receiving a descendant of the imam ʿAli, "welcomed him, bid him approach, greeted him, seated him beside him, and smiled at him,"[11] the prestige of the Hashemite clan being so great that the prince came down from his pedestal to pay homage to one of its members. Thus the example shows a prince who wanted to win over one of his former friends, a companion of the Prophet, who showed signs of reticence to authority: "I am still the brother I used to be. If you come to me when I am in an audience, sit down with me on my throne. If you come when I am not in an audience, sit down and wait for me to come to you."[12]

The beginnings of a dynasty or a reign were very enlightening in terms of the king's management of the *majliss*. The sound of the weapons still echoed; the competitors' claims were not yet silenced. The king therefore took care to appease them. He courted them, buying the support of his adversaries and those close to them. He cultivated the illusion of the king's benevolent friendship. Up until then, the royal throne had put up

[9] *Majma ʿal-amthâl*, II, 265.
[10] *Labîd*, 108.
[11] *Aghâni*, XXI, 130.
[12] *Aghâni*, XVII, 139.

with others mixing with the prince, who invited them in friendship to take their place beside him.[13] By contrast, with the reinforcement of the monarchy, the differences became greater, and the king adopted a nobility that he no longer deigned to share, even symbolically. He henceforth kept his distance from those in attendance.

To be near the king was to gain in nobility. The king's proximity elevated the chiefs and the great, consecrating them. Mo'âwiyya asked a certain notable: "'Who is the lord of your people?' The notable replied: 'The one you designate as sovereign, O commander of believers!' Mo'âwiyya then said: 'Then you are their lord.' And the notable replied: 'Let me sit beside you; rule my affairs and welcome me agreeably.'"[14] We can understand that the king was the center on which every gaze converged and toward which all requests were directed. He was the master who was the object of all attention and thoughts. The great jurisconsult and cousin of the Prophet, Abdallâh Ibn 'Abbâss, in the presence of the caliph greeted one of the great Omayyad governors of Kufa and Basra, without being greeted in return. He later heard the reply: "There is no ill will between us, by God's grace, but we are in a council where we answer to the commander of believers and to him alone!"[15] The presence of others served only to establish the one true presence, that of the king, whose presence confirmed their absence.

The regulation of the king's relationship with his servants appeared to work like the swinging of a pendulum. The repulsive attraction it created aimed to keep the servant in a constant state of fear and uncertainty. The *majliss* was a space where that regulation could be seen with the naked eye. Thus 'Obayd Allâh Ibn Ziyâd, one of the strong men of the caliph 'Abdelmalek Ibn Marwân, to whom he was close, was a living example of this. "It was he who cut off the head of Mos'ab Ibn Zoubayr, entered 'Abdelmalek's palace, and threw the head at his feet. Then 'Abdelmalek prostrated himself.... 'Obayd had a place next to the caliph on the couch that served as his throne. But after the murder of Mos'ab he turned away from him and pointed to a chair where he should sit."[16] Such a rearrangement occurred abruptly, without the one it concerned having time to prepare for it. When he entered for an audience as usual, 'Obayd was surprised to see someone else seated in his usual place. His place had

[13] Tabari, *Târîkh*, VI, 161; *as-Sîra*, I, 49.
[14] Baladhuri, 16.
[15] Baladhuri, 202.
[16] *Majma 'al-amthâl*, I, 485.

been taken from him intentionally to indicate his loss of influence and to reduce him to the status of a humble and common servant. Sometimes it happened that when a person was admitted to the council, he found no place for himself and remained at a loss. He very quickly became aware of the seriousness of the message and of its significance; it was a bad omen and possibly announced his political and perhaps even physical end.[17]

The *majliss* was a structure of order and disorder. It was an excellent vantage point for observing the regulation of control of the state's most powerful figures, circumstantial rapprochements, more lasting alliances, expressions of the relationships of power, and ongoing social transformations. The *majliss* accounted perfectly for the characteristic precariousness experienced by the multitude surrounding the king. An irrepressible, almost geological shifting was constantly at work in this enclosure, where it consciously and methodically pulled from the center to the periphery. The center was royal and allowed no permanence, only satellites. Behind the serene brilliance of the royal figure, behind the king's fits of anger that would suddenly flare up and then subside, a subterranean erosion worked to remove yesterday's favorites from the king's proximity.[18] The mechanism of the council conveyed the nature of the bonds that the king maintained with his environment. Like the turning of a wheel, it first welcomed, then elevated, and finally – irrevocably – lowered. And the process was continuously at work: the king smiling with a pleasant greeting, the king distant, the king haughty and inaccessible before the final downfall, when the veil forever removed the individual in question from the king's sight.[19]

Protocol varied during royal audiences, however, depending on whether they were open to the general public (*majliss al-ʿâmma*) or reserved for dignitaries (*majliss al-khâssa*). A prince said to his chief of police, who failed to comply with the order to appear in front of him: "Yes, indeed, that's how it is in the *majliss al-ʿâmma*, but there is no problem with that in the *majliss al-khâssa*,"[20] in which those of superior status gathered.

Such a privilege belonged to the great and to those close to the king. The king's attention was an obvious sign of his satisfaction with the chosen one. This vaunted attention was not awarded to just anyone; in fact, the comings and goings of most people generally met with indifference. And so one attempted to determine the king's state of mind before each

[17] *ʿIqd*, IV, 34–35.
[18] *Nihâya*, II, 519.
[19] Baladhuri, 242.
[20] Tabari, *Târîkh*, XI, 5.

audience in order to take note of his disposition toward those present. Slaves responsible for the ceremonies of the council knew all about the pardons and the disgraces that occurred in that space and thus were precious sources to whom one appealed to avoid missteps. The king's slightest actions and gestures thus formed the subject of a minute and very elaborate accounting. Those who were caught up in his anger did not lose hope as long as they retained the right to enter. The king, however, spoke not a word to them and did not even glance their way, thus publicly indicating the possible rejection in store for them.[21] The image was that of divinities who threatened their ill-advised adorers with punishment. In avoiding them, the king was simply following the example of God, who "on the Day of Resurrection ... will [not] speak to them"[22] and will not even "look at them."[23]

The king's good and bad moods set the tone for the entire council. If he showed the slightest sign of fatigue or annoyance, those present knew they should leave the premises right away.[24] If he became angry, stood up, and left the council room, those present had to stand up and wait for the specific order they would be given. If the order was late in coming, one still had to stand patiently. The women's chamber was nearby. The king might go there to calm his temper and return in a better mood. Sometimes he would go there while he was in the middle of holding his council.[25]

It was advised to advance with precaution and vigilance in the moving space of the *majliss*. Without going so far as to intentionally commit a reprehensible act, one had to demonstrate self-control even in situations that seemed to call for joking and relaxing. Thus a courtier, erroneously led on by the semblance of relaxation during an animated evening, naturally burst out laughing. Indignant, the king exploded: "He bursts out laughing in my council! Burn his neck!"[26] Such errors of judgment or uncontrolled zeal could be extremely costly. The king's jester himself could face the worst if he chose the wrong moment to tease his master.[27] As for the novice visitor, he was often the victim of his own inexperience and naiveté. One such visitor confessed that he was slapped numerous times,

[21] Râzi, III, Part I, 24.
[22] The Koran, 2:174.
[23] The Koran, 3:77.
[24] *Aghâni*, XXI, 132.
[25] *Aghâni*, XV, 225.
[26] *Jamharat ach'âr al-'Arab*, 75.
[27] *Aghâni*, XVII, 46.

struck in the face, dragged out in public, and humiliated in front of those in attendance to the point "that darkness reigned between the *majliss* and me."[28] Another was beaten with an iron bar right in the midst of an audience, and further examples abound.[29] In fact, angry kings did not hesitate to strike their victims themselves. The practice was established to the point that a certain type of whip was called *al-asbaḥiyya*, from the name of a king who no doubt used it excessively, Asbah al-Ḥimyâri.[30]

People familiar with the minefield of the *majliss* approached it prudently. A notable whom a caliph invited to sit on a cushion sat instead on the ground and explained: "A man recommended to his son: Do not overstay your visit with a sultan. Do not remain so distant that he forgets you. Do not sit on a rug or a cushion in his presence. Leave enough space between you and him for a person or two, as it is possible someone better suited for that place might arrive and you would be asked to get up for him, which would elevate him and diminish you."[31] A sort of natural selection seemed to operate in those places. To enter meant bending to the demands of court protocol, or in other words, submitting to the demands of servitude. The nobles had to give up their arrogance if they wanted to be there. Moʿâwiyya, seating a newcomer near him and pushing someone else away, admitted that he felt the debasement of the latter, noting on the same occasion that this method was well suited for training servants, that is, making them slaves.[32]

Ḥassâne Ibn Thâbite, the designated poet of the Prophet, was an expert on this subject. En route to a royal court, he encountered a man who attracted attention for his knowledge of the proper conduct in the king's presence:

I am going to show you how you must act with this man. When you encounter his keeper of the veil, announce yourself. Once you have informed him of your arrival, you will have to wait a month before receiving his reply; then he will ask for permission for you to enter. Upon your entrance before the king, you will find people who will ask you to recite verses, but do not do it until the king orders you to. When he does, then recite, and when you have finished, they will tell you to recite more, but do not do anything more until the king has ordered you to, and then wait for your reward.[33]

[28] *Aghâni*, XVIII, 209.
[29] *Al-Kâmil*, II, 574.
[30] *Al-Kâmil*, I, 589.
[31] Al-Jâhiz, *Al-Bayâne wa tabyînn*, 43.
[32] Al-Jâhiz, *Al-Bayâne wa tabyînn*, 307.
[33] *Jamharat ach'âr al-ʿArab*, 74.

As soon as one crossed the threshold into the king's audience, only the king could speak. One entered the audience anonymously. No one was introduced because the only name that was spoken was that of the master. He was the one who was listened to, admired, and praised.[34] The reception was ruled according to a ritual that made servitude official and public. In spite of the prerogatives and the consideration due to him by reason of his status, the notable, however great he may have been, bowed down before the king, in sight of all those who mattered in the kingdom. From the start, his progression was a semblance of an ascent planted with a thousand pitfalls:

> If the king gestures to approach, he takes three steps forward, and then stops; then three steps if he gestures again.... He must advance with his head lowered and then stop and raise it to wait for the signal.... If the signal does not come, that means he is at the end of his journey and in a place far from his Majesty. In the opposite case, he advances, arrives before the king, kneels down, and kisses his hands and feet. He rises again and goes to stand with the people of his rank. If the king gestures to sit, he sits. If the king speaks to him, he must respond softly with great economy of movement; if he is silent, he must immediately get up without greeting again or waiting for orders.[35]

It was public knowledge that "the one who goes to the doors of sultans gets up and sits down constantly."[36] The king's *majliss* was also called *qul'a*, or in other words, the place where no status was guaranteed. The demoted prince was called by this name; the king's council was thus the place where mastery eluded one. On the contrary, it was the space of instability, where the one who entered lost all initiative, was stripped of any possibility of expression, and for that reason was immediately demoted. "A council is *qul'a* when a member is obliged to give up his place to someone more noble than he, and this occurs over and over again."[37] In other words, to be there meant drifting gradually toward the periphery while becoming aware of one's distance from the master of the premises. In such a space, the king alone controlled the degrees of nobility and the criteria for classification. *Al-qallâ'*, literally meaning the one who uproots, was the informer who took pleasure in unseating the king's favorites of the day.

A space of intrigue, the *majliss* was also called *qun'a*, or council of servile begging. The first councils around the Prophet, at the very birth of

[34] *Bahjat al-majâliss*, I, 343.
[35] Jâhiz, *Tâj*, 6–7.
[36] *Bahjat al-majâliss*, I, 345.
[37] Tâj al-'Arûss, XI, 398.

Islam, basked in the ambiance of fraternity that prevailed among companions in misfortune, whose difficulties cemented their union. But this militant egalitarianism, common to the beginnings of all great and noble causes, very quickly gave way to the priorities imposed by the social game.[38] Even before the death of the Prophet, the social reality and the necessary alliances left their mark. His council showed no disorder of any kind. It was a high place of modesty where voices were not raised.[39] The verse on chambers clearly illustrates the preoccupation with establishing order around the Prophet, and the basic structures of the authority to come are very evident.

The courts of the kings would subsequently resume their earlier habits, reinforced by the influences of the great courts of the time. The power of the Muslim empire and the profits earned through wars and commerce filled the state coffers. The royal entourages thus became richer and the kings' authority stronger. It is precisely the entourage that is of interest here. What did proximity to kings really mean? What place did servitude hold there? In other words, what bonds structured the court?

THE COURT, OR *ḤÂCHIYA*

The term *ḥâchiya* is still used today to designate the court and the king's entourage. It deserves to be looked at closely, particularly in its origins, which will help us better understand its content. *Ḥâchiya* means the margin. Applied to fabric, it means the edges, whether fringed or not. Ironically, the word used for margins serves to delimit the royal court, or in other words, a center.

But the marginality of *ḥâchiya* is not limited to the realm of space; it also relates to the contents. Thus for the human body the word designated the least noble organs, those connected to digestion and defecation.[40] It meant everything the torso contains, except for the heart and the lungs. In the social hierarchy, it was applied to individuals without value or ambition; it still today carries this meaning in popular language.[41] In any case it always referred to a border; like the walls of a city or a palace, it existed by virtue of its interior. In terms of kinship, it encompassed the members of a family. Within the framework of royalty, the word referred to a much larger group.

[38] *Bahjat al-majâliss*, I, 40–41.
[39] *Fâ'iq*, III, 13.
[40] *Tâj al-ʿArûss*, XIX, 322–323.
[41] *Jamhara*, I, 539.

The word can thus only lead to confusion. *Ḥâchiya* also designated young camels moving around a group of adult camels and working their way into its midst.[42] Referring to little ones around adults, it did not mean young descendants naturally connected to the group, but a race of small stature.[43] Thus it was a question of inequality of status and more precisely of a base status, slaves being listed as minors regardless of their age and considered in that respect to be children, or *fityân*. The perfect servant circled around the king, ready to serve him; thus the entourage acquired a functional meaning that could be added to the toponymy: "[Y]ou shall see the angels circling about the Throne, giving glory to their Lord," says the sacred text.[44]

Indeed, both the court and the king's entourage were characterized by servitude, which is the key to understanding the bonds prevailing in that environment. Thus the history of the word *ḥâchiya* may help to better account for the apparent contradiction between its dual nature, simultaneously central and marginal. It is possible that in the beginning it encompassed followers who joined the processions of the powerful as they passed by. In fact, a great mass of common folk, motivated by their need, thus walked the great roads in search of sustenance. Some followed armies on campaign or hung around the encampments of kings, living off their leftovers and their alms. The term *ḥâchiya* clearly described these groups, as much for their placement vis-à-vis the processions as for their poverty and social marginality. But the term assumed a belonging; that is, it meant to be on the margins of something of which one was a part. And in fact the group's continual presence and its dependence on the procession for subsistence were its essential characteristics.

Subsequently, and given the very logic of the evolution of the monarchy, the meaning of the term evolved and changed in a way that left behind the marginality of its origins. As large kingdoms came into being, the kings' retinues swelled, going well beyond the few slaves and close relatives of the beginning. A number of *ḥâchiya* followers must have joined the entourage as servants of the king. At the same time, the royal institution's means of functioning, with the intent of establishing a perfect authority, imposed the *ḥijâb*, or the veil removing the king from the view of the population. The entourage, which had increased in size and importance by establishing its distance from the masses, thus became separated

42 *Majma ʿal-amthâl*, II, 67.
43 *Lissân*, XIV, 180.
44 The Koran, 39:75.

from its original meaning. Far from designating a margin or referring to a subaltern group, the *ḥâchiya* became integrated into the heart of the political system. It was marginal only in relation to the king.

Supporting such an evolution, another word designating the court seems to have followed a similar path. *Al-janâb a-charîf* is one of the adjectives used most often today to designate the palace in the sense of royal majesty. Like *ḥâchiya*, *janâb* or *jânib* was applied to the surroundings of the king, to his armed retinue, and to his followers in general, thus referring to his procession before coming to designate the king himself.[45] The margin served to emphasize the royal centrality but also revealed the spaces that royalty drew from to establish servitude. *Jânib* indisputably referred to the two poles of this bond, foreignness on one hand and proximity on the other. In its derivatives the word in fact encompassed the two meanings, designating at the same time the stranger to the group in terms of kinship and also his proximity, at first spatial and then relational.

An examination of the group known as *khâssa* seems to further support such a hypothesis. In addition to those who were close through kinship or through social status, here one finds others whom the language designates as rejects and intruders, *al-ḥachwa* and *ad-dukhlul*, literally the stranger to the group who has no connection to it other than servitude and worms his way into it without familial or noble legitimacy.[46] In general these were intimates of the king who had earned his complete confidence and belonged to the category of close ones considered to be his creatures. *Ḥâchiya* was thus a composite group that was not exempt from contradictions due to the very origins of its members. It was also stratified and composed of several circles.

The *ḥâchiya* of the king had nothing marginal about it except the term itself if it was applied to the entourage in the topographical sense, or to the statuses of its members as seen from the angle of servitude, that is, from the inside.[47] The margin had other adjectives and gathered true marginal workers. The royal court was henceforth locked up; access to it became more complex and costly. At that stage, the followers of the processions were nothing more than marginals living off of salaried work or begging.[48] As for the *ḥâchiya*, it consisted of subgroups that were not always connected. Some of its members were closer to the king than others, as in the case of those who made up the *bitâna*.

[45] *Tâj al-ʿArûss*, I, 381.
[46] *Tâj al-ʿArûss*, XIV, 322–325.
[47] *Fâʾiq*, II, 428.
[48] *Az-zaʾâniq*, see *Naqâʾid*, I, 29 and 212.

THE *BITÂNA*, OR FIRST CIRCLE

The close entourage of the king was the impassable border that protected him from the outside. This group was called the *bitâna*. In the common language it designates a lining, the material put inside a garment to make it warmer. Socially, *bitâna* belongs to the upper classes of society, those that were sufficiently endowed and had resources. The expression "thick lining" means a large fortune.

Bitâna here is the circle that enclosed the king, insulated him, and ensured the isolation essential to his personality. This group of confidants accompanied the king in defeat and protected him in failure and retreat. Without it the body of the king would be subject to the vicissitudes of fate.[49]

Such a grouping was the space in which the nascent monarchy came together within the tribal structure. Monarchical power in fact drew from that very structure and was supported by its foundations while rearranging them and using them to its benefit, following its own logic. Starting with the *fakhd*, the smallest division of a tribe, it enlarged its clan to the *batn*, which was a larger division. Already within this basic circle, familial relationships were no longer the only supports. The *batn* borrowed from the tribe and, calling upon blood ties, was henceforth transposed into the substance of the king. It included his *khâssa*, that is, his own men.[50] It consisted of those who knew his secrets and whose advice he sought in difficult moments. One of the expressions most commonly used to express confidence makes use of arteries and veins, including those that supply blood to the stomach.[51]

As one of the components of the *ḥâchiya*, the *bitâna* included members who had "infiltrated" it from the exterior and who were considered intruders by the king's relations. The group was heterogeneous and composed of security guards, confidants, advisers, courtiers, close servants, and close relatives who all shared, to various degrees, the confidence of the king. The inclusion of nonrelatives within a group initially constructed around kinship was based on that bond. *Ibtitân,* a synonym for adoption, conveyed the insertion of a newcomer within the framework of a family.[52] In pre-Islamic society, adoption could create a legitimate filiation.

[49] *A-Chi'ru wa chu'arâ'*, I, 67.
[50] *Tâj al-'Arûss*, XVIII, 61.
[51] *Aghâni*, VII, 191.
[52] *Aghâni*, II, 260.

If within the tribal framework the extension of such a bond could only strengthen the clan, in royalty *ibtitân* henceforth occurred on the basis of servitude. In any event, Islam limited the legal weight of adoption. Kinship continued to play an essential role, notably in the granting of positions and privileges, and the caliph ʿOthmân was greatly criticized for naming relatives to strategic positions. But the tribal logic was eventually demolished, even if the transition occurred slowly.[53] Furthermore, even in the tribal milieu, a chief's entourage included, in addition to relatives, followers such as servants and close guards. The expression *âl*, which usually referred to lineage and designated those who were close, encompassed, in addition to relatives, the *mawâlis*, that is, allies and dependents of all sorts.[54]

Close allies and servants were very soon found even at the heart of the entourage and on its front lines. Around Muhammad, the foundations of the authority of the Muslim state were placed outside of the familial circle and even beyond its territory. The *ʿitra*, or the family and the house, formed the heart of the close entourage, *al-jawf*, its center and its bowels. This is what the inhabitants of Yemen called the pavilions of their leaders, the large tents where negotiations occurred and decisions were made, and to which only intimates had access, or in other words, the interior of kings.[55] Granted, the content attributed to the term *ʿitra* is somewhat fluid.[56] In common usage, it referred primarily to a man's descendants, in the strict sense of the word. Later it included family members who were not subject to the canonical taxes. Other definitions attribute to it a broader content that, in any case, included those who were close but not related. Thus the caliph Abû Bakr, speaking in the name of the Quraysh, took this perspective by claiming to be part of the *ʿitra* of the Prophet, precisely the one that was simultaneously the fruit of his success and the product of his work.[57] The *ʿitra* was the basic unit of the conquest of power, and for this reason its composition is problematic.[58] The *Ansâr*, or inhabitants of Medina, were, Muhammad said, "my belly and my sack," that is, the holders of my secret and my confidence, according to the commentary of Zamakhchari, who equated it with the *bitâna*. The term rendered as "belly" (*karich*) is in fact literally the stomach, an interpretation

[53] Baladhuri, 537.
[54] *Tâj al-ʿArûss*, XIV, 33–34.
[55] *Tâj al-ʿArûss*, XII, 124.
[56] *Islâḥ al-Mantiq*, 28.
[57] *Nihâya*, III, 177.
[58] Adab al-kâtib, 32.

that limits its reach to descendants, whereas in the present case another logic clearly prevails, that of companionship.[59] The belly and the sack take this bond into account more fully. The belly refers to that of ruminants, who store their food in it, and the sack contains the clothing that covers the nakedness of the individual.[60]

The tribal *batn* gives us the *bitâna* of the king. It was no longer a central element regulated by kinship, but a satellite component of royal authority; it was nothing other than the entourage itself while also constituting its core. With the foundation of the new State and the enlargement of the empire, the tribal bases proved largely insufficient and inadequate to establish the new structure. The social base was growing, and concepts began to take on new meaning; thus Moʿâwiyya advised his son: "Consider the people of Syria; let them be your *bitâna*, your *ʿayba*, and your fortress."[61] *ʿAyba* refers to confidence. It was the sack in which the individual put his most cherished and precious possessions, and here it is the equivalent of the heart where one hides one's secrets.[62]

An entire vocabulary revolved around the body of the king, who thus became the center of authority. The king's entourage was listed and ranked according to proximity to him. In Mecca, the inhabitants who occupied the center, such as the great Hashemite, Omayyad, and other families, were considered the *batn* of the city, whereas those who lived on the heights occupied the *zahr*, that is, the back. Thus there were people on the inside and people on the outside; there were nobles and families of low status who were regarded with scorn.[63] Thus the *batn* and the *zahr*, the center and the periphery, the interior and the exterior, the visible and the invisible, formed the inside and the outside of a single thing. The *zihara* was the visible side of a fabric, and the *bitâna* was the hidden side.

The inner side was next to the body of the king, whose contours it took on; it was the group who had a view of the king, of his inside, who had access to his secrets, and who maintained continuous contact with him. Its members made up his *ʿayba*. By contrast, the *zihara* was made up of his allies of the same confederation as his tribe. It encompassed the distant allies whom he could call upon in the event of war or conflict.

The expression of proximity in corporeal terms is striking. Members of the royal entourage were called *as-sâmma*, from *as-sammu*, that is,

[59] *Fâ'iq*, III, 253.
[60] Al-Haroui, *Gharîbu al-ḥadith*, I, 88.
[61] Baladhuri, 145.
[62] *Lissân*, I, 634.
[63] *Tâj al-ʿArûss*, VII, 170.

the pores of the skin. Thus they were the king's windows to the outside, the filter that watched over his peace and shielded him from attacks and unpleasantness.[64] An author, comparing the king and his entourage to the body of a man, said: "You are his head, the vizier is his heart, your auxiliaries are his hands, your subjects are his feet, your justice is his soul, and without a soul there is no need for a body."[65] In the tribal milieu, the title of chief was derived from the word for head, but the chief was also called the neck, the hair, and the chest, and in relation to nobility, freedom, and rank, the members of the group were the hands.[66] The other subdivisions of the tribe were also inscribed within this corporeal structure.[67] The royal body indeed took the place of the tribal body.[68]

References to clothing were noteworthy. Expressing the intensity of the bond that existed between a caliph and one who was close to him, the chronicle reports "that he put him between his skin and his clothing."[69] Muhammad's supporters were called *al-chi'âr*, or undergarment. The term alludes to a great number and was thus applied to the royal entourage. It formed a protection reinforced by its numbers and density. The *chi'âr* was a synonym for dense vegetation or thick trees. This density was of course created here, in the case of the entourage, through confidence and loyalty to the king thanks to the extremely powerful bonds of blood or servitude. In one of its derivatives, the term also refers to the status of the slave.[70] The intensity of the bond and intimacy with the king also appeared in one of the meanings of the term, evoking sexual relationships between men and women. The husband and the wife were in fact called clothing for each other. The wife in particular was described as an article of clothing, *ḥaïk*, meaning mattress and blanket. She was thus the clothing that covered her husband and protected him during the night and in his solitude.[71] Here we find a contractual relationship freeing those involved from the veil, dedicating them to each other in their respective nakedness. Clothing expressed a very solid alliance; "to take people as clothing" was to be greatly and intimately attached to them. The alliance in question took place with the authority of which clothing

[64] *Tâj al-'Arûss*, XVI, 364.
[65] Jâhiz, *Sirâj*, I, 214.
[66] *Kachâf*, III, 560.
[67] *Nihâya*, III, 451, and *Tâj al-'Arûss*, II, 114.
[68] *Tâj al-'Arûss*, II, 114.
[69] Jâhiz, *Tâj*, 55.
[70] *Tâj al-'Arûss*, VII, 30–33.
[71] *Tâj al-'Arûss*, VIII, 457, and IX, 160.

was one of the symbols, and the allies were its pillars. Addressing the Prophet on the subject of his vocation and the gift of authority that God had granted him, his wife ʿAisha speaks of the "chemise with which God has clothed you."[72] The *qamis* in question was a body-hugging undergarment without an opening, and also referred to the membrane that surrounds the heart.[73] Clothing expressed investiture as well as demotion; the expression "to pull back one's hand from obedience" came from the act of taking off a piece of clothing, *al-khal'*. In pre-Islamic society, the father denied responsibility for the misdeeds of his children by using this terminology and having it announced by the town crier. The only possibility a wife had to free herself from the marriage contract was by buying her freedom within the framework of the *khul'*. This shows the place of the metaphor of clothing in the expression of relationships of authority.

Reference to clothing is found in other expressions. Thus the *bitâna* also was called *khimla*, which refers both to fabric with fringes like a dense forest and to a secret, but also to the absolute submission evoked by the fringes dangling from the fabric when a man covers his body with it. Submission in this context was so perfect that such an attitude of submissiveness was given as an example in prayer.

The language referring to the king's close entourage accounts sufficiently for the turbulent coexistence of its members. Conflicts raged, and low blows were common occurrences. In this world of crime and hatred, like the woods whose name it carried and that it resembled, the law of the jungle held sway. It was a place of fear, obscurity, intrigues, and assassinations in spite of the smiling expression that decorum imposed.

Also found in this place were those whom the king's family and the great noble families called parasites. *Al-mubâtin* was one of those dubious figures who infiltrated the *bitâna* and was structurally a part of it, as the name indicated. He was a *dakhîl*, from the verb "to enter," understood here as someone of unknown and thus servile origin who claimed a kinship that was not his own. The term was derived from *dakhl*, meaning defect or vice. And it was in fact (originally) that vice, that impurity, on which the king's interest in him was based, as his nobility would only be greater because of it!

Set into base matter, gold only shines more brightly. But it also purifies, and the king thus nurtured those intruders with his protection. Like God he pardoned the fallen man, the repentant servant granting his servitude

[72] Ibn Mâja, *Saḥîḥ*, I, 55.
[73] *Tâj al-ʿArûss*, IX, 348.

and proving it in his absolute submission. The relationship was a symbiotic exchange of services that was largely beneficial to the two parties, even if the well-established lineages saw this only as parasitism. For them, the *dakhîl* in question was nothing but an intruder insinuating himself into a universe where he was a stranger and benefiting from the dense, interlacing legitimate familial bonds to unduly penetrate it and thereby demonstrate that those bonds were not as tight as they should be. A being from the darkness, he was compared to feathers embedded under the skin, never seeing the light of day. The image sums up the obscure and unknown origin, the dubious color, and the lack of virtue that people attributed to those close to the king![74] They circulated in the darkness of night like the vectors of death that they were.

Al-du'mûss was the black worm found in ponds. The word was also used for foreigners without noble ancestry who meddled in public affairs and approached the kings.[75] Such vocabulary illustrates the struggle of the clans and the terrible competition, often ending in bloodshed, that took place in that universe. Nevertheless it is equally informative regarding the functioning of the *bitâna* and the central role that servitude played there. In choosing these intruders, the monarchy crossed a threshold, violating the role of kinship and *'asabiya*, or tribal solidarity, as the bonds that were privileged with proximity to the king.

The question bearing on the dominance of servitude in the king's relationships with his family is an important one. The violent criticism of foreigners who enjoyed de facto primacy stressed the possible disadvantages that could result from it for the king's close relatives despite the established etiquette giving them priority and the false sense of order that this could sometimes suggest. A number of elements indeed suggest that the familial circle in fact bore the brunt of the situation. The efficacy of servitude must have convinced many of its members to adopt that course of action in their approach to the king to insure that they would receive his blessing.

Strong evidence supports this alternative. Thus the group of *ḥafada*, which today designates exclusively grandchildren, seemed to have previously been much more open, with less clearly defined boundaries. The term originally designated primarily the one who diligently carried out orders, thus the faithful servant. Yet some variation remained in the

[74] *Tâj al-'Arûss*, XIV, 232. The word *ḥachwa*, which is discussed in the section on *hâchiya*, was also used.

[75] *Tâj al-'Arûss*, IX, 282.

definition of the group in question. It consisted of the grandsons or the children of a wife from an earlier marriage,[76] to which Ibn Kathîr added the daughters' husbands.[77] According to some authors, this group contained servants but also the wife's male relatives, notably her father and brothers.[78] It therefore appears that the members of the household were all, on different levels, encompassed by servitude. The notion of *ḥafada* was applied to that population under the patriarch's command and in his service. Diligence in service was common to this close entourage made up of descendants, relatives, allies, and slaves,[79] especially at the beginning of the formation of the royal court, which needed to mobilize all its members. There was thus some confusion between the foreign servants and those belonging to the royal family. The good slave, a commentator stressed, was on the order of a son,[80] and "the male and female slave were also called *walîd* and *walîda*,"[81] which were very close to *walad*, or son.

Servitude and a lowly status seemed particularly to involve the wife's relatives. *Al-khawal* designated servants who were acquired by unknown means, perhaps purchased or acquired as the spoils of war; the word's similarity to the term designating the husband's brother-in-law is striking.[82] For many authors, furthermore, *al-khawal* were different from classic slaves because the term did not necessarily imply ownership.[83] The close relatives of the wife did not belong to the *dhawi al-qorbâ*, or the close relatives of the husband, which made their status all the more fragile.[84]

But beyond the particular status relating to the wife, the enlargement of the base of the royalty and the fear of potential competitors worked in favor of the composite nature of the groups surrounding the king and the insertion of family into the mechanism of servitude. *Al-facîla*, which included those who were close by blood, could be less useful than *nâhida*, which was the supporting family who aided the king in trials and included the most faithful of his servants.[85] Thus the *ḥacham*, which for the common man could also include relatives of neighbors, was limited for the

[76] The Koran, 16:72.
[77] Ibn Kathîr, *Tafsîr*, II, 753.
[78] *Kachâf*, II, 596, note 4.
[79] Tabari, *Târîkh*, VII, 616–620.
[80] Râzi, XII, Part I, 186.
[81] *Kachâf*, I, 423.
[82] *Jamhara*, I, 621.
[83] *Nihâya*, II, 88, and Ibn Hilâl, 244.
[84] Râzi, II, Part I, 152.
[85] *Tâj al-ʿArûss*, X, 174.

king to his wives, concubines, and slaves.[86] A certain caliph restricted it to the wives, the children, and the closest of his slaves[87]; it thus encompassed the core of unconditional allies.[88] In fact, the close entourage was larger; a certain caliph went out "with his family, his *ḥacham*, his *ghâchiya*, and his friends,"[89] thus indicating the malleability of those different groups. The *ghâchiya* designated the protective entourage; the term referred to the contrast between light and darkness and meant the veil, or in this precise case, the caliph's black guard. These different terms far from exhaust the subdivisions that made up the royal entourage, only the dynamics of which concern us here. The lexicon dealing with this entourage is, without a doubt, an important indication of the evolution of the royal institution itself.

In any event, the progressive predominance of servitude that accompanied the rising power of the monarchy is clear. It is evident in the number of affected individuals in the royal entourage but also in its regulatory function, in which it dictated to other bonds the fundamental logic of royal proximity. Even when other logics seemed to be at work, as the discourse might lead one to believe, servitude was sure to intervene. In this regard, it is very enlightening to examine the relationship of kinship alongside the membership of the group encompassed by royal friendship. What did it mean to be a friend of the king?

A FRIEND OF THE KING

The friend in question was designated by the term *muḥibb*, which was often used by kings to distinguish exceptional personalities that the word placed beyond the logic of authority. *Al-ḥubb* was love, friendship, affection (*al-maḥabba*, *al-ḥibbu*). The *muḥibb* was the loved one, more commonly called *maḥbûb* and very rarely *muḥabb*.[90] To convey that meaning one also used *al-ḥibbu*, a word that is found again in connection to Zayd Ibn Hâritha, "*ḥibbu Rassûli Allah*" that is, the beloved of the Prophet, and that also applied to male-female relationships, ʿAisha thus being *ḥibbatu Rassûli Allah*, his beloved.

[86] *Kitâb al-alfâdh*, 348.
[87] Tabari, *Târîkh*, XII, 63.
[88] *Tâj al-ʿArûss*, XVI, 152–153.
[89] *Aghâni*, II, 129.
[90] *Tâj al-ʿArûss*, I, 392, and *Siḥaḥ*, I, 161.

Thus it seems natural that the word came to be applied to family relationships, to relatives of various sorts, to spouses, to lovers, or quite simply to friends, that is, when it evoked the most common social relationships. The problem, in the relationship that concerns us here, arises in its use for associates who lacked the type of bond that could justify the use of such a term.

Was there any correlation between service to the prince and his friendship? To put it more bluntly, could one be both a servant and a friend of the king? And could one be a friend of the king, in his kingdom, without being his servant? In other words, to what did such a term refer beyond its common meaning?

Muḥibb calls forth an image borrowed from the animal world. It designates the camel that, stricken by illness or immobilized with a broken bone, remains on its knees, fixed to the ground, no longer able to stand up or move. Like a statue, the animal is incapable of getting to its feet; it stays there as if dead, without any apparent prospect of recovery.[91]

Love is a fixation on something, an impassioned attachment that turns one away from everything else, and even from what is essential, that is (in the lexicon of authority), from the love of the master. The Koran says of Solomon: "We gave Solomon to David; and he was a good and faithful servant. When, one evening, his prancing steeds were ranged before him, he said: 'My love for good things has distracted me from the remembrance of my Lord; for now the sun has vanished behind the veil of darkness.'"[92] He remained subjugated, petrified by the elegance and beauty. To love something means to pay attention to and think of nothing but it.

Such is the case of the *muḥibb* camel, held to the ground by an injury that saps its strength and leaves it no ability to move. Such a posture, even involuntary in its origin, suggests the posture of the perfect adorer, the lover who loves to the point of forgetting all movement, forgetting himself, and letting himself go. From this posture comes the fantasy of the master, who saw in it the image of what his servant should be, imagining him thus incarnated in the camel and, like that animal, prostrated at his feet. And so a transfer occurred: the word itself, *muḥibb*, which should have designated the lover, then named the beloved, the friend whom the king constantly sought, the one of every master's dreams! One understands better the offer of "friendship" that the king advanced to the recipient: to be the friend of the king, his *muḥibb*, meant to be his adorer!

[91] Ibn Chajari, 286.

[92] The Koran, 38:32.

Prophetic tradition attributes this assertion to God: "The faithful one approaches Me through the strength of prayer until I love him."[93] We must, however, agree on the wording; the language is in fact determinative here and is, it seems, one of the great problems posed by the translation of the Koran. Let's translate the passage more literally in order to remain closer to the cultural context: "The slave will not cease to be close to me through the strength of *ʿibâda* until I love him." We are thus in the realm of servitude, in which postures take on another meaning because these words had a precise meaning for the Arabs of that time, in a society in which slavery was much more common than is generally believed and, certainly, was decisive in the construction of political structures.

Love and adoration went hand in hand in the realm of authority. Adoration, or *ʿibâda*, let us emphasize, comes from *ʿubûdiyya*, that is, a reduction to slavery. The slave was at the lowest level before his master; he was on his knees ready to hear him and to obey him. The adorer, the texts remind us, was closest to God in the posture of prostration.[94]

The term, should proof be needed, is filled with solicitations that these multiple facets corroborate. *Al-ḥubb* designated a large jar, the one that the Bedouin dreamed of on desert paths.[95] This brings us directly to the realm of mirage. A derivative (*ḥabâba*) described the noise of little waves that enticed the gaze of the dreamer and broke at his feet as if marking an unconditional surrender. The lack of water that hurt animals wandering thirsty in the great deserts was called *al-huyâm*, that is, mad love.[96] But among these terms with fresh and tender connotations, bad fairies could slip into the cracks; *al-ḥubâb* designated simultaneously a grass snake and a demon![97] Friendship in the high spheres of servitude was a very peculiar thing. Lady Macbeth says to her husband:

Your face, my thane, is as a book where men
  May read strange matters. To beguile the time,
  Look like the time; bear welcome in your eye,
  Your hand, your tongue: look like the innocent flower,
  But be the serpent under't ...[98]

[93] Râzi, XIII, Part I, 26.
[94] An-Nassâi, *Sunan*, 12, 41.
[95] *Aghâni*, XX, 218.
[96] *Tâj al-ʿArûss*, III, 95.
[97] *Siḥaḥ*, I, 163.
[98] Shakespeare, *Macbeth*, Act I, Scene V.

Still in the same family, a closely related term designates the way babies move when crawling on all fours, incapable as they are of standing upright. To get around on all fours also related to a baser, nonhuman register. We thus remain in the kneeling posture of the *muḥibb* camel, but this fixation to the ground brings to mind the way reptiles move, the result of an original curse.[99] According to legend, in the beginning the grass snake was "a four-legged animal similar to the camel and one of the most beautiful of beasts." But following Satan's intrusion it was cursed, lost its legs, and was condemned to crawl on its stomach and search for food in the dust.[100] The camel on its knees is described as having its chest on the ground; here dust recalls degeneration and death.

Resorting to animal typology to illustrate submission to the king has the advantage of being both didactic and very colorful. The image of the perfect servant is again provided by man's faithful animal companion, by the submissive animal, by the animal who stands attentive to the master's needs, attuned to his comings and goings, by the animal confined to a pen or chained to the threshold, who waits and is not allowed to wander at will in the pasture.[101]

The association with an animal thus proves to be more eloquent as to the true content of the social bonds. The *muḥibb* camel, an image that brings to light that which, in this very specific friendship, remains unsaid, cloaked in the condescension of language, is of precious help in decoding the bonds of power. Other terms that designate the same posture are less romantic and more explicit. *Al-qu'âd* was a disease that attacked the hip, making both men and animals incapable of movement. To remain on the ground deprived of any ability to move, in a position that placed a being at the lowest rung and put it at the service of others at the height of their strength, was the complete meaning of a word that described a social bond as well as the posture itself. The standing position, moreover, symbolized power and the domination of masculinity in contrast to femininity, which was the symbol of dependence and servitude.[102] Furthermore, it also referred not only to the disabled camel but also to the working animal that was always within arm's length of the shepherd. The servant animal in question was called the *qâ'ûd*, as was, among humans, the companion of the powerful, who did not leave the entourage and never failed

[99] *Jamhara*, 1017.
[100] Râzi, II, Part I, 15.
[101] *Nihâya*, III, 250.
[102] The Koran, 4:34, and Râzi, XIV, Part II, 113.

to respond to the call of duty. This faithful availability, masked by the semblance of friendship, was in fact strict dependence and servitude.[103]

Of course, in this pedagogy of servitude, recourse to the master-slave relationship was very common since the terminology (*'abd, 'ubûdiyya, 'ibâda*) was taken from that register. But to call upon the animal realm, and notably the camel, shows, in addition to familiarity with this animal, the interest in having recourse to a species that was undeniably inferior to man, a species that man could use as he wished. The bond of total domination that was inspired by the relationship to the animal raised no moral quandaries and was subject to no limits. It is reported in prophetic tradition that "man does not become pious until he is baser than a beast of burden who bellows at any attack," which, in the case of the camel, was a sign of submission![104]

One of the characteristics of submission was immediate, unhesitating obedience. Into the animal's nose one put a stick that was attached to the bridle so that the mount was forced to respond promptly to the rider's orders. When one considers the importance of the nose, extending from the face like a prow, as a symbol of nobility for Arabs, one becomes aware of the debasement that such a procedure implied if the parallel with the ideal attitude of the servant is drawn.[105] The category of *ar-rikâb*, or docile camels that knelt and allowed the master to kick them while riding, were trained to accept this attitude, unlike difficult camels (*al-'asîr*), which were not easily subdued in that way.[106]

Such examples say a great deal about how men were trained for servitude; they remind us of the process that led to the servile attitude and consolidated that bond. And like animals, men devoted to a servile career could be trained to the point of instilling an almost animallike obedience. The master was the symbol of majesty and elevation; he reigned over his subjects. A powerful man presiding over his council, who was begged to follow a recommendation of the Prophet, took care "to get off his couch, sit on the ground, and show himself to be humbly submissive."[107] As for the animal, it was already on the ground, its back ready to bear the load and endure the whip, while the master stood tall, or even, let us say, on high, in the heavens.

We are thus not in the realm of the love between two individuals, in the framework of the attachment that binds one person to another,

103 Râzi, XV, Part I, 70–71. See also *Tâj al-'Arûss*, V, 194.
104 *Nihâya*, IV, 87.
105 *Nihâya*, III, 33.
106 Al-Sakkari, *Chi'r al-Akhtal*, 254; *Diwân al-Hotay'a*, ed. Ibn al-Sikkite, 227.
107 *Nihâya*, IV, 344.

and from which one cannot escape. We are within the framework of a fundamental social relationship, a relationship of domination, a hierarchical and unequal relationship, a relationship of servitude. It is the relationship that connects the king to his close servants, to his *khâssa*, to a given moment in one particular phase of that bond, for it had its own dynamics. Those dynamics intensified with proximity: those closest to the Prophet on the day of the Resurrection, those whom he "loves the most," were those who let their guard down and, when they were approached, listened with kindness, unlike the prideful with their forked tongues.[108] *Al-ḥaba'* (plural *aḥibba'*), a derived and synonymous term, designated the very close companion of the king, the one within reach who had the pleasure of enjoying that distinction and who lived in the shadow of the king, who bestowed his largesse upon him.

In the bond of servitude, the status of "friend" was dictated by the master who granted that privilege. It was God who chose Abraham as a *khalîl*. It was the ultimate stage of servitude, in which the servant was entirely devoted to adoring and serving the master. Symbolically, the chronicle reports in Islamic tradition that the angel of death visited Abraham and told him: "I am the angel of death; I have come to give you the good news: God has chosen you as *khalîl*."[109] The envoy in question was precisely the one who took life away, who demonstrated to men their mortality. The friendship in question should not be confused with friendship between mortals, which presumes that equivalent sentiments are exchanged. Servants could not boast in their writings about the friendship of the king because "those he commands move only in command, / Nothing in love."[110] The prince's friendship was thus a category of its own order. In Shakespeare's *Richard III*, King Richard, close to death, wonders about friendship after a nightmare:

It is now dead midnight.
  Cold fearful drops stand on my trembling flesh.
  What do I fear? myself? there's none else by:
  Richard loves Richard; that is, I am I.
  Is there a murderer here? No. Yes, I am:
  Then fly. What, from myself? Great reason why:
  Lest I revenge. What, myself upon myself?
  Alack. I love myself.[111]

[108] *Fâ'iq*, IV, 68.
[109] Tabari, *Târîkh*, III, 50.
[110] Shakespeare, *Macbeth*, Act V, Scene II.
[111] Shakespeare, *Richard III*, Act V, Scene III.

In the friendship between master and servant, the inequality was obvious: it was between heaven and earth, between the all-powerful and the most extreme weakness. The *khalîl*, the status granted to Abraham by God, was a poor man in a difficult condition. Like a bird with meager plumage, he was unsheltered from the wind. Granted, poverty was a sign of detachment from material goods, and seen from that angle, the *khalîl* was precisely the *muḥibb*, whose adoration was not sullied by any defect.[112] The detachment in question here is a renunciation of pride. The blessed man recognized the essence of his human condition. The Koran speaks of the "needy man in distress"[113] to say how great his destitution was! He was like a slave because he was enslaved to the poverty that deprived him of the freedom to move about and fixed him to the ground. The poor whose only refuge was the earth were called "children of the dust."[114] The Koran refers to the dust and to the ground because the poor man "has nothing above to cover him nor anything underneath on which he can lean."[115] Born from dust, man returns to it; here dust recalls fragility and calls for submission.

Such renunciation in service of adoration in such a bond meant obedience without fail. But let us further examine the question of poverty. *Al-faqîr* did not mean just destitution but also the annihilation resulting from it, a physical annihilation that leads us back to the station of *muḥibb*. This status was inscribed, in fact, in a social bond of which it was the product. Let's once again call upon the camel, which says so much about the human condition! The *faqîr* was the animal that suffered a broken vertebra in the course of being tamed. But one also proceeded in a more classic way. The animal's nose was shaved with an iron, stripping it to the bone; then one made notches into which ropes were placed such that the pain immediately caused the mount to collapse. If the beast was still untamed, three cuts were made, one of which was very close to the lips, where the rope was placed; the mastery of the animal was then absolute.[116]

The seated position of the camel, or the position of the adorer, of the *muḥibb*, was originally the product of a trial of strength. Posture was essential in a reading of the social bond. The absence of a hierarchy among tribal chiefs gave rise to symbolic jousts in the form of posturing,

112 *Tâj al-ʿArûss*, XIV, 209.
113 The Koran, 90:16.
114 Al-ʿAskari, *Al-Mu'jam fi baqiyat al-achya'*, 119.
115 Râzi, XVI, Part I, 169.
116 *Tâj al-ʿArûss*, VII, 355–356.

in which each of the competitors tried to imbue himself with a legitimacy beyond the true extent of his command. If talent, courage, and feasts set before the starving populations all were qualities praised by the poets, posture was the central element needed to affirm an elevation in status. During great tribal assemblies, such as the great communication fair *Souq'Ukâz*, the powerful made their voices heard through their established criers, who proclaimed their status by listing their great deeds. The chiefs themselves sat comfortably, their feet extended in a sign of serenity and of a nobility that bore no trace of servitude.[117] The chronicle speaks of a lord "wearing his turban that served as a crown, and around whom people knelt on the ground."[118] Thus even before the distance between the two positions confirmed the difference in statuses, the chief/subject postures were expressed in the contrast between the extended knee and the bent knee.[119]

The king's friendship was well inscribed within the framework of servitude. There was, however, a much larger concept encompassing all of the king's dependents, regardless of their statutory differences; this was the *mawlâ*.

THE *MAWLÂ*

No other term better expresses, or more fully obscures, the significance and the strength of the bond of servitude in Islamic Arabic society than *mawlâ*. The term is derived from proximity.[120] It encompassed all personal bonds from kinship to friendship and to slavery. *Mawlâ* had some twenty-one synonyms, most of which are found in prophetic tradition, a sign, among others, of the captivating strength of such a bond at the time of the establishment of Islamic authoritarian structures. Among them one finds the master, God, the owner, the lord, the benefactor, the liberator, the one to whom one turned and from whom one sought assistance, the friend, the client, the neighbor, the first cousin (son of a paternal uncle), the ally, the grandson, the son-in-law, the slave, and the freedman.[121]

The many synonyms of *mawlâ* were a sign, also, of the rapid emergence of a centralized state in a tribal society that did not have the opportunity to evolve gradually by means of a progressive internal hierarchization

[117] *Aghâni*, XXII, 59.
[118] *Aghâni*, XXII, 336.
[119] At-Tha'âlibî, *Fiqh al-lugha*, 238.
[120] Râzi, IX, Part I, 101–102, and VII, Part I, 15.
[121] *Nihâya*, IV, 228.

over the long term, spurred on by vigorous economic pressures, toward structures better suited for the establishment of a new state power. In that context the very extensible bond of *mawlâ*, encompassing a wide gamut of social relationships, proved efficacious in harnessing the bonds quickly formed in a society that was increasingly open to the outside world.

Migrations in the wake of conquests, consisting of a significant influx of foreigners into large cities that were seats of central power and flourishing commercial centers, swelled the ranks of the *mawâli* seeking various bonds of dependence with Arab families. The rapid urban expansion was accompanied by a movement of detribalization and by a new logic of social relationships that encouraged such an evolution. The increasing wealth of the servants of the state and the growing prosperity of merchants enlarged the circles of *mawâli* of all kinds. In a sure sign of prosperity, households began to include more slaves and dependents. In the city of Kufa, the inhabitants' wealth was such that "a man there goes out in the company of ten or twenty of his *mawâli*."[122] The powers that be took control of the social fabric by extending their sway, either directly or indirectly through dominant families, over those foreign groups that would play an increasingly important role in the exercise of power. The *wala'* became an essential key to social and political domination. A famous hadith of the Prophet, beneficiary of Shiite obedience, also stresses the importance that the nascent state granted to that bond: "The one for whom I am the *mawlâ*, the lord, 'Ali is also his."[123] This statement thus reveals the ambiguities of the term and its various meanings.

It was necessary for newcomers, foreigners, and those who arrived without families to find a means of support in order to integrate lastingly and effectively into society. Proximity to notables could open the door to a comfortable situation. Regardless of how one achieved this, it was first necessary to find a place in the entourage of the great and their friends. Thus the *ḥalîf*, or ally, was certainly someone close and in that capacity was a contractual *mawlâ*, but in fact he was seen as a member of the family, in the same way that the slave and the freedman were.[124] For the latter, close proximity was confined to kinship due to the closeness of the bonds and their density in daily life. Prophetic tradition confirmed this on many occasions; it was in fact said that "man descends from his father and the *mawlâ* from his masters."[125] This tendency of the *mawlâ*, regardless of his

[122] *Al-Kâmil*, I, 259.
[123] *Nihâya*, IV, 228.
[124] *Aghâni*, XVIII, 280.
[125] *Al-Kâmil*, II, 729.

rank, to obtain the closest proximity possible, tended in fact to confuse him with the servile statuses by reason of the nature of the bond. The impenetrable nature of the despotic space in the hands of dominant Arab lineages made servitude the only path of ascension for those who did not belong to them. In a basically unsettled and horizontal universe, the surest mode of vertical movement was *wala'*.

Great confusion thus surrounded the nebulous *mawâli*, to the point that each translator renders the word in a different way.[126] Such a situation encouraged authorities to restrict the content of this social bond. Thus the caliph 'Omar Ibn 'Abdel'aziz decreed that "the *mawâli* are of three orders: the *mawlâ* through kinship, the *mawlâ* through enfranchisement, and the contractual *mawlâ*. The relative inherits and is inherited; the freedman is inherited but does not inherit. As for the contractual, he does not inherit, and his inheritance goes to his paternal relatives."[127]

In the social reality, the essential elements that constituted such a bond remained kinship, ownership, and authority. Action words reveal the subtle meanings that the term conceals when detached from its origins. Thus *al-walâya* particularly encompassed broad kinship, alliances, and enfranchisement; *al-wilâya*, by contrast, was restricted to authority; and *al-walâ'*, which is still commonly used today to render allegiance, was restricted to the freedman and to close relatives. *Al-muwâlat* referred to a variety of statuses, notably followers and various dependents.[128]

The powerful bonds of kinship, ownership, and authority were thus quite distinct from others, encompassing various cliental bonds, some stronger than others. But indisputably servitude was at the heart of that social bond: it ultimately unified it by lending its tint to all the theoretically different bonds designated by the term. Any foreigner, brought as a captive or arriving on his own, who had no legitimate claim to a free Arab lineage had no choice but dependency, which was the price one paid for proximity to the great and an ensured means of subsistence and protection. Freedmen were at the heart of this category.[129]

The *walâ'*, here the equivalent of the right of patronage, was at the time a bond as strong as slavery. It was the object of transactions: certain

[126] Thus in one of the French translations of the Koran (Masson) the word is rendered by "companion": The day when no friend will be able to do anything for companion" 44:41. Râzi renders the word here as "coreligionnaire," "relative," or "freedman." *Tafsîr*, XIV, Part I, 214.

[127] *'Iqd*, IV, 397.

[128] *Tâj al-'Arûss*, XX, 312.

[129] Tabari, *Târîkh*, VIII, 214.

mawâli were exchanged between lineages or abandoned to others[130]; former masters did not hesitate to sell their rights over their freedmen.[131] Among the various bonds of dependency, the status of freedman was less scorned than others that harbored a claim to equality in their dealings with free families. Thus servitude, without leading inevitably to high positions, at least proved to be a less undesirable state than freedom attained in destitution and social marginalization. To be a freedman or of a similar status, even without having been a slave, which was a relatively common phenomenon, provided insurance against the status of a reject without family ties (*laqît, manbûdh*).[132] A well-known singer refused to be affiliated with the family of his patrons as an adopted son, alleging "that to be a respectable *mawlâ*, close and faithful, is preferable to affiliating myself with a father who is not mine."[133] Of course, freedmen did not inherit, but they accumulated social capital as a function of their patrons' social milieu and by that fact became favored intermediaries on the path of upward mobility. Thus masters took care to derive the greatest benefit from them. Seen from that angle, the *wala'* was a privileged means to strengthen one's bonds with the dominant groups. Thus when a slave married a freedwoman and had children with her, the children's right of patronage fell to the wife's masters. But when the slave's owner freed him, he thereby obtained the patronage of the children. Thanks to a seemingly charitable gesture, the master enlarged his circle of dependents and, through them, entered indirectly into a relationship with the family that held the patronage before him.[134]

The verb linked to *walâ'* meant to approach someone,[135] in the sense of a vital proximity that often granted survival and could procure honors and benefits. It is useful to note that *walyu*, a synonym for proximity, designated the successive rains of the wet seasons, a vital substance that arrived just as it was needed to ease the pain of a drought! As in social relationships, foreignness was needed. Thus just as water arrived when one least expected it, the individual arriving from elsewhere and seeking refuge encountered a protector. In the relationship of servitude, the shadow of death hovered near, and it was submission that masked its presence; in the desert society, a reference to water to signify proximity

[130] *Aghâni*, VI, 79.
[131] *Aghâni*, I, 312.
[132] *Aghâni*, XIX, 235.
[133] *Aghâni*, III, 70.
[134] Al-Haroui, *Gharîbu al-ḥadîth*, II, 162.
[135] Râzi, XI, Part I, 154–155.

was essential. It emphasized the strength of the bond that also worked to the benefit of God.

Thus kings were careful to maintain their bonds with their slaves and their freedmen. These bonds were modeled upon familiarity, as Jâhiz stresses regarding the Abbasid caliphs:

> They granted their *mawâli* the privilege of coming to their table, of enjoying themselves in their company, and of maintaining familiar relationships with them. The did not exclude the black man for his blackness, nor the ugly man because of his ugliness, nor the one who had a base profession. They advised their eldest sons to watch over them. They took care to preside over the burials of many of them and to offer prayers on those occasions in the presence of uncles, cousins, and brothers.[136]

Experience indeed showed that the *mawâli* were the most faithful and sure supports. The Abbasids and the Omayyads used them profusely. In addition to their loyalty, the *mawâli* were adapted to all tasks. No task repulsed them, unlike faithful relatives who did not deign to undertake certain tasks for fear of lowering themselves socially.[137] "Take your *mawâli* into consideration. Grant them benefits. Ensure that they are close to you, and increase their numbers. They are your faithful support in difficulty," a king advised his heir.[138] Kinship was of course a powerful factor of proximity, but by its very nature it continually called into question the uniqueness of the king, his sui generis existence. This is why the king favored among his entourage the proximity of servitude, which, through recruitment from within a particular category, fortified his serenity as absolute and single master. The *mawlâ* was foremost the stranger of servile or assimilated status[139]; he served the master without any seed of discord threatening that peaceful servitude.[140]

> Al-Mansûr had a slave who was pale verging on brown, rather talented. One day he said to him, "What is your race?"
>
> He responded: "Arab, O Commander of the believers!"
>
> "And from which Arabs do you come?" al-Mansûr asked.
>
> "From Khûlân," replied the slave. "I was raised in Yemen. One of our enemies took me and castrated me, and I became a slave. I passed into the hands of an Omayyad and then to you."

[136] Jähiz, *Rasâ'il*, I, 23.
[137] Tabari, *Târîkh*, IX, 276.
[138] Tabari, *Târîkh*, IX, 291.
[139] The texts speak of *mawlâ taba'a* (follower) and of *mawlâ 'atâqa* (freeman); Tabari, *Târîkh*, VIII, 214.
[140] Tabari, *Târîkh*, XII, 64.

Al-Mansûr said, "Know that you are a perfect servant, but I cannot admit an Arab into my palace in the service of my harem. Leave, and may God keep you in good health. Go where you wish."[141]

In certain spheres, absolute servitude was the rule. In that framework the servant was cut off from his original milieu, which he no longer knew or of which he was simply stripped. Freedmen were thus very sought after for having a relationship to the master founded on the basis of ownership. It was recommended to place them in strategic positions, notably that of chamberlain.[142] Jâhiz became a spokesman for them:

We give sincere advice, offer solid friendship, and are the most worthy of confidence in difficulty. The defects of the lower *mawlâ* necessitate that he love the *mawlâ* above (the master) because the nobility of the master reflects upon him, the master's generosity increases his own, and his little renown lessens his worth. He wishes to see his master display all the virtues of good people because the greater, more noble, and more considerable the master is, the more he derives glory from him. The *mawlâ* is less envious of his master.[143]

Servitude was hardly ever questioned; the efficacy of the master-servant duo was praised without revealing the extent to which the freedom and nobility of the one assumed the debasement of the other. Revisiting the allegation confusing *walâ'* and kinship,[144] Jâhiz, unlike other black intellectuals of the time, defended the established order that made servitude the twin of authority. It is true that the dominant house saw its authority increase thanks to its slaves and to its *mawâli* of various statuses. This shows how much they, along with relatives, belonged to the inner core. From there their bonds with the chiefs continued to develop. They derived their strength not only from blind obedience and great loyalty but also, as Jâhiz notes, from the fact of serving both father and son, thereby serving as a living, breathing reminder of the continuity of the lineage.[145] They spent their days in proximity to the kings whom they had cared for as children and accompanied in their games. They could even enter into kinship with the house in the event of marriage of one of their daughters with one of its powerful members. Thus kings showed a conciliatory attitude toward them, as the prophet Muhammad did toward one of his own, whom he called "friend, son of a friend."[146]

141 Tabari, *Târîkh*, IX, 288.
142 Tabari, *Târîkh*, VIII, 145.
143 Jâhiz, *Rasâ'il*, I, 23.
144 Jâhiz, *Rasâ'il*, I, 12.
145 Jâhiz, *Rasâ'il*, I, 23.
146 This concerns Oussama Ibn Zayd, Jâhiz, *Rasâ'il*, 25; see also on a similar subject Râzi, XIV, Part II, 112.

The circles of proximity, as shown in the various profiles we have looked at, had servitude as the dominant force in spite of the diverse origins and unequal statuses of their members. Servitude was the common cement that constructed the solid bond to the king; indeed it was found in everything that the majority of people in proximity claimed.

PROXIMITY TO THE KING

Proximity, notes an author, is "delicious, and is all the more so when the king is important."[147] Those close to the sultan were believed to enjoy his complete confidence. They were the *ḥawâriyûn*, literally those of immaculate whiteness,[148] that is, with unfailing loyalty. Such purity won them intimacy with the king and made them the elect whom he chose for his service. Thus "the king said: 'Bring [Joseph] before me. I will choose him for my own.'"[149]

They were "worked" to that end by the king himself.[150] It was the condition necessary to cross the threshold of the king's own space, like that which took place in heaven. Moses, the interlocutor of God, reached that degree of proximity because God chose him for that purpose and endowed him so that he would be capable of it at the desired moment; as the sacred text says, "I have [created] you for Myself."[151] More than a simple choice, it was a question of a re-creation. The Arabic word rendered here by "to create" or "to work" is *istanaʿa*, the language used by the slave master who "worked" his own and notably his concubines of choice, of whom he took great care. The term is also used by horse breeders, for whom training was fundamental.[152] We are thus in the presence of creatures over whom the king had complete control.

Not only could he put them to death for a real or assumed crime, but he was believed to have given them life: he made them what they were, his faithful. The whiteness and purity attributed to them were synonymous with transparency, suggesting the idea of ghosts surrounding the king. Their status associated a fragility with their elevation that could be confused with the dead. They were the *qurbân*, those close to the king

[147] Râzi, XV, Part I, 72.
[148] *Kachâf*, IV, 516.
[149] The Koran, 12:54.
[150] *Jamharat rasâʾil al-ʿArab*, III, 445.
[151] The Koran, 20:41.
[152] *Tâj al-ʿArûss*, XI, 285; *Nihâya*, III, 56; *Tâj al-ʿArûss*, XI, 284 and 288–89.

but also, literally, offerings ready to be sacrificed, whose lives no longer belonged to them.[153]

This circle of those close to the king was very diverse and had various vocations. It included the palace bureaucracy consisting of viziers and other scribes whose function was to unburden the king from the management of daily affairs.[154] It also included companions as well as the *ḥâmma*, that is, close relatives.[155]

Kings brought close to themselves those "whom they love and those whom they fear so that the latter did not join the ranks of their enemies."[156] Indeed, proximity to the king was not the fruit of a privileged connection; it also proved to be a means by which the master controlled the great of the kingdom, keeping them within his reach. This is how the caliph ʿOmar kept the companions of the Prophet within reach in Medina.[157] In this way, any vague desire of close relatives to seize power was cut short. When the caliph al-Amîn caught wind of the growing renown of his brother al-Mâmûn, then governor of Khurâssan, he attempted to bring him into the fold. "The commander of the believers," he wrote to his brother, "has become convinced that your presence near him will better protect the borders, will do more good for the troops, will increase the spoils, and will be more profitable to the population than your stay in Khurâssan, deprived of your family and distanced from the commander of the believers."[158]

Proximity consisted of crossing a threshold, a line of demarcation, the veil that created the mystery of royalty. So many levels of servitude marked the ladder that extended from the common subject, simply servile, to the favored servant. The highest degree of servitude, the one that caused people to plant themselves at the foot of the throne, allowed them to reach the secret of mastery, and opened the path to all honors and privileges, was reached with proximity, which "was the beginning; the rank is the continuation."[159] To cross that threshold was to belong to a particular category, appointed to the king's company and direct service; it was "to be authorized to come close to him in the *majliss al-unss*," the special council made up of the close of the close, *khâssatuhu wa saffiyatuhu*,

[153] Ibn Chajari, 169; *Siḥaḥ*, I, 299.
[154] *Kachâf*, III, 59.
[155] *Jamharat rasâ'il*, II, 409.
[156] Râzi, XV, Part I, 72.
[157] Taha Hussein, *Al-Finatatu al-kubra*, I, 46.
[158] *Jamharat rasâ'il*, III, 306.
[159] Râzi, XI, Part I, 77.

those who saw the king and supported him. The verb *ânasa*, which gave this council its name, means to see and to hear or, in this case, to cross the invisible barrier to reach the place where the king finally conceded a bit of his grandeur to humans.[160]

The jurisconsult could not resist drawing a parallel with the divine. He identified two large categories of people who were close to the king (*al-muqarrabûn*). The *mukallafûn* (which gives us *kulfa*, or duty) were assigned tasks determined in his proximity; they received his orders without seeing him. The others benefited from his largesse, served as his companions in leisure and in the council, and saw him without having a specific responsibility. This latter group was similar to angels, those to whom God was not hidden, even if they were not supposed to look at him.[161] Angels in fact enjoyed proximity to God without him expecting anything from them but complete and total adoration.[162] Furthermore, the word "angel" itself designates what is royal in the sense of proximity and service to the king.[163]

Such a similarity should not cause confusion about the extreme servitude of the individuals in question. The king's gravitational pull in fact deprived one of all autonomy, giving the master control over one's every movement. The courtier was thus the *qa'îd*, the *nadhîm*. He was a being in continual repentance, closely attached to the royal proximity, stuck in place like an inanimate object – an image that brings us back to the dust that served as glue sticking the miserable powerless one to the earth. He was there at the feet of the master like a lifeless statue.[164] The imagc of the camel kneeling on the ground, now with the implication of a magnetic pull, is more fitting than ever.

Extreme proximity meant belonging completely to the master; it consisted of devoting oneself to his adoration by "going to the extreme of servitude and submission." It was an elevation "of servitude to the *'indiyya*, meaning the true accomplishment of servitude."[165] It was the realm of the elect, those closest to the master. The proximity could be spatial, as the Koranic text states for the divine entourage: "His are all who dwell in the heavens and on the earth. Those who stand in His presence do not disdain to worship Him, nor are they ever wearied. They praise

160 *Siḥaḥ*, III, 61–63; *Tâj al-'Arûss*, VIII, 186–192; Râzi, XI, Part I, 77.
161 Râzi, XV, Part I, 138.
162 Râzi, XV, Part I, 129.
163 Râzi, XIV, Part II, 266.
164 Râzi, XV, Part I, 74 and 86.
165 Râzi, VIII, Part II, 12.

Him night and day, tirelessly."[166] It could also be a proximity of consideration and ennoblement such as we find again in the Koran: "This is the word of a gracious and mighty messenger, held in honour by the Lord of the Throne."[167] *Al-ʿindiyya* is derived from *ʿind*, an adverb of place and time meaning "the presence of a thing and its (mastered) proximity" and conveying the most extreme form of proximity in terms of possession and authority.[168]

Servitude, the royal path of proximity, had as its price a total renunciation of one's self, an effacement synonymous with sacrifice. *Al-bughbûr*, the name given to the kings of China, designated the stone on which one made burnt offerings to the divinities.[169] Human sacrifice to the divine was at the time still familiar to the population. The chronicle reports that the grandfather of the Prophet vowed to sacrifice one of his sons to the *Ka'ba* if his wish to have ten sons should come to pass.[170]

Servitude was the crossroads to which that abandonment led. *Al-mutayyam* meant one who was impassioned to the point of losing his mind; a related word, *taym*, meant slave and in the feminine form designated the sheep whose throat was cut during times of famine.[171] Prayer was a sacrifice, and that of the dawn even shows it in its name, *naḥr*.[172] Adoration or *ʿibâda* was also called *nisk*, a word that gives us *al-minsak*, that is, the place where burnt offerings were made, a meaning that later extended to encompass all the rituals of pilgrimage.[173] Let us stress that *nisk* also meant an ingot of pure silver, whence its application to the adorer *al-muta'abidd*, who submitted himself without regret or doubt.[174] Thus Abraham's sacrifice, which was the perfect prayer of the faithful, was a symbol of pure obedience to the All-Powerful. We will speak of this again in looking at death, servitude being a sacrifice in suspense, a death in remission; it was the crossing of the first threshold that founded the king's authority. Animal sacrifice during pilgrimages or feasts functioned for the faithful as a sacrifice of his own person: "He who sought proximity [with God] by spilling the blood of an offering sees this act as redeeming himself in return. It was as if he exchanged the animal for

[166] *ʿIndiyyat al-makân* or spatial proximity, the Koran, 21:19; Râzi, XVI, Part I, 68.
[167] The Koran, 81:19–20.
[168] *Tâj al-ʿArûss*, XIII, 130–131.
[169] *Tâj al-ʿArûss*, VI, 103.
[170] *As-Sîra*, I, 151–155; more generally, *Kachâf*, II, 66–67, and Tabari, *Târîkh*, II, 182–183.
[171] *Lissân*, XII, 75.
[172] *Kachâf*, IV, 802.
[173] Râzi, XII, Part I, 57.
[174] Râzi, VII, Part II, 10.

his soul with the aim of pleasing God, the All-Powerful."[175] Through the sacrifice, the servant showed his submission by mimicking his own death; he demonstrated his ability to die for his master by serving him faithfully. This immolation was the obligatory route to pass beyond the veil; it recognized one's status as a royal creation.

THE KING'S CREATURES

The debasement of that near-death existence was the essence of the servile relationship. The servant risked death if he ever ceased to fear the master.

> Living constantly in opulence, the slave became insolent. He thus lost his dignity and no longer took into consideration the favors that had been granted him. He attributed those goods to his abilities, to his own merit, to his family, his clan, his tribe. But as soon as the vicissitudes of fate fell upon him and his vision cleared from the blindness caused by his confusion in the presence of authority, he humbled himself in submission, greatly regretting his misdeeds.[176]

Threats and calls to order were thus constant and stressed the extent to which servitude was a blend of voluntary and forced submission. The "children of the house," or creatures of the king, had no point of reference but him and were to defer to him alone. The caliph wrote to a certain governor that "the commander of the believers has honored you with the governorship of Iraq without your belonging to one of the great houses or being of ancient nobility."[177] The real status was unveiled in the dialogue between the master and the servant, in which the caliph threatened to "chain his hands to his neck."[178] This was the opposite of the process described by the expression that referred to the freeing or liberating of the neck.

In Arab tribal society, servitude provided the framework that placed the king in a position, thanks to and through his creatures, that enabled him to hold together a segmented society. It provided the ideal modality for the king to transgress the inherent territorial and social limits of tribal solidarity. In response to the concern expressed by a certain Nuṣayr, whom he had earlier named governor of Khurâssan, and who complained of his lack of family support, the caliph said: "How can you lack support when

[175] Râzi, XII, Part I, 26.
[176] Letter from Hichâm Ibn ʿAbdelmâlik in *Jamharat rasâʾil*, II, 345.
[177] *Jamharat rasâʾil*, II, 347.
[178] *Jamharat rasâʾil*, II, 355.

I am your family!"[179] The sovereignty of the king prevailed over others and transcended them. Servitude engendered a dynamic that produced a hierarchy and an authority in a tribal milieu hardly inclined to give rise to them itself. The servant scarcely had need of a tribe; he lived by the logic of servile affiliation, serving as his master's shadow, right hand, and standard-bearer. Almost transparent, the servant existed only for the master. Such an argument was used to convince one who was afraid to conduct a prayer due to his servile origins and whom the caliph bluntly told: "Was it in your name or in the name of your father or grandfather that you were going to conduct the prayer? It would have been my place if I had been present! But if I am absent, you are the best suited for it due to your position close to the sultan."[180] Such words were especially true in light of the servant's absence despite his physical presence that harbored the shadow of the king.

One found these creatures notably in the royal guard that swore only to the king. Thus the king an-Nu'mânn had a guard consisting of five squadrons. Among them were the *wadâi'*, a squadron of a thousand Persian men, thus free of the dependency engendered by Arab tribal affiliation, whom the suzerain sent to Ḥira for the security of his king. The word referred to something kept in store, but also to an alliance. The second squadron consisted of the *achâhib*, white men and worthy warriors belonging to the royal family. Beyond those two groups, whose loyalty was guaranteed by the foreign origins of the first, which deprived it of local legitimacy, and by the family ties of the second, the remaining squadrons fell within the framework of the servile relationship. Thus was the case of the *rahâ'in*, or hostages left by the tribes of the kingdom. Received each year by the king, who renewed their land holdings, the tribal notables were obliged to leave with the court some soldiers who were assigned to exterior missions. Individuals of little value, as sources assert, they were of base status both by nature and by virtue of the recruitment process itself. The *Dawsâr* came from the tribes, especially those with a confirmed reputation as warriors. They were mercenaries in the hands of the king, his men of action who derived their name from murder, *adasr*. They were his creatures recruited to conduct his defense and inflict his blows. Finally there were the *sanâ'i'*, or creatures who were recruited within the framework of the process that distinguished among individuals, mentioned earlier in this chapter, and were often those who

[179] *Jamharat rasâ'il*, II, 358.
[180] *Jamharat rasâ'il*, III, 141.

had been excommunicated. Without faith or law, they had no legitimacy except in service to the king, for whom they formed the closest guard.[181]

Proximity to the king enlarged his entourage; it did so all the more in that it worked to the benefit of the most devoted, or to put it more prosaically, those who managed to cast themselves aside and live only for and by the master. The apogee was the viceroy who was believed to occupy the highest rank and at the same time to live in almost total obscurity because of his constant contact with the chief. Such was the existence of the *ridf*.

A certain 'Attâb Ibn Ḥamriya Ibn Riyyâh was the *ridf* or viceroy. When the king rode, he rode behind him (on the same mount). When the king sat, he took a place next to him (on the throne), to his right; if he went to war, a quarter of the spoils came to him, and when the king drank, he drank from the same glass after him.[182] Some said that this viceroy represented the secondary but powerful tribes.[183] 'Othmân, under the caliphate of 'Omar, apparently had the name *radîf*, literally meaning, according to Tabari, "the man who is after the man"; this is what Arabs called the one whom they wanted as their future chief.[184]

Didn't the viceroy's lieutenancy offend the royal all-powerfulness and the exceptionality of the king, constantly flanked by an all-too-present double? In fact, the word that designated the viceroy also conveyed a transfer of power indicating the omnipresence of the king even in his physical absence. This transfer of power, like the succession of day to night, enhanced the light's value by succeeding it with a shadow that emphasized its absence.[185]

The profundity of the fact that the king and his lieutenant rode the same mount was the great proximity between the two figures. The royal logic of proximity could not conceive that a dependent, a servant of such high rank, should be detached from the master's convoy. The king brought close to him those whom he loved and those whom he feared. So the magic of vocabulary placed the lieutenant behind the king, on the saddle of the royal mount, which served as a moving throne. The *ridf* was thus an extension of the royal person; he was in the king's shadow, erased by him. The great poet al-Akhtal drew upon this vocabulary to speak of

181 *Al-Akhtal*, 95; *Majma 'al-amthâl*, I, 163; *Al-Kâmil*, I, 328–329; *Naqâ'id*, II, 238, and *Tâj al-'Arûss*, XI, 517; *'Iqd*, V, 221; *Jamhara*, 905.

182 *Aghâni*, XIII, 143. For the tax see also *Naqâ'id*, I, 53.

183 *Naqâ'id*, I, 217.

184 Tabari, *Târîkh*, IV, 3.

185 *Al-Kâmil*, II, 769.

women who were kidnapped during raids, because the horsemen took them and rode away with the women behind them on their horses.[186] The kidnapped woman was then called *al-murdafa*. Royal proximity thus was a state similar to captivity.

This feminization of servitude is also found in other statuses of proximity, extending as far as the circle of agents in service of the reign. Such was the case of the *khadîm*. The term in question is used today in Morocco to designate agents of the state, agents of authority, and others responsible for various administrations, in their relationship to the king. At the beginning of the century those agents were of two statuses: that of *khadîm* (plural *khuddâm*) and that of *wassîf*. The first was reserved for agents of free status; the second, for slaves and freedmen of the sultan.[187] The second has disappeared from official acts with the intervening transformations and the gradual disappearance of slavery.

The large Arabic dictionaries do not mention the *khadîm*. They mention *khadîm* designating the male or female domestic slave (also called *khâdima*), and the plurals *khuddâm* and *khadam*.[188] The word is thus of recent usage and perhaps arises from a desire to distinguish domestic slaves from those meant for high administrative and military offices. Its servile sense, however, is indisputable.[189] It is possible that the word was borrowed from the adjective *khadhîm*, which, when applied to the ear, means that it is pierced[190] or has a piece cut off,[191] which was common for camels in Arabia and, most applicable to our purposes, for black slaves. The word is derived from *al-ikhdâm*, which means the lack of a sense of honor and debasement.[192]

Thus we return to the original meaning of *khâdim* and of service, or *khidma*. They come from *al-khidâm*, which means the *khalkhâl*, or the silver bracelet that oriental women wore on the ankle.[193] The anklet in question acquired this name due to its circular shape, for the word

[186] *Al-Akhtal*, 54 and 422.

[187] M. Ennaji, *Soldats, domestiques et concubines*, 145–170.

[188] *Tâj al-ʿArûss*, XVI, 195; *Lissân*, XII, 166; *Jamhara*, I, 580; *Kitâb al-alfâdh*, 346; Kazimirsky, I, 547.

[189] J. B. Belot, *Al-Farâ'id al-darriya* [Arabic-French Vocabulary], Beirut, 1899, 153; the author gives *khadîm* and *khaddiîm*, which he defines as slaves.

[190] *Lissân*, II, 597.

[191] *Lissân*, XII, 169.

[192] Ibid.

[193] *Kachâf*, IV, 581; Al-Haroui, *Gharîbu al-ḥadîth*, II, 179. The *mukhaddam* is the placing of the anklet on the leg; it is also the place where women tied their trousers. *Tâj al-ʿArûss*, XVI, 195.

originally meant a group of people in a circle. In literature the term conveys the situation of panic and fear when women took flight during an attack and uncovered their legs in their haste. One also finds the same image of a woman, not in the disarray of flight, but attacked, mistreated, and taken by force, her nakedness visible as she was led captive toward an unknown destiny.[194] The symbol of submission and of reduction to slavery is reinforced by the feminization of the victim in the Koran: "On the day [when their legs will be naked] and they are told to prostrate themselves, they will not be able."[195] Giving a lesson in obedience to one of his servants, the caliph ʿOmar Ibn ʿAbdelʾaziz notified him that it consisted of "taking from your mustache until your lips are visible and from your clothing until your heels appear."[196]

The *khadîm* was the one who circled around a man, inquiring of his needs and serving him diligently. He was the *tâʾif*, "the one who goes around"; according to the jurisconsults, it was precisely for this reason that one did not apply the term to God. One clearly perceives the similarity between this circular movement and the anklet on the female leg.[197] The word was later applied to domestic servitude in general due to the incessant circulation of those who waited around for the king's orders. One fought to obtain proximity to the king and trembled at the idea of losing its advantages; indeed, a servant never recovered from the shame of distance.

If the king held a servant at a distance, the latter immediately felt the agony of solitude. For the one accustomed to the rituals of servitude, nothing could replace the presence of the master. Observe this poet's supplication to a grand vizier, which speaks eloquently of the requester's state of abandonment:

> Your wrath toward me, together with your abandonment of me and the negligence that you show toward me, profoundly affects me to the point that I can neither rest nor move, whether in sleep or awake. It is as though I am neither truly alive nor truly dead and delivered. I beg you not to view what you see from me as simply prayer, submission, humiliation, or weakness. Such attitudes are not in my nature. Nor are they the product of artifice or ruse. They are the humiliation, submission, and prayer of someone who is submissive, base, and weak only in opposition to the one to whom it is glorifying, elevating, and ennobling to address a prayer.[198]

194 Al-Akhtal, 54.
195 The Koran, 68:42.
196 *Al-Kâmil*, I, 248.
197 Al-ʿAskari, *Kitâb al-furûq*, 243.
198 *Jamharat rasâʾil al-ʿArab*, III, 149.

This was a claim of servitude as both a privilege and an end in itself. The poet al-Mutannabi, of legendary pride, however, conveyed the mortal sadness that being distanced from the prince caused even when it was not accompanied by disgrace.[199] For the close servant, the pressing need to regain the favors of the master never left him. Those outside the circle of servitude who had not experienced its delights could not grasp the importance of it. Responding to one of his friends, who advised him against approaching the sultan and his entourage, a notable was quick to stress: "If the sultan calls to me, I rush to him; if he is late in doing so, I go before him."[200]

Those banished from the king's proximity suffered from it. A certain individual "was forbidden from appearing before the king, who sent him away and no longer paid him any attention."[201] The fear of banishment following a disgrace was an obsession that haunted the servants. Even when they were solidly in the heart of the entourage and benefited from royal solicitude, they never ceased to think of it, as is noted by Jâhiz: "In spite of their position they are troubled and embittered by the fear of the master's attack, the companion's punishment, a change in government, and the advent of difficulties. And if those events occurred, as they often did, they became all the more unhappy, inspiring pity in their enemies, not to mention in those close to them."[202]

The banishment in question could occur without the slightest warning. A certain courtier, not up to date on the customs, angered the king, who "became angry and insulted me," said the one concerned, "and gave the order to drag me by my feet and send me away, which was done. And he forbade me access to his audiences."[203] These were not isolated acts; in fact, it often happened that a courtier would be thrown into the street, beaten with a stick, and definitively forbidden from staying at the palace.[204] Such expulsions all had in common the experience of public humiliation.

Regardless of the risks of expulsion, the desire for proximity to the master remained intact. Despite the king's restrained ire or openly expressed anger, an irrepressible desire to regain the royal esteem gave rise to endless requests for mercy. "I was punished," reports a man, "by the

199 *Al-Mutanabbi*, I, 175 et seq.
200 *Jamharat rasâ'il*, III, 173.
201 *Aghâni*, XIV, 185.
202 Jâhiz, *Rasâ'il*, II, 255.
203 *Aghâni*, V, 88.
204 *Aghâni*, XI, 363.

commander of the believers, who deprived me of coming near to him. A month passed, then I received the good news that he granted me his pardon and authorized me to present myself to him. He gave me his hand, which I kissed."[205] This was a happy outcome; many others were not. The outcome varied depending on king's moods, the rank of the incriminated, and his degree of servitude. It could be limited to the stripping and crushing of the individual. One man received two hundred blows and had his head shaved as well as his beard and his eyebrows.[206]

Was this pure whim, believed to be the king's right? In reality, the king's supremacy rationalized his deeds and gestures. The king's secret was to be seen as unpredictable in the imaginations of his subjects and those close to him. The servitude at the foundation of his command fed on this uncertainty that dwelled in them and frightened them. Thus the back-and-forth of rejection and recall, of exile and repatriation, accompanied by the constant fear of a permanent exile or a mortal disgrace, was one of the forces at work in servitude. Proximity thus contained its own rupture. Great was the ordeal of the king's audiences for the important figures who occupied the highest ranks one day and found themselves distanced the next. A certain provincial governor, asked how he felt about exercising his authority, listed the advantages and then concluded: "I detest it because of the fear that the arrival of messengers instills in me and the persistent fear of death that threatens destitution."[207] Thus was spoken the word by which kings claimed the status of gods.

[205] *Aghâni*, VII, 225.
[206] Ibid., XVI, 116.
[207] *'Iqd*, I, 99.

7

The King's Threshold, or the Weapon of Forced Servitude

DEATH TAMED

Death lurked around the king. The servant moved within a space where he was ultimately destined to die. The king's grandeur allowed no grandeur around him; it was satisfied only with shadows. Abû Muslim al-Khurâsânî knew this well enough and wrote to the caliph al-Mansûr: "The commander of believers – may God heap rewards upon him – no longer has a single enemy that he has not conquered through divine grace. And it is said, according to the chronicles of the Sassanid kings, that some viziers are feared the most after the appeasement of the crowd! Thus, alarmed, we keep our distance from your proximity, faithful to our engagement as long as you respect it, committed to hearing you and obeying you, but from afar, in order to remain safe."[1]

Such fear of death was ingrained in the relationship with authority, including the relationship with God. Going near him was to have a meeting with death. The immortality of God took on meaning only in its juxtaposition with human mortality. For that reason, the feeling of an impending end never left the believer-servant. It was natural "for those who fear God to be convinced that death could take them at any moment."[2] The constant imminence of death filled the heart with fear and inspired submission. Death was inscribed in the logic of servitude as proof of the All-Powerful.

[1] *Jamharat rasâ'il*, III, 27.
[2] Râzi, II, Part I, 48.

Whether they were great dignitaries or common folk, servants had a keen awareness of death's presence in their everyday lives. Yahya Ibn Khâlid, summoned urgently to the palace by the caliph al-Hâdi, thought he was lost: "He said his goodbyes to his family, anointed himself [in the way one anointed cadavers], and put on new clothes, no longer doubting that he would face his death."[3] And that case was certainly not isolated. A certain jurisconsult, having decided to lecture the caliph, took care, before going to meet him, to carry out the customary mortuary preparations. He went to the caliph's home shrouded in white clothing and smelling of *ḥanut* (*ḥinat*), the aromatics always used for the dead.[4] The *ḥanut* in question, with which one embalmed shrouds and cadavers, was a mixture of powdered cyperus to cleanse the cadaver, musk, amber, camphor, sugarcane, and santal oil extracted from *rimth* flour, which in its ripe state had a white color verging slightly on yellow, and a pleasant odor.[5] Prepared in such a way, the dead person was rid of impurities and crossed the threshold essentially whitened.

But one did not have to go as far as lecturing the king to deserve death. A notable, summoned to the caliph Hârûn ar-Rachîd and fearing for his life, recounted: "I put on my mourning clothes and prayed to God that he would show me the mercy of death by the sword." It was the fear that gnawed at his stomach each time the royal veil was lifted that made the servant so ready for death. Approaching and retreating from death's door created a sensation of rebirth and of owing one's life precisely to the one who was feared for his ability to take life away. The king's ability to give life came from the extraordinary ability to cause death that was his alone. When the above-mentioned notable received news of his promotion, he threw himself at the feet of the caliph and kissed him: "I felt as though I had just been removed from a shroud or freed from prison."[6] As we can see, death haunted these high places. Abû Muslim did not breathe until he saw his master murdered and cut up into pieces: "As God is my witness, never once did I rely on him since I began to accompany him! Not a single day did I go to him without saying my final wishes, putting on my shroud, and anointing myself!"[7]

Death lay in wait for the elect and went hand in hand with their success. The ascension that increased their power also highlighted their

[3] Tabari, *Târîkh*, X, 38.
[4] *'Iqd*, V, 51.
[5] *Tâj al-'Arûss*, X, 224.
[6] *'Iqd*, V, 60–61.
[7] Tabari, *Târîkh*, IX, 128.

fragility. The highly coveted places they entered and flaunted were fraught with danger. Enemy eyes, envious and jealous, watched their every move.[8] Proximity to the prince revealed to his familiars his *'awra*, that is, his humanity, or to put it simply, his weaknesses and defects. The one close to him in fact became a suspect who could be toppled by the slightest doubt or faux pas. Al-Hajjâj, upon being shown the head of one of his familiars, whom he had just put to death for treason, looked at it for a long time and then exclaimed: "So many secrets I confided to this head that escaped it only when it was brought to me cut off."[9] To see the head of an enemy, where so much praise and so many plots were conceived, detached from its natural support, disarmed, so to speak, aggrandized the king in the face of his adversaries. The spectacle of decapitated servants, reduced permanently to the height of the ground, captured the attention of the living.

The king's power to inflict death was outrageously displayed. It was the message of a conqueror asserting his power. During a conquest in which the number of captives reached four thousand, according to the chronicle, the commander in chief got out his litter, sat down on it in public, and gave the order to execute the captives. One thousand were killed in front of him, one thousand to his right, one thousand to his left, and one thousand behind him. Such a sense of symmetry meant that the king was at the center of a killing machine. The veil that surrounded him was deadly, and its order was primordial. And death was an eventuality inscribed in the public memory right from the start.[10] It was an eventuality that the king's men were careful always to remember. Indeed one evoked, in that regard, "signs of the final judgment," which presaged the apocalyptic end that filled them with fear. They were the *achrât*, a term close to *churat*, which designated the king's police by the insignia they wore and which made subjects tremble. The king's extraordinary nature fed on such messages.[11]

The spectacle of death was part and parcel of the ritual that surrounded it. In full audience, and unanticipated by those in attendance, the order could fall: the *nat'* and the sword joined the indisputable voice; the *nat'* was the leather ground cloth on which the throats of the condemned were cut! Putting someone to death could take place instantaneously without

[8] *Aghâni*, V, 130–131.
[9] *Aghâni*, XI, 313.
[10] Tabari, *Târîkh*, VIII, 36.
[11] *Nihâya*, II, 460.

any response from those in attendance.[12] Whether in possession of all his faculties or dead drunk, the caliph remained the *qayl* whose word had the executionary power to maintain life or inflict death.[13] ʿAbdelmalek Ibn Marwân, seeing before him a man from the tribe of the Banû Tamîn, felt only "the desire to kill him because of his look and his corpulence!"[14] with no other apparent reason than the distaste the visitor inspired in him and above all his power to annihilate him.

The "immortality" of the king, that is, his endurance and his authority, fed on the virtual death of his subjects. That death, a mark of absolute servitude, appeased the fury of the king, whose ogre's appetite was then sated. The death of competitors sealed the monarch's undisputed authority; his consuming flame reduced them to ashes. The king's anger in fact obliterated everything in its path; it took out the living just as it could be unleashed against the dead, who were taken from their graves if needed[15] in order to make them the objects of cruelty.[16] In a lighthearted tone that the entourage knew was far from joking, an entertainer declared of the king: "Don't you know that all that rains from the sky and all the fruit of the earth are his, that everything of this world is in his possession and in his hands, at his disposal. And even more extraordinary is the order that was given to the Angel of Death: Everything that he says to you, you shall carry it out."[17]

One understands why high dignitaries often wore, hidden beneath their ceremonial clothing, the garments of the dead. Sudden and brutal death could, indeed, arrive without warning. The fear of royal fury terrorized them at the slightest sign of disgrace. A certain poet described a night endured in the throes of agony following the threats of the king an-Nuʾmânn Ibn al-Mundhir. From that moment, "to spend a night of Ibn al-Mundhir," or a night of the king, became an expression that referred to those difficult nights full of fear and suffering.[18]

It was reported that upon his conquest of power and after putting his Omayyad competitors to death, Abû al-ʿAbbâs as-Saffâḥ covered their dying bodies with a rug and called for his midday meal. "He sat on top and began to eat while they were still writhing beneath him. Sated, he

[12] *Aghâni*, XXV, 161.
[13] *Aghâni*, XXV, 156–157.
[14] *Fâʾiq*, III, 272.
[15] Tabari, *Târîkh*, X, 98.
[16] *Aghâni*, XI, 342.
[17] Tabari, *Târîkh*, X, 124.
[18] *Tâj al-ʿArûss*, VII, 518.

said: As far as I recall, I have never eaten a meal that was as beneficial and agreeable to me as this one." It was as if his victims' remains were part of the feast and he was to absorb the life that still was in them. The meal in fact symbolized the irreversible seizure of power. The king acquired the intimate conviction, deep down inside, of their irremediable end and of his victory by throning upon them! Next came the public demonstration: "When he had finished, he said: Drag them by their feet and throw them in the street so that people will curse them dead as they cursed them alive." The chronicler reports that he saw dogs pulling at their feet, nipping their silk trousers. They were abandoned on the ground until the smell became unbearable; then a grave was dug and they were hastily thrown in.[19] Another version reports that the caliph crucified them in the palace gardens and asserted, despite the insupportable stench, that the odor was more pleasing to him than the finest perfume.[20] The display of cadavers as a memento mori was a statement of the king's undisputed and uncontested power. Like so many messages of remission, the display signified to the public how fortunate they were to remain among the living thanks to the clemency of the master.

When al-Mahdi succeeded his father al-Mansûr, he had the storerooms to which he had been given the keys opened: "It was a great vault full of the bodies of people who had been assassinated, with a note affixed to their ears showing their affiliation. They were great in number and included children, young people, adults, and old people. Upon seeing this, al-Mahdi was terrified."[21] This was his inheritance, among so many other storerooms filled with riches of all sorts. A message from the dead king, received at the dawn of a new reign, it was an explicit reference to a fundamental assumption of the monarchy: the death upon which it was based. This message of the king to his entourage, his servants, and his subjects on the relationship of royalty to death was conveyed by the legendary tale that was its genesis.

It again involved an-Nu'mânn, the king who founded the monarchic tradition in popular memory in Arabia. The tale begins with a common incident in the royal house: Two courtiers committed a gaffe that sent the king into a terrible fit of anger, after which he ordered that they immediately be buried alive. He was later seized with regrets and had two buildings constructed for the victims, which according to legend were

[19] *Aghâni*, IV, 341.
[20] *Aghâni*, IV, 346.
[21] Tabari, *Târîkh*, IX, 292.

situated in Kufa near the mausoleum of the imam ʿAli.[22] He then set aside two days each year: one day of good deeds and one day of misfortune. On each of these days he went and sat beside the buildings. The first person who came to him on the day of good deeds was given a gift of great value: one hundred black camels of a rare and highly prized breed. The first person who appeared on the day of misfortune received the head of a skunk before having his throat cut and his blood spread over the mortuary buildings.

The day of life and the day of death, symbolizing both sides of all-powerfulness, sealed the destinies of subjects through chance encounters. The king inflicted death like a fatality external to his own will, like a harmful but inevitable destiny: "I am no longer king if the people contradict my orders."[23] He went so far as to inflict death upon a very close relative on the day of misfortune. He had the sentence carried out and consequently broke the bonds of kinship and friendship that naturally affected human beings. The necessity of keeping his distance from his status as a man loomed large; those close to him, like other servants, were the *qurbân*, or sacrificial offerings. Death was a given in the bond between the king and his subjects.

One day of misfortune, one of the victims showed up "shrouded, anointed, and accompanied by his wailer."[24] Seeing this sign of total submission and the readiness of his subjects to sacrifice themselves to the king, the latter suspended the execution.

It was a suspension of the execution, but not of the sentence – a remission rather than anything else. Death was ever present, and the sword waited to slit the throat of the next person. In fact, by suspending the execution the king gave himself the divine privilege of giving life when he could inflict death. He granted himself the ability to master one's destiny, to decide the time of death. Like God, he was the master of his world. Furthermore, the scenario of the death of the two courtiers at the beginning of the tale is revealing. They were buried alive so that they would realize the extent of their master's power. This procedure established two thresholds, the first illustrating the king's will and his ability to inflict death, and the second ensuring that the royal decision to put them to death was carried out. In the space or interval between the two thresholds, only the king had the power to strike. He held this power for

[22] *Tâj al-ʿArûss*, XX, 12.
[23] *Aghâni*, XXII, 95.
[24] Ibid.

the victims buried under the earth and even more so for the living witnesses.[25] The king thus assumed supreme power; the decision of death, a central attribute of divinity, became his. The earth and the sky henceforth came together in his person.

The royal authority indeed used and fed on this interval. The king, through his pardon, by postponing the date of execution, seized the right of death; he made the privilege to grant remission his own. To postpone the act of giving death was not a human shortcoming, some sort of weakness, but an edict supporting the divinity of the king. Life threatened and then given back was the same as a re-creation; it was like a transfer of power between heaven and earth.

Examples of similar actions by the kings abound. Such was the case between ʿAbdelmalek Ibn Marwân and ʿAmr Ibn Saʾîd Ibn al-ʿÂss: "He spent several years trying to kill him. Once he deferred his death, another time he became angry at him; yet another time he held back and then struck. And he ended up giving him the ultimate blow."[26] The interval, constantly repeated, was the secret of power. The person who was the object of such a threat was called *hâma*, a word that was applied to an old man at the end of his life, to the dying man, and to the lowly individual who received no consideration and was like the living dead, in other words, a ghost.[27] The term illustrates the weakness of the mortal man in the face of the one who controlled his destiny, that is, the king. Thus the subject was continually in the crosshairs.

Thus, regarding kings, the holy Koran insists on this divine ability: "Have you not heard of him who argued with Abraham about his Lord because God had bestowed sovereignty upon him? Abraham said: 'My Lord is He who has the power of life and death.' 'I, too,' replied the other, 'have the power of life and death.'"[28] The term used for "giving life" is *iḥyâʾ*, which in fact means to spare a condemned man from death or to restore life to a barren terrain. This is what Nimrod responded to Abraham. But according to tradition, Nimrod was the first king, which thus puts us in the presence of the fundamental and original conflict with God. Against the royal claims Abraham contrasted the divine power to make the sun rise and set, thus setting forth in a certain way not really a negation of the king's powers, but a spatial delimitation of his abilities.[29]

[25] For the tale in question, see *Aghâni*, XXII, 91–95.
[26] Jâhiz, *Tâj*, 64.
[27] Jâhiz, *Tâj*, 106.
[28] The Koran, 2:258.
[29] Tabari, *Tafsîr*, III, 26–277.

Recall that the kingdom of Alexander extended from where the sun rose to where it set, a spatial extension that evoked the integral power of life and death attributed to God.[30]

The power to give back life was recognized in the kings and even in powerful chiefs, such as the one who saved from death girls whose parents intended to kill them (*maw'ûda*) and bought back captives by paying their ransom.[31] A power lauded by the poets,[32] the king's mastery of the interval extending from the threat of death or a virtual death to actual death endowed him with this extraordinary ability. In addition to the threshold irreversibly crossed when vital functions came to a halt, the authority put into place an initial threshold that was crossed not only by those condemned to death but by all of the king's subjects, who could be led by his sentence to the kingdom of night. The night was indeed a foretaste of death, a threshold crossed each day in daily life.

THE NIGHT, A THRESHOLD FORETELLING DEATH

The night was a crossing of the first threshold. It was a warning, a call to order: "The night is another sign for men. From the night We lift the day – and they are plunged in darkness."[33] In certain Arabic dialects night is called *ghayb*, that is, the invisible, the hidden; the very word names the realm belonging to God, or his mystery. Night was the time of a heavy absence[34]; it surreptitiously introduced the realm of death. The chronicle reports that God created Adam on a Friday and gave life to his head without animating the rest of his body as the day was already drawing to a close. Adam then begged God to hurry before the sun set.[35]

One feared the night. Thus one avoided saying the prayer for the dead at sunset for fear of upsetting their universe.[36] Arab society was concerned, like so many other societies were, with the upheaval of the night. The threshold foretelling its advent was scrutinized and divided into levels. *Al-sadaf*, the first level, was the coming of darkness, after which came *al-malth*, in which there was no more light and which was followed by *malass*.[37] Despite the hopes that were attached to the last rays of light still

[30] Râzi, II, Part I, 139.
[31] *Ichtiqâq*, 239, and *Aghâni*, XXI, 283.
[32] *Mutanabbi*, I, 163.
[33] The Koran, 36:37.
[34] Râzi, IX, Part II, 152.
[35] Râzi, XI, Part II, 148.
[36] Al-Haroui, *Gharîbu al-ḥadîth*, II, 320.
[37] *Tâj al-'Arûss*, III, 267.

bearing life, the intrusion of nocturnal darkness immediately sowed fear and anxiety.[38] The moment of reddening light, or *chafaq*, was compared to the agony of the dead; it was the moment when the sun's final rays extended onto the graves.[39] Indicating a specific moment of hesitation, a threshold held at bay, the word *chafaq* denoted a great fragility when applied to objects, but also, bearing on feelings, suggested a sensitivity and a tenderness like that of departure and separation. The classification as light coming out of redness or whiteness was heavy with uncertainty. It was a moment apart, "a state different from that which preceded it, that is, the light of day and that which it preceded, or the darkness of night."[40] It was the interval between the prayer of the *maghrib*, or the setting of the sun, and that of the *'achâ'*, the moment of fear and upsetting, of entrance into darkness or *'atama*, and furthermore which designated the mediocre. It was also the *ghassiq*, or nightfall, when vision no longer distinguishes anything and when the cold settles in, a meaning of the term in question that makes a clear reference to death. The *ghassaq* was also the eye overflowing with tears, signaling the invasion of the world by darkest night.[41]

The individual was then delivered to the unknown. Arab tribes took their guests' baggage but left them their weapons at night.[42] The fear of darkness was profoundly anchored in one's consciousness. When it occurred with the extraordinary event of an eclipse, the population was terrified. The Prophet called for prayer on that occasion: "There was an eclipse at the time of the Prophet, may God bless and honor him. When it happened he fled, frightened, to the mosque and did not stop praying until the end of the eclipse."[43] Among the rituals of the tribe of Quraysh, when a baby was born at night, it was to be covered with a pot until daybreak for fear of the evil forces connected to darkness. It was reported that this happened when the Prophet came into the world.[44]

The angel Gabriel spoke to the prophet Muhammad at night, pulling him out of sleep, that is, from death to life: "You that are wrapped up in your mantle, keep vigil all night, save for a few hours; half the night, or even less: or a little more – and with measured tone recite the Koran."[45]

[38] *Al-ghabâchîr* is the light that persists in the darkness; *Tâj al-'Arûss*, VII, 292.
[39] *Tâj al-'Arûss*, XIII, 240.
[40] Râzi, XVI, Part I, 99–100.
[41] Râzi, XVI, Part II, 178, and Part I, 15.
[42] *Aghâni*, XXII, 223.
[43] An-Nassâi, *Saḥîh*, 16, 16.
[44] *Ichtiqâq*, 8.
[45] The Koran, 73:1.

At the very beginning of the revelation, believers were supposed to recite their prayers at night before this practice fell into disuse and the five daily prayers were decreed. The individual was alone at night, isolated in the face of the divinity and in total submission to it. This was the perfect interval for communication with the Authority.

The night was synonymous with fear. "By the heaven, and by the nightly visitant!"[46] said the holy text. The nocturnal star was called *at-târiq*, but the term encompassed everything that came out at night, whether a star or anything else. In any case, it never came during the day. Whether it was a bad omen, a forewarning of misfortune, or misfortune itself, people invoked the protection of God against it. The fear was such that the Prophet had advised against arriving at others' homes at night.[47] Houses were kept closed, and the visitor was forced to knock on the door. The term also related to disturbance or to the impure, like water dirtied by the excrement of animals.

The absence of life that surrounded the populations at night was the equivalent of that which occurred in graves. The night was a reminder of submission, an edifying example of the power of life and death. It was like the royal sentence whose execution was constantly postponed. "It is He that claims you back by night, knowing what you have done by day, and then rouses you up to fulfil your allotted span of life,"[48] recalled the supreme master to his creatures. The suspension of the punishment was explicit: "God takes away men's souls upon their death, and the souls of the living during their sleep. Those that are doomed He keeps with Him, and restores the others for a time ordained." The sleeping man was thus stripped of what made him a feeling and intelligent being; he was in the same condition as the dead. Disagreement among exegetes on this state of death during sleep was not limited to questions of details. For some jurisconsults, during sleep God recalled a man's mind and intelligence without touching other vital functions, whereas for others the sleeping man was completely dead.[49] In sleep "feeling spirits leave the visible part [of the body] for the interior. As a result the apparent senses are no longer functional. In the state of sleep, the visible part of the body loses some of its functions, whereas in death the entire body no longer functions. From this comes the parallel between sleep and death and the reason

[46] The Koran, 86:1.
[47] Râzi, XVI, Part I, 115. *At-tarq* or *at-turûq* arrived at night.
[48] The Koran, 6:60; Râzi, XVI, Part II, 7.
[49] *Kachâf*, IV, 126.

why sleep is called death."[50] Sleep was thus a ritual announcing death, a staging in which the master reminded the servant of his forceful presence by annihilating his vital forces, by disarming him prematurely, in a way. The miracle of resurrection that reanimated the body and enabled its departure from sleep arose from divine mastery, as did the king's pardon of the condemned man and his magnanimous regard for his still-living flock. The key to this pardon was the servitude that consisted of exalting the master for his gift of life.[51]

To die was also to be lost, to be recalcitrant to authority, to obedience. Thus heretics were like the dead in spite of their senses that were still alive.[52] The announcement of death in fact took on meaning only through the threat of hell or the promise of paradise after resurrection. Pre-Islamic Arab society believed strongly in resurrection well before the advent of Islam. It was customary to attach a camel directly to a dead person's tomb; the animal was supposed to serve as a mount on the day of resurrection, without which the deceased would be condemned to travel on foot with the multitudes. This mount of the resurrection, or *baliyya*, was intended to die and was therefore given nothing to eat or drink.[53] According to another source, the animal was buried alive in a hole dug for that purpose next to the grave of its master.[54]

In fact, in servitude the relationship to the master carried with it a virtual death. The power and the authority of the dominant one had as a corollary the obliteration of the dominated, the annihilation of his own will, his personality. He became no more than a shadow, an organ of execution. In the *ʿubûdiyya* the servant lived with his own death that he bore within him. Death and servitude were moreover synonymous, no doubt due to the malleability of the debased and completely subjected man.[55]

TO STARVE AND TO FEED

Such a relationship was largely favored by the conditions of the time. In a universe haunted by the threat of hunger, the harshness of the elements, and the uncertainty of fate, death was a fixture of the décor. A rapidly approaching apocalyptic end of the world was not a shocking idea in

[50] Râzi, VII, Part I, 11.
[51] Râzi, I, Part II, 139.
[52] The Koran, 27:80.
[53] Ibn Hichâm, *As-Sîra*, I, 140, note 9; Kûrâ', 31.
[54] *Tâj al-ʿArûss*, XIX, 216.
[55] *Jamharat al-lugha*, I, 299.

the mentality of the time. From the most humble to the most powerful, Arabs feared death, which could come at any moment.[56] "The day of the final judgment will arrive before the white death and the red death appear."[57] A terrible and terrifying death thus constantly watched for its victims. When a storm's wind blew, the Prophet paled and admitted that he "feared the hour," that is, the imminence of death. Death lurked close by for the populations who feared its arrival at any moment.

White death was the unforeseeable death that carried a man off without any sign foreshadowing an imminent end.[58] Red death resulted from a murder in which blood flowed in abundance. In another version, that color came from the visual sensations that the attack of a lion produced, evoking the image of the carnivore jumping on its prey. Such an image was also evoked as black, a color representing the disturbance of sight and the vertigo that took hold of an individual seized with terror.[59]

The fragility of man in these conditions abolished the borders between life and death, which came so close that they blended together in daily life. Such was the experience of a fever. It was the first threshold serving as a foreshadowing of death on earth. It "was an incursion of Gehenna here on earth," as the prophetic tradition reported; it was the door to death.[60] It was God's prison on earth, where he put "his sinning slave." It was thus a demonstration of God's life-and-death power, just as the prison was for the king.[61] With frequent epidemics, death was present in a massive way, and its daily victims were many; it was called the impetuous storm, a term justly used for the plague.[62]

The populations' vulnerability in the face of the elements constituted a powerful advantage for authority, whether celestial or terrestrial. The control over essential riches, including water sources and pasture lands, gave the powerful a means of control over their subjects by holding real power over their survival. Hunger was always one of the favored weapons of masters.[63] "Starve your dog and he will follow you," said a proverb attributed to a king of Ḥimyar, a pitiless tyrant who let his subjects die

[56] *Tâj al-ʿArûss*, XI, 229–230.
[57] *Nihâya*, I, 172–173.
[58] *Fâ'iq*, I, 142.
[59] *Majma ʿal-amthâl*, II, 358.
[60] *Tâj al-ʿArûss*, XVI, 178.
[61] *Fâ'iq*, II, 90.
[62] *Jamharat al-lugha*, I, 463.
[63] Tabari, *Tafsîr*, IX, 235.

of hunger.[64] Times were indeed difficult. Those who were in a position to have two meals a day were already living in luxury![65]

Kings were acutely aware of the strategic role played by their mastery of the cycle of production and distribution of goods. Appointed by the king, Joseph advised him: "It is your right to keep food in storerooms. Then people will come to you from everywhere to buy it, and you will amass riches like no one before you. Thus he sold food to the populations of Egypt during the years of drought, for money during the first year, according to legend, for jewels the second, then for animals, then for their furniture and property, until they no longer had anything to exchange except their own bodies. He then made them his slaves."[66] The mechanism has been in place since the dawn of time. The chronicle reports that the first king on earth, Nimrod, asserted his authority through his ability to feed, that is, to give life. While selling his grain he questioned the populations: "Who is your God? They responded: You."[67] Servitude was the prerogative of the one who dispensed food and shelter.

The well-advised servant was like the camel in a pen: he was kept where he was assured of having something to eat.[68] To assure one's vital needs was a sure means of enslavement. Mo'âwiyya, speaking to Husayn, son of the caliph 'Ali, who was considered the most noble of all: "I scarcely clothed you and I did not humiliate you." To clothe here obviously means to cover nakedness, which meant weakness in the language of the time, thus rendering the recipient beholden to servile obedience.[69]

To feed was one of the most important signs of nobility in Arabia. Arabs called the lord who fed the surrounding populations "the great bowl."[70] The great poet Labîd promised to feed people as long as the wind blew in times of cold and drought. He placed two giant vats at the disposition of the poor of his clan, from which he earned the reputation as "feeder of the wind." Rare were the generous few who had the right to such a name.[71]

The reputation of a great house was measured by the size of its ecuelles and by their provisioning in moments of strong winds and great fear. The

[64] *Majma 'al-amthâl*, I, 220.
[65] *Kachâf*, III, 26.
[66] *Kachâf*, II, 464.
[67] Tabari, *Tafsîr*, III, 27.
[68] *Nihâya*, III, 250.
[69] *Nihâya*, II, 92.
[70] *Nihâya*, I, 280.
[71] *Labîd*, 168.

poet sings this theme to glorify his lineage; he describes the starving populations appeasing their hunger, prostrated before the bowls "as in prayer before a divinity."[72] We can understand how the rich powers who were so inclined thus consolidated their position: "Al-Mughîra – another great one – placed bowls along the roads and among the tribes, thus giving the populations something to eat."[73]

To feed in such a context was to save from death. The great feeders were recognized as sources of life, *manâ'ich*, or "resuscitators," to use the term of the time.[74] Having nothing left, a man led his wife and children to the edges of a royal encampment and said to them: "Stay here near the king; something will come from his bounty while you wait for me to return."[75] Chronic difficulties and the deprivation they left in their wake, the constant threat of death in places that life seemed to abandon, pushed populations to throw themselves at the feet of kings, to submit themselves avidly to their authority. Al-Farazdaq sings in honor of the caliph: "Toward you, commander of believers, the worries of need and our wandering in the great solitudes have directed us."[76]

The king's nourishing function, vital and direct in the early phases of the court, consisted of providing for his entourage and his followers and is clearly connected to the names applied to the land granted to the servants. Thus *ukl*, or eating,[77] or *tu'ma*, synonymous with food, designated the conceded regions; the concession of a part of the *kharâj*, or land tax, also bore that name.[78] Moreover the *rizq*, or revenue, that is, the means of subsistence, was called *tu'ma*. God was indeed the Dispenser (*ar-Razzâq*).

The bloody tyrant al-Hajjâj gave his people abundant food to eat: "Every day he served a thousand tables. On each one there was *tharîd*, half a sheep roasted on a spit, and fresh fish. He was carried on his litter among the guests and asked about people's problems.... Servants poured them water, honey, and whey."[79] A certain lord, whom the Arabs called God, sacrificed "thousands of animals and distributed thousands of tunics" during the great annual feast.[80] The chronicle speaks of the huge

72 *Naqâ'id*, II, 15.
73 *Aghâni*, XVI, 295.
74 *Al-Akhṭal*, 381.
75 *Aghâni*, XVIII, 255.
76 *Naqâ'id*, II, 10.
77 *Naqâ'id*, I, 117 and 207.
78 *Tâj al-'Arûss*, XVII, 437–438.
79 *Al-Kâmil*, I, 208.
80 Ibn Hichâm, *As-Sîra*, I, 77, note 2.

palace by the name of *al-khawarnaq*, a term that originally designated eating and drinking, thus making them reemerge as primordial redistributive functions of the king.[81] These functions were the object of great competition among the lords who provided nourishment.[82]

Times were difficult. Famines were terrible, and their many names highlight their atrocity. One was the *makmasa*, or deprivation that left people in a skeletal state. There was also *al-ḥâtûm*, or terrible year, which destroyed everything and gave its name to one of the doors of hell.[83] There was the year of ashes, so named because seeds, trees, and palms were burned and reduced to ashes,[84] creating a sick and desolate earth, devoid of life and in which no movement could be discerned, like an immobile world in suffocating heat.[85] There were moments of great fear when individuals were reduced to eating carrion.[86] It was an ambiance of apocalypse, to be sure, where the macabre reigned and people were sent into despair. Burning hunger and need made death seem preferable. Even in the heart of the Prophet's tribe, families ruined by famine went to a desolate place, closed themselves up in a tent, and prepared to die.[87] Death thus appeared as a choice forced upon them by the elements. Thus many newborns, having barely come into the world, were sacrificed in such circumstances. The midwife carried out their "drowning," to use the expression of the time, *at-taghrîq*, by allowing them to absorb the amniotic fluid.[88]

Fear of the day of resurrection was not a pure image invented from scratch by the prophecy; it came from the familiar language of the world below. *Al-ḥachr* was the assemblage engraved in the collective memory of a population confronted with poverty and need. During great catastrophes when droughts wiped out the herds, populations moved in waves toward the cities that were the seats of power, seeking food either sold or distributed by the kings. *Al-ḥachr*, which in the holy text was the name of the Resurrection, took on its meaning from those images of populations haunted by imminent death, approaching to bend their knees before the authority.[89]

[81] *Tâj al-'Arûss*, XIII, 113.
[82] *Aghâni*, XXI, 285; see the tale on this subject.
[83] *Tâj al-'Arûss*, XVI, 171.
[84] Al-Haroui, *Gharîbu al-ḥadîth*, II, 5.
[85] *Al-Akhṭal*, 39.
[86] Râzi, X, Part II, 103.
[87] Râzi, XVI, Part II, 100.
[88] *Tâj al-'Arûss*, XIII, 373.
[89] *Lissân*, IV, 191.

Years of suffering were perceived as so many punishments: "Wait for the day when the sky will pour down palpable smoke, enveloping mankind: a woeful scourge."[90] Following a curse by Muhammad against his tribe, the Quraysh, misfortune struck his people:

> Then the rain ceased and the earth was dry. The famine was so severe among the Quraysh that they ate bones, dogs, and carrion. The people were so strongly wracked by hunger that they saw smoke veiling the sky.... In fact, that smoke was the darkness in their eyes caused by starvation. Ibn Qutayba has proposed two different commentaries on the smoke in question. First, during the years of drought, the earth dried out from the absence of rain, causing dust to rise up in great quantities and darken the sky as though it were filled with smoke. One henceforth called a drought-filled year the dusty one. Second, Arabs called misfortune "smoke" ... because in a situation of great fear and weakness, man's view is darkened and he sees the world as filled with smoke. But there is another commentary on smoke. It tells of the smoke that will appear on the earth as a sign of the Resurrection.[91]

We can see the extent to which natural difficulties and obedience were connected in the mentalities of the period. These mentalities made the populations more inclined to submit.[92] The desert and suffering seemed to provide the ideal setting for the perfection of mastery, at the birth of God. The Prophet constantly called people to order and warned against difficult times. "If only you knew," he said, "what dusty hunger and red death there will be among the people."[93] The commentator is explicit: "Difficult times softened the heart and turned heads toward God."[94] The verb "to soften" here translates *taraqqaqa*, a derivative of *riq*, that is, slavery!

This is because poverty and need debased people and made them potential slaves. "God, protect me from poverty, precariousness, and humiliation,"[95] the Prophet said. To experience poverty was like death: "'Praise be to God who gave me life again after poverty,' said a man."[96] Need unceremoniously led to servility. Poverty annihilated the individual, landed him powerless on the ground due to hunger (*mublit*, *muflaj*), stuck him in the dust to the point of bearing its name (*matraba* for poverty),

[90] The Koran, 44:10.
[91] Râzi, XIV, Part I, 7.
[92] *Kachâf*, II, 139.
[93] *Nihâya*, III, 337.
[94] Râzi, VII, Part II, 175.
[95] An-Nassâî, *Saḥîḥ*, XIV, and XV, 50.
[96] Idem.

and reduced him to nothingness (*'adam*).[97] Servitude ended these problems and gave back life after one crossed the necessary threshold. One can measure how important servitude was by looking at the death and fear that it inspired. Look at the earth, in a state of humiliation, reported the chronicle, stripped bare in the autumn and desperate until God sends rain that covers it with grass and flowers: "God sends forth the winds which set the clouds in motion. We drive them on to some dead land and give fresh life to the earth after it has died."[98] Authority took advantage of that miracle of life by framing the multiple thresholds as so many signs and sermons: night, illness, famine, the anger of the elements, and the need for survival. The heavens and the earth made use of them. Within this framework, among the privileges that supported the king's ability to give life, prison was an essential piece; it made him the condemned man's only recourse.

THE PRISON: A NEW INSTITUTION?

Al-ḥaddâd was the doorkeeper, the jailer. He was foremost the one who forbid, punished, and deprived of freedom, the word having the same etymology as *ḥudûd* or punishment in Islam.[99] In fact, in the beginning punishment par excellence consisted of holding someone in anticipation of torture. And escape was highly unlikely. Placed under arrest, the prisoner had few illusions about his fate. The word *as-sabr*, which commonly designates watching, waiting, and resignation, was synonymous with imprisonment and more precisely with the corridor to death. It applied to anything that was kept, and today it means the preservation of food for later consumption. It includes the deprivation of freedom and constraint, particularly by chaining.[100]

To imprison someone in order to force him to swear an oath was called "the oath of the guard." The term applied to captives as well as to prisoners condemned to execution or to a slow death in what took the place of a cell.[101] It meant "that the man was taken captive and was later executed. He was not killed by treachery or ruse, but was taken without a guarantee for his safety."[102] The term was applied to various situations,

[97] *Kitâb al-alfâdh*, 16–18.
[98] The Koran, 35:9; Râzi, IX, Part I, 14–15.
[99] *Jamhara*, 95.
[100] *Lissân*, IV, 438. The condemned was called *masbûr* and *sabûra*.
[101] Al-Haroui, *Gharîbu al-ḥadîth*, I, 157; *Siḥaḥ*, II, 393.
[102] Al-Haroui, *Gharîbu al-ḥadîth*, II, 56.

all of which ended in death. Thus one called a person whose throat had been cut *sabran*,[103] that is, after a period of incarceration under a watchful guard, or one spoke of a captive of the battle of Badr in the time of the Prophet, who was "kept to be executed."[104] The term was applied to those who were chained up as prisoners and condemned to die.[105] The term was also used for animals who were kept penned up for one reason or another.[106] If originally it meant "a stay in prison until being put to death," it was later applied to the sentence given by the judge.[107] For in the beginning it was indeed a decision, the decision to inflict death, the term covering any person killed except in battle or by mistake.[108] Upon his conquest of Mecca, the Prophet enjoined that no members of his tribe should henceforth be subject to such a condemnation: "As of today, no Quraysh will be killed *sabran*."[109] The practice nevertheless continued and was still found under the Omayyad reign.[110] The chronicle reports that under the governorship of al-Hajjâj, a listing of *sabran* deaths, that is, those condemned to death, amounted to 120,000 individuals![111]

The term eloquently expresses the authoritarian nature of incarceration. It conveys the prince's power to make one wait, to force resignation, to deliver to death while leaving a hope for life. The king condemned as a powerful tyrant, at the same time using duration to create the illusion of being a magnanimous prince. Among the ninety-nine beautiful names for the many attributes of the divine, God was *as-Sabûr*, the one who knew how to make one wait by keeping his sword suspended, the sword that could inflict death at any moment while showing no hurry to do so.[112] Prison was the fearsome weapon of the kings. It was their instrument of the mastery of death and, at the same time, the mastery of people's lives.

Prisons were very basic in the beginning, resembling the places where animals were kept, and they even had the same name: *maḥbas*. This similarity no doubt stressed the temporary nature of the imprisonment, the prisoner often being, in the beginning, a foreign captive whose destiny was

[103] Tabari, *Târîkh*, III, 233.
[104] *Aghâni*, I, 23.
[105] *Aghâni*, III, 64.
[106] Kazimirsky, I, 1305.
[107] *Fâ'iq*, II, 242 and 276.
[108] *'Iqd*, III, 265.
[109] *Nihâya*, IV, 13.
[110] Tabari, *Târîkh*, VI, 147.
[111] *'Iqd*, V, 46.
[112] *Lissân*, IV, 437.

decided without much delay after his capture. The basic aspect was nevertheless counteracted by the fact that the captives were typically chained. The same name was used for the jailer and for the blacksmith belonging to a guild of artisans who worked over fire and thus had the dirtiest faces, evoking the watchmen of hell.[113] The prisoner was, for his part, synonymous with the bound. He was called the chained one, *al-makbûl*, from *kabl*, or chain, which evokes the very active participation of the blacksmith, suggesting that true guarding depended on the sureness of the chaining.[114] Chains were so integral to the life of the prisoner that the poet al-Akhtal, incarcerated, wrote, regarding his family: "Inform them, if you see them, that the irons, at nightfall, sing for me,"[115] that is, make their dull clanking sound, the song of prison life! The sound of chains has left its imprint in modern language. Arrest by the forces of order is called, in current language, *i'tiqâl*, in other words, the act of binding or chaining. Indeed, in ancient Arab society, on the occasion of a murder, those close to the murderer paid a ransom in the form of livestock. The animals were led into the house of the victim and were held there instead of the murderer. Even if ransoms were later paid in money, the initial formula of payment definitively marked that compensation. It gave its name both to the family of the murderer and to the payment itself, *al-'âqila*, the origin of which was "binding," or *'iqâl*.[116]

In fact, imprisonment could take place in various locations. Prisoners could be held outdoors, at the mercy of the sun's harsh rays. The parallel with hell was striking, "We have made Hell a prison-house for the unbelievers,"[117] stressed the Koran. But prisons could also be dark holes that the sun never reached. Those prisons were more elaborate and meant to last. Or prisons could be simple wells. Al-Hutay'a, a cursed poet, imploring the caliph 'Omar to take pity on the fate of his abandoned children and release him, said to him: "You have thrown their protector into a dark well."[118] Likewise, prisons could consist of tunnels dug into the ground or of buildings closed off from the light and called *al-mudammass*.[119] But the prison was also the house or the palace itself.[120] Thus we get *maqsûra*,

[113] *Nihâya*, I, 353.
[114] *Jamhara*, 476, and *Tâj al-'Arûss*, IV, 411; al-Haroui, *Gharîbu al-ḥadîth*, II, 119.
[115] Al-Akhtal, 381.
[116] *Mu'jam al-'Asma'î*, 283.
[117] The Koran, 17:8.
[118] *Al-Hutay'a*, Ibn Sikkite, 192.
[119] *Jamhara*, 648.
[120] The Koran, 55:72.

or a small house where women were kept, which gives us the concubine by the same name.[121]

According to the chronicle, there was no building reserved specifically for prisoners in the time of the Prophet and even until the reign of the caliph ʿOmar. Captives were held, depending on the circumstances, in the mosque, in an animal pen, or in an underground place. The prophet Muhammad ordered imprisonments without specifying the modalities or the places.[122] The intent to establish a penal institution did appear symbolically with the conquest of Mecca and the affirmation of the Prophet's message. It is reported that ʿOmar acquired, at his own expense, a place for that purpose[123] – a prison house, adds a commentator.[124] It is even specified that he paid four thousand dirhams to the owners.[125] Penitentiary establishments already existed at the time of ʿOthmân. One was noted on the occasion of a visit by the caliph to the prisoners, an apparently turbulent visit during which a prisoner attempted to stab him, which suggests a primitive organization with striking inefficiency.[126] There are similar accounts, such as the case of a prisoner "who remained locked up until he was stricken with a stomach illness. He became putrid and died in the prison of ʿOthmân."[127] Also mentioned is an establishment in Kufa, outside the city walls, the management of which was conferred to a Christian, which provides further evidence of the novelty of the institution, which was still gaining momentum at the time and must have been on a par with the nascent state.[128] It has been established, in any case, that the caliph ʿOthmân was the first to name a chief of police, which goes along with the institutionalization of a security system.[129] It is likely, however, that at this time it remained a shaky institution rather than a stable establishment. Most sources attribute the construction of the first prison of the nascent Muslim state to the caliph ʿAli; he called it *Nâfiʾ*, or The Useful. It was, however, a building of doubtful efficacy; with bars made of reeds, it offered so little resistance to the prisoners that they escaped without difficulty. He had another built in Kufa by the name of

[121] *Jamhara*, 743.
[122] *Bahjat al-majâliss*, III, 107.
[123] Râzi, XII, Part II, 22.
[124] *Kachâf*, III, 148.
[125] Az-Zamakhchari, *Al-Fâiq fi gharîbi al-ḥadith*, II, 416.
[126] *Naqâʾid*, I, 162.
[127] *Naqâʾid*, I, 162.
[128] *Aghâni*, V, 156.
[129] *ʿIqd*, IV, 264.

al-Mukhayass, or place of degradation and debasement.[130] More a matter of the institution than of the building itself, the state prison thus made its appearance, breaking with the captive-holding pens that by the very status of their residents were not meant to last.

To tell the truth, the captives' fate was unenviable, as the death of many of them was commonplace at the time. One paid little attention to their fate if it seemed unlikely that their families would buy them back or if their sale was not expected to bring much profit. The tale of a captive who was brought trembling before the Prophet and then was killed by mistake due to an incorrect interpretation of the instructions given is enlightening in this regard.[131] The available descriptions and eyewitness accounts of captives show their pitiable condition. They were condemned to the elements, exposed to the sun, dehydrated, and most often reduced to the condition of domestic animals Their hands and feet were tied with wet leather cords that, when dry, cut into the skin, causing it to become inflamed and infected.[132] With the expansion of the empire under the caliphate of ʿOmar, the use of iron chains became more widespread.[133] Captives condemned to death were marked on the arm with saffron or other dyes having a base of saffron.[134] They were smothered to death, or more elaborate means were used to kill them, such as burning them en masse.[135]

Their disastrous psychological state was worsened by chronic malnutrition. The captive suffered endlessly, slept little, and was stricken with illnesses characteristic of his condition, the signs of which were similar to the condition of a dying man and were called *al-ʿalaz*. The symptoms were "worrying that deprived him of sleep, a great weakness, fear, anxiety, agitation, and convulsions."[136] At the advent of Islam, captives were to be fed by canonic alms while waiting for their fate to be decided: death, liberation, or slavery might await them, but most often they ended up in servitude.

THE PRINCE'S ROLE

With the Omayyads, the power of the state was consolidated, and the repressive structures were expanded and perfected. Far from the first

130 *Jamharat rasâʾil al-ʿArab*, IV, 183.
131 *Jamhara*, 113.
132 Ibid.
133 *ʿIqd*, I, 65.
134 *Majma ʿal-amthâl*, I, 196.
135 *Tâj al-ʿArûss*, XI, 124, and *Ichtiqâq*, 344.
136 *Tâj al-ʿArûss*, VIII, 10.

prisons constructed in haste, it was now more a question of fortresses.[137] The incarcerated population reached its peak, as seen in the numbers occasionally gleaned from the chronicle. Upon the death of al-Hajjâj, some eighty thousand prisoners were freed from his prisons in a single day.[138] Another source suggests thirty-three thousand prisoners not condemned to death.[139] These numbers are corroborated by the fact that the condemned usually went to prison without any hope of liberation, which depended on the goodwill of the prince and the ability of the prisoner's family to intercede as required. In any case, the incarcerated population was considerable.

The new canonical legislation encountered many obstacles. The still solid tribal social structure did not facilitate the centralization of justice by the reigning power. Furthermore, the slave institution opposed for many reasons the government's application of penalties to slaves, preferring, following its own logic, that this role fall to masters judged more legitimate.[140] In the view of a state that intended to extract the individual from other tribal, clan, familial, and enslaving powers, the application of such punishment could have in reality only an ideological and publicizing effect. The assertion of the state's authority came through its strong hold over the society and its principal networks, notably through the recognition of the prince's power over life and death. More than any other punishment, imprisonment was the most efficacious means of influence in that direction. The judge was marginalized in such a system. To imprison was an act of the prince, whose power indeed consisted of the uncertainty he left to hover over the condemned and bring the prisoner's family to their knees. His wrath and his mercy determined the length of incarceration, prolonging it indefinitely or bringing it to a swift end. Without his mastery over the thresholds, the king was no longer a king.

Obviously this discussion leaves some room for doubt concerning this fearful power. In fact, from time to time, especially during a change in regime, when kings sent their regional chiefs long letters filled with directives, advice, and lectures, a certain concern for the legality of the governors' actions emerged. Thus in one such letter, the governor is instructed to draw up an act of liberation for each prisoner, taking care to note his identity and to document the reasons that led to his being freed. It was

137 *Fâ'iq*, II, 124.
138 *Al-Kâmil*, II, 534.
139 *'Iqd*, III, 484.
140 Râzi, VI, Part I, 180, and IX, Part I, 107.

also recommended to proceed with inspections of the prisons, note the prisoners' condition, find out the reasons for their incarceration, try to free those whose imprisonment should end, and keep those who should stay forever. The governor was supposed to consult with competent jurisconsults on their account and consequently to apply the punishments dictated by the law.[141] Similar recommendations, made at the beginning of a reign, attested, in reality, more to the weak hold of the judges on a penal system completely controlled by the king's agents than to a true concern for legalization.

The length of incarceration did not seem to be the object of particular attention. To go to prison did not necessarily mean one would leave it. Hârûn ar-Rachîd's chief of police, having seen the caliph accede to his intercession on a prisoner's behalf, had second thoughts and replied: "If you have had him put in prison, O commander of believers, I do not see how it is fitting that he be freed in the short term."[142] The principle was to "educate," to bring the wandering sheep back to the right path, and it fell to the prince to determine, at his convenience, the appropriate moment for release.

Tribal practices were moreover still present in the management of imprisonment. Intercessions were customary; the only difference was that they were inscribed in the affirmation of royal all-powerfulness that shifted between mercy and the threat of death. Money could help to hasten an otherwise improbable release.[143]

A number of caliphs, including Sulaymân Ibn ʿAbdelmalek as well as his successor ʿOmar Ibn ʿAbdelʾaziz, gave edicts, at the beginning of their reign, for a general pardon.[144] The prince marked his ascension to power with the gift of life, which gave proof of his clemency toward his subjects. In reality, in this way he announced his right over life and death. Authority could not only prolong the length of incarceration at will; it was also able, if it saw fit, to coldly execute prisoners without any procedure being followed. Many sources mention killings that took place during the night in numerous establishments.[145]

Beginning with the orthodox caliphs, a custom came into being that consisted of putting every suspect into prison for a few days before presenting him to the governor.[146] Such a practice seemed to have been

141 *Jamharat rasâʾil al-ʿArab*, IV, 294.
142 Tabari, *Târîkh*, X, 97.
143 *ʿIqd*, IV, 390.
144 *ʿIqd*, IV, 387–389.
145 *ʿIqd*, IV, 436.
146 Baladhuri, 275.

instituted to avoid quick executions accompanying a conquest. This reaction by the caliph ʿOmar following the execution of an apostate is reported: "You could have locked him up in a house and thrown him bread for three days; he might have perhaps confessed.... God be my witness, I neither ordered nor approved that."[147] Such a statement confirms the absence of a penitentiary establishment at the time and the summary justice that sometimes escaped the central power itself. But the prison was very quickly asserted as a necessity for the new state. Punishments, or *hudûd*, such as amputation, gave way to incarceration, a clearly more efficient method of social control. Even if society had not broken with ancient practices such as crucifixion, prison imposed itself as a solution without closing the way to any other recourse. Thus, regarding robbers and thieves, who would have been crucified, killed, or sent into exile, the caliph ʿOmar Ibn ʿAbdelʾaziz ordered one of his agents: "If the proof of what they are accused of is established, put iron chains around their necks and make them disappear, while naming the prison indicated for that end."[148] Exile, considered very harsh and undesirable,[149] and which had great significance with the tribes, lost its intensity with the new social structures. The expansion of the empire stripped it of its meaning; exiling lost its punitive value in a world that was now larger and offered recourses other than the tribe. As for prison, by guaranteeing isolation it offered a convenient and preferred place of exile. With it, and for useful purposes, authority kept the prisoner within reach.

Among the official prisons, most frequently mentioned are those of Sijn ʿArim (Zayd ʿArim).[150] Muhammad Ibn al-Hanîfa was imprisoned there. The establishment was founded by ʿAbdallah Ibn Zoubayr; then it passed into the hands of al-Hajjâj. In his dictionary, Yâqût is not sure of its location and leans toward Tâʾif.[151] Its name came from a slave of ʿOmar Ibn Zubayr, called ʿÂrim, who was imprisoned with his master and for whom had been constructed a special cell of four square cubits, where he was locked up with other prisoners until their death.[152] Other establishments were no less famous: Sijn Bab Châm in Baghdad,[153] Sijn Ibn

[147] *Fâʾiq*, III, 61.
[148] Tabari, *Tafsîr*, IV, 559.
[149] *Kachâf*, I, 615. Zamakhchari gives the names of the places of exile.
[150] Tabari, *Târîkh*, VI, 179.
[151] *Aghâni*, IX, 21.
[152] Baladhuri, 315.
[153] Tabari, *Târîkh*, XII, 35.

Mâlik in the same city,[154] and the Mutbaq near Bab Châm, which will be discussed below.[155] A prison used only for women is also mentioned.[156]

The king was the absolute master of his prison and his prisoners. In tales reported by the chronicle, there was very little concern for legality. It was an instrument of his power and placed him in the godlike ranks through the right of life and death that it granted him. A weapon par excellence of forced servitude, it effectively compensated for the subtleties of the ideology.

A prisoner wrote to Hârûn ar-Rachîd:

> "You have neglected my affair, O commander of believers, shunned my memory, and paid little attention to my arguments and my repentance. I am at the end, exhausted by all prejudice of your prison." The caliph's response is enlightening: "By taking the path of ignorance you have merited death. Your rebellion against me and against yourself led you from the opulence of the world to a tomb of the living. He who ignores the recognition of benefit sees his endurance reduced. So accept the consequences of your sins and the harm caused by your errors.... If you are determined to put an end to your rebellion and have chosen to obey me and to regret your insubordination, then you may continue to hope for a pardon from me."[157]

There was no question of proof or of legal procedure, and even less of the authority of the judge. The text refers to the bond between master and servant and to the first threshold leading to death; we are in the arcana of servitude.

Prison was indeed the tomb that the great caliph clearly mentions. In the confrontation between God and the king, the power over life and death was indeed the aspect in question. In his response to the divine challenge, Nimrod gives proof of his ability to give life by freeing a prisoner.[158] For this reason, prison was the punishment preferred over all others, for the delay it allowed before the death sentence was carried out, a delay that delighted the king who based his majesty on it, like the one Jâhiz mentions, whose jailer submits to him a macabre list of the dead.[159] The caliph Marwân Ibn al-Hakam wisely advised his son not to slit throats too quickly in anger, noting that "the one who first put prisons

[154] Tabari, *Târîkh*, XI, 203.
[155] *Aghâni*, XX, 192, and *Tâj al-'Arûss*, XIII, 288.
[156] Tabari, *Târîkh*, XI, 255.
[157] *Jamharat rasâ'il al-'Arab*, III, 442.
[158] Râzi, IV, Part I, 34.
[159] *Bayân*, 313.

in place was merciful and knew how to wait."[160] For behind that wait, which only appeared to be clemency, shone the sharp edge of the sword. That sword formed the basis for royal authority, which was expressed in the first prisons by the importance granted to the well, continued even by the modern powers because of its unequaled symbolic power. The mattamore, an underground storehouse, derives its sound from *ṭamara*, which quite simply means "to bury."[161] The well in fact symbolized a tomb, its depth instilling a distance whose verticality sealed the evidence of the royal highness and clearly emphasized the contrast between light and darkness, between white and black, between noble and servile. In many respects the divine model seems, here, to be based on the model of a king whose mighty force has not been disproven. The masters of language teach us that among the ancient Arabs, a very deep well was called *Jahannam*, the word used most often to designate hell.[162] The jailers were like those described in the sacred text as "rude and violent,"[163] which recalls the king an-Nu'mânn's jailer 'Iqabb, whose very name means short, corpulent, and of great coarseness.[164] The prince's control of the prison was so essential to the exercise of his power that one found, in addition to the "official prisons," others that were completely out of view, private prisons in a certain sense.

The private prison was still in use. The family home itself could be used as a space of confinement in some cases, for neither imprisonment nor the application of punishment was yet an exclusive monopoly of the public powers. Thus the case of the adulterous wife was an example of this: "If any of your women commit a lewd act, call in four witnesses from among yourselves against them; if they testify to their guilt, confine [the guilty ones] to their houses till death overtakes them."[165] The private prison was inscribed in the family sphere and more precisely in the conjugal framework, where the husband's power was equivalent to that of a master. Legislation would subsequently abolish imprisonment in favor of stoning and exile.[166]

In spite of the institutionalization of the prison, which depended in large part on monarchic will, alongside official and recognized prisons

[160] *'Iqd*, I, 591.
[161] *Tâj al-'Arûss*, VII, 144.
[162] Râzi, VIII, Part II, 96; on the term and its origins, *Tâj al-'Arûss*, XVI, 125.
[163] The Koran, 66:6.
[164] *Tâj al-'Arûss*, II, 260.
[165] The Koran, 4:15.
[166] Râzi, VI, Part I, 180.

there existed improvised prisons that seemed to prolong the tradition of private prisons. Some still existed under the Omayyad dynasty.[167] As for the caliphs, they used this practice for high-stakes prisoners, such as pretenders and competitors whose support they wished to cut off by keeping them in absolute secret.

The caliphs took care to lock up these people near them. Thus the pretender locked up in Samana, in the house of Masrû in a narrow cell measuring two cubits by three. He stayed there three days before being transferred to a more spacious location. A certain prestigious chief in the army of the caliph al-Mu'tasim was locked up in al-Jawssaq. Care was taken to construct especially for him a cell at the top of the palace that was called the pearl. It resembled a lighthouse with its center just large enough to hold the prisoner in a seated position.[168]

The al-Jawssaq palace was an example of the prince's privatization of incarceration.[169] It was an integrated complex that included the king's living quarters, the treasury, close servants, the guard, and the prison for high-risk figures. The royal power watched over everything.[170] The word *qasr*, or palace, meant oppression and domination, and it enclosed people judged to be minors, most notably women.[171] Cases of the imprisonment of familiars were mentioned under the reign of al-Mansûr. A concubine wearing a tunic of wool fastened tightly at the neck was locked up for an entire month in dark latrines and was fed bread, water, and salt that were pushed under the door.[172] On a structural level, the carceral model had not yet definitively broken with the family prison, that of the warlords. They were still found, in keeping with the strict sense of the term, in the homes of the great with their private guard.[173] Power was still constrained by a strongly segmented society with its dissentions, alliances, and misalliances. The rupture of the model occurred equally on the level of the central power as on the regional level.[174] It also denoted the system's finality and its mode of functioning, which consisted of a summary justice entirely devoted to the service of the prince, who held it firmly in

167 *Al-Akhtal*, 3, note 3.
168 Tabari, *Târîkh*, XI, 118.
169 On this place see Yâqût, *Mu'jam al-buldân*, II, 214.
170 Tabari, *Târîkh*, XII, 17.
171 *Tâj al-'Arûss*, VII, 401.
172 *Aghâni*, XXI, 79.
173 Tabari, *Târîkh*, XII, 203.
174 Tabari, *Târîkh*, XII, 18.

his hands without the judge being able to intervene except in a marginal way of little consequence.[175]

The "political prisoners," who were pretenders and close figures in disgrace, were subjected to the most severe treatment. Thus a man close to the Abbasid caliph al-Mahdi was sent to prison to die. The caliph had in fact ordered "to incarcerate him in Mutbaq and for no one to speak to him any more." The individual in question himself reported: "I was then incarcerated. They chose a well for me and lowered me into it. I stayed there a long time without knowing how many days had passed. My vision was affected, and my hair grew so long that it came to resemble that of animals."[176] Released when the following reign came into power, he died shortly afterward.

Isolation was standard in those cases. Thus in the prison of the *Zanâdiqa* (free thinkers), where one also found great men in disgrace, the poet Salâḥ Ibn ʿAbd al-Qudûss, incarcerated and forgotten in prison, wrote: "We left the world and have no contact with men – we belong neither to the living nor to the dead. When the jailer visits us for some reason, we are stunned and say: he comes to us from the world."[177]

Prisons made to order for great servants practically constituted a custom. One great servant was closed up "in a cell and walled in. Each day he was thrown some bread and a cup of water."[178] To plunge the disgraced one into a silence that announced his coming death particularly satisfied the prince's desire for all-powerfulness. To isolate the prisoner, deprive him of basic necessities, and wear him down both psychologically and physically emphasized his solitude, setting him apart from others, like the sinner before God on resurrection day. To starve the prisoner, then give food in abundance, and then later deprive the prisoner of water to the point of death was a common practice.[179] Locking one up in a well increased the distance from the king, who became untouchable in his height except through a supplication curiously similar to prayer. Furthermore, wells were dug with small openings just large enough to throw in a minimum amount of food. In some cases, after that long torture the wells were flooded.[180]

175 Tabari, *Târîkh*, XI, 155.
176 Tabari, *Târîkh*, X, 8.
177 Râzi, VI, Part I, 171.
178 Tabari, *Târîkh*, XI, 100–101.
179 Tabari, *Târîkh*, XI, 100.
180 Tabari, *Târîkh*, XI, 101.

For those close to the king, the reversal of one's situation was terrible. The descent into hell could prove endless. A former vizier in disgrace was stripped of his property and thrown into prison. For the first few days he was left free to move; then came the order to put him in chains. He then refused to eat and no longer consumed anything. He sat devastated in his cell and cried all the time, speaking very little and often meditating. He stayed like that for several days; then he was forced to stay awake, his jailers withholding sleep by poking him repeatedly with a large needle. This treatment continued for a day and a night, after which he was allowed to sleep. When he awoke, he asked for grapes and other fruit, which were brought to him. He ate and then was again deprived of sleep. Then he was put into a large wooden receptacle filled with nails. After that, having received no further news, we do not know whether he died there or was beaten to death. In the case of such figures, the effect of public demonstration was considered very important. Their bodies were crucified and then displayed on bridges, sometimes with the head and torso displayed separately for greater effect.

Public exhibition posed some "technical" problems that were difficult to resolve, particularly in relation to the preparation of bodies. The case of a certain notable is particularly enlightening on this subject, the head having already reached an advanced stage of decomposition. "They asked for someone to cut up the meat [*sic*] and take out the ocular globe and all the internal contents [between the skull and the neck]. No volunteer was found. The butchers had fled. They asked among the members of a sect who were in prison, *al-kharramiya*, or throat slitters, but no one dared except for a worker in the new prison by the name of Sahl Ibn al-Sa'di. He undertook to remove the brains and the eyes and did everything by hand. Then he washed the head and put it in cotton. He put plant essences, musk, and camphor in it."[181] In the face of such situations, one can understand that prisoners did not hesitate to escape if the occasion arose.

ESCAPE, A COMMON PRACTICE

Frequent were the attempts to escape. Some of them were massive. The processes varied and drew from the classic methods found just about everywhere. Digging tunnels, in spite of the effort it required, was common.[182] It was often accomplished through family solidarity or the

[181] Tabari, *Târîkh*, XI, 212.
[182] Tabari, *Târîkh*, IX, 299.

intervention of men who worked on the prisoner's behalf. Such was the case of one notable, a certain Ibn Husayn, who ordered his slaves to dig a tunnel that ended under his bed. He took flight at night, horses having been posted for that purpose at the other end of the tunnel.[183] Other similar cases are pointed out.[184]

Another pretender took advantage of the festivities that ended the fast of Ramadan to escape. It is said that he used a rope to escape from the roof at night. Without a doubt he must have had strong accomplices to do such a thing right in the royal palace. This highlights how a close and evidently faithful entourage harbored many turncoats who acted against the royal order when they were solicited with a lot of money.[185]

Sometimes it even happened that prisoners would plead their case. This was the case when they sang at the top of their lungs in a sign of protest. Some cases of revolt were severely punished and resulted in a man's death.[186] The mobilization of powerful clans could overcome the guards' resistance. The ʿArim prison mentioned earlier was thus attacked by Shiites who broke down the gate and liberated members of the Hashemite clan.[187] It is appropriate to mention here that the security mechanism itself sometimes left much to be desired and thus facilitated escapes.

Troubled times and periods in which a power vacuum existed were the most propitious to revolts and to mass escapes.[188] Watchmen unsure of how to behave showed their indifference. It even happened that in the event of a revolt, the residents of a city, fed up with harsh treatment, took the initiative themselves to open the doors of the establishments perceived to be emblems of tyranny.[189] Dated examples include the events of 1 Safar AH 248 (approximately April 4 of 862 CE). People took to the streets of Baghdad en masse, shouting for revolt. They were quickly joined by the youth of the city and by mercenaries, who for their part complained of unpaid salaries. They opened the doors of the Nasr Ibn Mâlik prison and freed the prisoners, and then proceeded to do the same at al-Qantara in Bab al-Jisr. The same year, moreover, people attacked the prison in Samana and allowed the prisoners to escape.[190] It was not

[183] *ʿIqd*, II, 155.
[184] *Aghâni*, XXI, 315, and *Al-Kâmil*, II, 534.
[185] Tabari, *Târîkh*, XI, 57.
[186] Tabari, *Târîkh*, XI, 19.
[187] *ʿIqd*, IV, 387; for another case see *Al-Kâmil*, II, 618.
[188] Tabari, *Târîkh*, X, 184.
[189] Tabari, *Târîkh*, XI, 108.
[190] Tabari, *Târîkh*, XI, 208.

always necessary for the population to get involved. In one case, the men of an army company whose wages had gone unpaid took matters into their own hands and whipped up a mob to attack the Sijn al-Châm prison at night.[191] In 278 AH (891 CE), during a transfer of power, revolt broke out again, "the prison doors were broken down and holes made in the walls, and all the prisoners escaped, notably those from Mutbaq."[192] Revolts were, however, harshly punished. The leaders were locked up in special cells called "cells of darkness" where visitors were forbidden and prisoners were heavily chained and deprived of *sadaqa*, or the alms distributed to the prisoners, and thus were sentenced to death by starvation.[193] The condition of the "common" prisoner, locked up for nonpolitical reasons, was already quite unenviable.

LIFE IN PRISON

The worst was the underground prison, which was nonetheless in common use. Texts often mention someone being arrested and then "chained and imprisoned in the dungeons."[194] One famous example, the Mutbaq, was a gloomy subterranean prison under the Abbasids.[195] Al-Hajjâj had a prison called the tunnel, or *al-diymâss*, whose darkness made it truly tomblike.[196] But even when they were not subterranean, prisons were deprived of light. Cells were called *dhullal*, zones of shadow or, more prosaically, dark zones.[197] A Bedouin, a highway robber by trade whom nostalgia had turned into a poet, begged his guards, upon seeing a few rays of light, to open the door slightly just so he could see it better.[198] The *ḥaddâd*, or jailer, was also the name of the guardian of the doors of hell, which said a lot about the prisoners' destiny.[199] The jailer, or *sajjân*, who seemed to have some leverage in the choice of the prisoners' treatment, was reputed for his corruption. One of them was appropriately nicknamed Dinar, no doubt conveying his susceptibility to bribes of cold, hard cash.[200] He ended up being executed, however, for releasing a

[191] Tabari, *Târîkh*, XIII, 36.
[192] Tabari, *Târîkh*, XII, 208.
[193] Tabari, *Târîkh*, XI, 136.
[194] Tabari, *Târîkh*, XII, 233.
[195] *Aghâni*, XXV, 91.
[196] Az-Zamakhchari, *Al-Fâiq fi gharîbi al-ḥadith*, I, 438.
[197] *Tâj al-ʿArûss*, XV, 456.
[198] Yâqût, *Muʿjam*, I, 83.
[199] Râzi, XV, Part II, 180.
[200] Baladhuri, 519.

prisoner who had been arrested for murder. In general, the power of the jailers was considerable. They went so far as to grant freedom of movement to the least dangerous prisoners, as in the case of one prisoner who was permitted to leave the establishment at night and come back in the morning,[201] a decision that no doubt benefited from a tacit agreement from above. Such power was, moreover, a testament to the strength and stability of the penitentiary institution.

The prisoner was well shackled. He was chained at his feet and neck, and lived most of the time in darkness.[202] Prisoners were treated harshly, often like animals. Brutality was a daily occurrence, and the adjective *sijjîn*, derived from the word for prison, was synonymous with harshness.[203] In any case, the living conditions in prison were deplorable, as a number of indications suggest. Someone close to the caliph Moʿâwiyya, who was worried about prisoners escaping, reminded him that they "left naked from head to toe," suggesting in complete destitution.[204] The expression reflected one of the descriptions that the Prophet gave of people at the resurrection.[205]

The various words for prison foretold the great solitude of the prisoner and the suffering he endured.[206] For its population, the prison was "a cemetery of the living," a world between life and death. Guards who came into contact with the prisoners seemed to them like visitors from another world. This tells how powerful was the link between prison and death.[207]

Regular eyewitness accounts confirm the indisputable fact that one's social standing, wealth, and relationships could soften the stay in prison and perhaps even improve it.[208] Notables, at least those who were not irrevocably condemned by the system and kept in isolation, seem to have benefited from privileged treatment. Thus in a prison in Damascus, certain prisoners went so far as to receive their servants[209] and were provided with suitable bedding, rugs, and even accessories.[210] Abû Nûwâss is mentioned as playing chess and receiving many visits in prison.[211] This

[201] Tabari, *Târîkh*, VI, 159.
[202] Az-Zamakhchari, *Al-Fâiq fi gharîbi al-ḥadith*, II, 416.
[203] Yâqût, *Muʿjam*, I, 134.
[204] Baladhuri, 47.
[205] Ibn Mâja, *Saḥîḥ*, III, 392.
[206] *Tâj al-ʿArûss*, XI, 67–68.
[207] Al-qurtubî abî Yûsuf ibn ʿAbdillah, *Bahjat al-mjâliss wa unss al-mujâliss*, II, 108.
[208] Tabari, *Târîkh*, X, 97.
[209] Tabari, *Târîkh*, IX, 92.
[210] Tabari, *Târîkh*, IX, 4.
[211] *Aghâni*, XXV, 79 and 109.

image is, however, misleading due to the particular status of this important poet of the court.

Food consisted of alms and must have been quite sparse. For those who had the means, relatives provided food when they had a way to ensure that it reached the prisoner. The sanitary conditions were extremely bad. In order to take care of their needs, the prisoners were let out in chains and closely watched. In Medina, where the prison was basic, they could only do so at night, outside.[212] In general, the prisons that held many inmates were cramped to the point of overflowing.[213]

From time to time there were inspections of prisons, but they were far from commonplace.[214] In certain prisons, registers were kept that included lists of the condemned and the punishments that had been inflicted on them, lists that were burned following a revolt.[215]

Even if we do not have a breakdown of the incarcerated population by types of crimes, the revolts that revealed the deplorable conditions in prison also show that the prisons housed robbers and criminals alongside the notables who ended up there because of the prince.[216] The prisoners' harsh living conditions were even worse for those who had a brush with authority and were subjected to torture.

TORTURE INSCRIBED IN THE SYSTEM

The object of torture was to intensify the feeling of destitution and solitude before authority that was caused by crossing the first threshold toward death. That destitution was multiplied by the public humiliation that notified the rest of the subjects and servants of the royal power. A certain poet, incriminated for having mocked the caliph, was dragged in front of the ruler, who called for a *nat'* and a sword. The poet "then denied the poem in question and swore to all his gods.... he began to cry, to beg, and to kiss the ground at the caliph's feet. The caliph then spared his life and had him beaten until he defecated. He was then placed on his back, his mouth was forced open, and he was made to swallow his feces." He was later released and was poisoned when he was already far from the capital.[217] Scenes of great cruelty unfolded under the eyes of the

[212] *Aghâni*, XXIV, 149.
[213] *Al-Kâmil*, II, 338.
[214] Tabari, *Târîkh*, X, 233.
[215] Tabari, *Târîkh*, XI, 208.
[216] Tabari, *Târîkh*, XII, 36 and 233.
[217] *Aghâni*, XX, 200.

caliph. While al-Mo'tassim was seated in the garden of the palace, slightly tipsy, a condemned man was brought to him. He gave the order to strip the man of his clothing and to whip him while a hole was dug. Once the hole was complete, he ordered that the man be struck again on his face and body with sticks until he lost consciousness; he was then thrown into the hole, where he died.[218]

Intensifying the prisoner's physical suffering through the use of a whip and other instruments of torture was the first step. *Al-miqtara* or *falaq*, which derived its name from a procession of animals harnessed together, was a long plank with a line of holes into which the prisoners' legs were inserted, thus depriving them of movement.[219] The *tannûr* was a type of oven covered with hot nails into which a prisoner condemned for dreadful crimes was placed.[220] Specialized professional torturers were also used. Prisoners were sent to one of them, in the city of Tâ'if, to be sliced up until they died.[221]

There were many examples of torture. One individual was tied to a sugar cane and had his body sprinkled with salt and vinegar until it dried out. He moaned audibly until his death.[222] Public exhibition of torture was part of the landscape. Another man, after being tortured, was covered with a goat hide glued to his skin, which gave him a diabolical appearance; he was then dragged into a public square and tortured again.[223] Women with shaved heads were also dragged through the streets on camelback and were thus exposed to public condemnation.[224]

Special treatment was reserved for great figures of the state, as well as for pretenders and those close to the king who had fallen into disgrace. A fallen caliph was thus deprived of water and food for three days. Then he was put into a gypsum tunnel just large enough to hold him, and the opening was shut. He was found dead the next day.[225] Indeed the prince's objective was to force a person to cross the threshold leading to certain death with a keen awareness, during that long period of agony, of the true power he held over life and death.

[218] Tabari, *Târîkh*, XI, 100.
[219] *Tâj al-'Arûss*, VII, 406.
[220] *Aghâni*, XXIII, 78.
[221] *Aghâni*, XIII, 106.
[222] *Al-Kâmil*, II, 685.
[223] *Aghâni*, IV, 233.
[224] *Aghâni*, XIX, 144.
[225] Tabari, *Târîkh*, XII, 29.

Torture with fire was an ancient practice. The king Muḥarriq, or the burner, specifically of men in this case, was the first to be known for it.[226] Fire could be a radical and efficient means to dispose of prisoners who were grouped together in a pen and burned alive.[227] But death could also be rendered sparingly, notably by prolonged and public exposure to the sun.[228]

To inflict death was an ancient practice; to prolong the victim's agony by having him tortured in the half-living, in-between state in which only the king could give back life, and to do so publicly, proclaimed to the living the presence of the Authority and his all-powerfulness, as did the sultan's treatment of the disgraced caid that was described at the beginning of this book.

After all, servitude was the state of the forlorn, depersonalized individual dependent upon the mercy of his master; it was a partial death. A master demonstrated so in his use of the sword and especially the prison. His means were the monopoly over punishment and his discretionary use of it. The state born from Islam was no exception in this regard.

[226] *Ichtiqâq*, 435.
[227] *Ichtiqâq*, 495.
[228] Tabari, *Târîkh*, XI, 99–100.

Conclusion

Between Heaven and Earth

The history of the Arab world is charged with weighty events that obscure our view. Memory abounds with the sacred and with mythic or accursed characters. History is held captive by religious discourse and its representations. The real society with its everyday concerns and its contradictions, the hard labor of ordinary people, the constraints of material life, and the inherent difficulties of an unforgiving natural environment are almost absent from it. The sacred draws a veil over the functioning of society and hides its everpresent dynamics. The orthodox caliphs, stripped of their social and historical dimensions, occupy the scene, and politics appear futile in a universe where conflicts were resolved or eliminated with the swift application of Koranic verses and decrees borrowed from the prophetic tradition. The present age forcefully reminds us of the power of such arguments.

Thus it is imperative to desacralize the historical approach to that period and those that followed it. To desacralize must be understood in the sense of breaking down the barriers between the political and the religious, and reading that period, which corresponded to the essential moment of the formation of an effective royal state, as we read all others, according to the overall logic of the functioning of society – a state founded on a social bond that imbues it with its earthly logic.

To proceed in that way is to escape the hold of the events in question, which, despite their importance and their density, give a false perception of Arab social dynamics. It is to write the story on a human scale that enables us to better reveal the ghosts that haunt the present.

It is to read the history of a period that flowed from the preceding ones without a radical break: there was no real revolution that affected the economic and social structures. I believe I have proceeded in this way while attempting to uncover the nature of the bond of authority from an open perspective.

The Muslim state grew out of the ruins of the ancient Arabian kingdoms. Putting their heritage to use, the rituals of royal protocol were quickly established. While the caliphate was crumbling from the inside, exhausted by internal struggles and attempting to contain social upheavals, the monarchy waited in the wings, preparing for its advent per se by feeding on the very contradictions of the existing rule. In practice, the caliphate, despite its mythical representation by Muslim ideologues, remained encumbered by economic and social structures. Even in the accomplishments for which it was most highly lauded, such as the creation of the *shûra*[1] committee that was believed to democratically define the modalities of succession, one finds the imprint of the dominant clans. Wealth once again came to play a determining role in the distribution of power, as it did in earlier periods and as it would continue to do in the future. In any event, the caliphate evolved by itself toward a hereditary reign that not only corresponded better to the dominant social structures but proved to be the best guarantor of a system in equilibrium.

In addition to a more extensive and lasting economic base, the state that was thus put into place benefited from religious foundations that allowed it to claim a legitimacy transcending its tribal origins. The same laws and the same logic that governed the formation of states in the small pre-Islamic Arab kingdoms were in fact at work here, with the sacred filling the gaps and compensating for the shortcomings of the other institutions, thus accelerating historical time.

But in fact it was the social milieu of the time that fashioned the authoritarian mode. In its expression, its content, and its mechanisms, the earlier modes of the exercise of power, from the master-slave bond to the monarchical bond, clearly contributed to the structure of the political space and at times the celestial space. As it increased in importance, the bond of authority, originally terrestrial, henceforth dealt in the extremes of all-powerfulness and insignificance; the Master and the faithful were thus stripped of terrestrial contingencies, rid of any impurity that threatened the Authority or the servant's adoration of it. In heaven Authority attained its perfection, and servitude its ultimate realization. In return, the political became imbued with the arcana of religion, and despite the

[1] A committee designated by the caliph ʿOmar, one member of which would be chosen as his successor.

continuity in the nature of authority and its servile content, the religious modified the modes of legitimation and of access to power. Thus the religious field became a central space in the clans' struggle to claim power. A secular reading of religious texts therefore proves essential to an understanding of power. One must decode, or unveil, the sacred language for it to convey its true message.

Thus we see a strong continuity between the old and the new. Theological discourse posits a radical rupture, introducing as its sole criterion an ahistorical sacred that breaks with the past and denies the period before the advent of Islam, a period presumed to be one of darkness and ignorance, of its legitimate status as a historical antecedent – and this despite its obvious and decisive legacies, notably in the area of social domination and struggle for hegemony. Efforts at understanding the present through historical reason were put aside. The sacred became the protagonist in a series of periods said to begin with the advent of Islam. This advent certainly constituted an important moment of transition: favorable conditions were created for the establishment of a state, for its endowment with considerable material wealth, for its widespread territorial expansion, for its reworking of the social fabric, and for its foundation on a social structure that was no longer limited to the clan or the tribe. These conditions are, however, far from a radical break with the earlier social and political forms.

Servitude indeed appeared on the scene as a mode of authority borrowed from private social bonds. In the tribal milieu, the master-slave relationship proved the most effective means to establish and affirm the power of the chief. The king's relationships with his entourage, his servants, and his subjects were formed around this common core. The religious realm, which conceived of the relationship to the master solely as a relationship of absolute authority, sought to legitimize the indisputable authority of the king by transforming its terrestrial origin into a delegation granted from heaven.

Principal Sources

Ibn ʿAbdu Rabbih, *Kitâb al'iqd al-farîd*, Dâr al-kitâb alʿarabi, Beirut, 7 volumes.
Ibn al-Aflili, *Charḥ chi'r al-Mutanabbi*, Moassassat ar-rissâla, Beirut, 1998, 4 volumes.
Ibn al-Athir, *An-Nihâya fi gharîbi al-ḥadîthi wa al-athar*, Dâr al-fikr, Beirut, 4 volumes.
Al-Baladhuri, *Ansâb al-achrâf*, Franz Steiner Verlag GMBH, Wiesbaden, 1979.
Ibn Durayde, *Kitâb jamharat al-lugha*, Dâr al-ʿilm lilmayinn, Beirut, 1987, 3 volumes.
Al-Ichtiqâq, Dâr al-jîl, Beirut, 1991.
Al-Jâhiz, *Al-Bayânn wa tabyînn*, al-maktaba al'asriyya, Beirut, 1999.
Kitâb al-ḥayawânn, Dâr al-kutub al'ilmiyya, Beirut, 1998, 4 volumes.
Rasâ'il al-Jâhiz, Dâr al-jîl, Beirut, 1991, 2 volumes.
Al-Jawhari, *As-Siḥaḥ, tâju al-lugha wa siḥaḥu al-ʿarabiyya*, Dâr al-kutub al'ilmiyya, Beirut, 1999, 7 volumes.
Ahmad Ibn Hanbal, *Musnad*, Dâr al-kutub alʿilmiyya, Beirut, 1993, 8 volumes.
Al-Haroui Abi ʿUbayad al Qâssim Ibn Salâm, *Gharîbu al-ḥadîth*, Dâr al-kutub al'ilmiyya, Beirut, 1986, 2 volumes.
Ibn Hichâm, *As-Sîra an-nabawiyya*, al-Maktaba al-'ilmiyya, Beirut, 4 volumes.
Ibn Hilâl al-ʿAskari, *Kitâb al-furûq*, Beirut, 1994.
Ibn Kathîr, *Tafsîr*, Muassassat ar-Riyyân, Beirut, 1996, 4 volumes.
Abi Faraj al-Asfahâni, *Al-Aghâni*, Dâr al-kutub al'ilmiyya, Beirut, 1992, 25 volumes.
Ibn Mandhûr, *Lissân al-ʿArab*, Dâr Sâder, Beirut, 15 volumes.
Ibn Mâja, *Saḥîḥ*, Maktabat al-ma'ârif linnachr wa tawzî', Riyadh, 1997, 4 volumes.
Al-Mubarrad, *Al-Kâmil fi al-lugha wa al-adab*, Dâr al-fikr al'arabi, Beirut, 1999, 2 volumes.
Ibn al-Muthannâ, at-Taymi al-Basri, *Kitâb an-Naqâidh, naqâ'idh Jarîr wa al-Farazdaq*, Dâr al-kutub al'ilmiyya, Beirut, 1998, 4 volumes.
An-Nassâi, *Sunan*, Maktabat al-matbû'ât al-'islâmiyya, Beirut, 1994, 5 volumes.

Ibn Qutayaba, *A-Chi'ru wa chu'arâ'*, Dâr al-ḥadîth, Cairo, 1998, 2 volumes.
Ibn Sidah, *Al-Mukhassass*, Dâr ihya' at-thurâth al-'arabi, Beirut, 1996, 5 volumes.
Ibn Sikkite, *Kitâb al-alfâdh*, Maktabat Lubnân nâchirûn, Beirut, 1998.
Islâḥ al-Mantiq, Dâr al-ma'ârif, Cairo.
At-Tabari, *Târîkh*, Dâr al-fikr, Beirut, 1998, 16 volumes.
Tafsîr ou Jâmi' al-bayâne fi ta'wili al-Qur'ân, Dâr al-kutub al'ilmiyya, Beirut, 1996, 12 volumes.
At-Tha'labi, Ghayât Ibn Ghaout, *Chi'r al-Akhṭal*, Dâr al-fikr al-mu'âssir, Beirut, 1996.
At-Tha'âlibî 'Abdallah Ibn Muhammad, *Fiqh al-lugha wa sirru al-'Arabiyya*, Dâr al-Jîl, Beirut, 1998.
Fakhr ad-Dîn Châfi'î ar-Râzi, *At-Tafsîr al-kabîr aw mafâtih al-ghayb*, Dâr al-kutub al'ilmiyya, Beirut, 1990, 16 volumes.
Az-Zamakhchari, *Al-Kachâf* ..., Dâr al-kutub al'ilmiyya, Beirut, 1995, 4 volumes.
Al-Fâiq fi gharîbi al-ḥadith, Dâr al-fikr, Beirut, 1993, 4 volumes.
Ahmad Zaki Safwat, *Jamharat rasâ'il al-'Arab*, Dâr al-matbû'ât al-'arabiya, Cairo, 4 volumes.
Jamharat khutab al-'Arab, al-maktaba al'ilmiyya, Beirut, 3 volumes.
Az-Zubaydi al-Hanafi, *Tâj al-'Arûss min jawâhiri al-qâmuss*, Dâr al-fikr, Beirut, 1994, 20 volumes.

Thematic Index

Index of Places and People